Like Rolling Uphill

Realizing the Honesty of Atheism

Dianna Narciso

Wayward Cat Publishing

Second Edition 2014
ISBN 978-1-938999-16-1
Library of Congress Control Number: 2014916316

First Edition © 2003 Dianna Narciso

Wayward Cat Publishing
Palm Bay, Florida
www.waywardcatpublishing.com

Cover art copyright © 2014 Wayward Cat Publishing
Photo of landscape © Bartosz Hadyniak via istockphoto

Like Rolling Uphill
Realizing the Honesty of Atheism

Snark: snide sarcasm

Snarked: having been snarkly fisked

Fisking: criticizing or commenting at length or point-by-point

Offsnarked: offended by the use of snark

Whineoffsnarking: letting someone know his snark has offended you

F*c%snarkoff: a statement or gesture letting someone know you don't care if your snark has offended him

Snarkpology: an apology for offending someone with your snark with the full intention of continuing to do so

Introduction to Second Edition
(Cue: Todd Rundgren, "Hello It's Me")

It goes like this, pretty much: I like to write fiction. I realize I'm an atheist. I get mad at some Christians. I decide to be an activist. I get less mad. I write *Like Rolling Uphill: Realizing the Honesty of Atheism*. I get mad at some atheists. I quit atheism. I write fiction. I decide to take said book off the market. Then I decide to release it again because, well, I wrote it and it ought to be out there. I look at it and realize there's something wrong with it. What was the problem? Well, as I was reading it, I didn't recognize the author. *I'm* the author. But I kept saying to myself, "Who is that person?"

The author of the first edition of *Like Rolling Uphill* is more than ten years younger than I am. She wants to be taken seriously by god only knows who...the world, I guess, but damn it she's an atheist so that's not going to happen. She's had it up to *here* with being accused of things, labeled incorrectly, and dissed by the religious. She wants to lay it all on the line with the expectation that she won't have to talk about it anymore afterward. (It worked. Pretty much.) She's trying to sound conversational...not snooty and intellectual as she often comes across when she writes about the subjects of religion and atheism. She's trying to be *nice*. Like, when a nurse has to give you a shot and she gets all, "This might hurt a bit." It's fake. It might not have been fake at the time, but it sounds fake now.

I couldn't just reissue this book with my name on it when it doesn't represent me anymore. So I decided to write a different book—a wacky memoir of a sort—on growing up and realizing I was an atheist. I thought I'd include the entire *Like Rolling Uphill* book inside it (at the end, rather), only this time critiqued by me. No, I mean it. A crazy memoir and then *this* book, totally fisked. But I started on the memoir and realized it just wouldn't work. The memoir is wild. Uncontrolled. Batshit crazy. And *Like Rolling Uphill*...well, it isn't. They don't go together. I don't want them together.

That settled it. I had to release it on its own—a second edition. But I had to put the new me into it somehow. I thought I could just rewrite it. Completely. But I know how that turns out—a completely different book. I wanted to somehow preserve what I wrote back then—who I was and who I was trying to be—and still hack the crap out of it. So that's what I did. And that's what you're going to get: the old me with a stick up her butt and the new me snarking her for it. We should call this, *Like Rolling Uphill: Snark Edition*.

2

I've also addressed any grammatical, spelling, or factual issues I came across. Nothing major. Silly stuff that drives me nuts. Like the fact that 2003 me was apparently not as enamored with the Oxford comma as I am today.

Let me apologize in advance for offending you. Christians, believers, agnostics, atheists, anti-semicolonists, anti-exclamationmarkists: sorry about that. No, really. Really sorry. Somewhere inside there's a sorry part. Oh, and sorry I say, "snap!" a lot. I'm kind of a nerd.

Chapter One

To Begin With

I remember well the first time I came out to a Christian family member; my body tingled with fear and my face grew hot. I didn't know what she would do or say–I didn't know what I should do or say. I carefully avoided the "A" word, saying simply that I didn't believe in God. Her reaction was mild surprise and a question: "Are you an atheist?" My response was a mumbled, "yes" followed by weak support for Jesus as "okay by me" thrown in as an apologetic afterthought. [*What a coward.*] She was curious and open; though she didn't seem to mind that I didn't believe, she felt I was wrong and recommended a book on the subject. I agreed to read it and let her know exactly what I thought of it. *Big mistake.*

Maybe it wasn't entirely my fault. Perhaps she hadn't actually read the book she recommended, the one that said atheists were immoral, irrational, hopeless, and depressed. She may not have known it was merely an angry diatribe against nonbelief and instead rather hoped it would lead me to see things from her perspective. But I reacted as if she, herself, had written the book; I was hurt and insulted and let my thoughts be known. [*Let my thoughts be known? You can see why I don't like the original version, right? What I did was write her a series of emails picking apart the books she gave me, telling her in no uncertain terms how wrong and unsubstantiated (love that word) they were (are?). At one point, I think I told her that if her God came down here I'd throw the Bible at him or smack him with it or something. It was good stuff. It just wasn't the sort of stuff you write to someone you're related to and might want to chat with at a family get together later. What I should have done was to just nod politely while she was talking about Jesus and sing a song in my head. Cue: The Who, "Baba O'Riley."*] Clue to the clueless: most people don't really want to know what you think; they want you to think like they do.

Humanity is a silly species. [*Really? Silly? How about batshit crazy?*] It's a good feeling to be able to say that now, because for so long I didn't find anything remotely humorous about it. Early on I thought people were rather stupid, but for the most part well-intentioned. After realizing atheism, I went through a phase when I thought people were hateful, cruel, and ignorant–certain book recommendations didn't help. I noticed, though, that there were others like me in the world who weren't fuming...they were entertained. These people watched John Hagee and Benny Hinn for a good belly laugh when I couldn't stand to listen to them. [*I'm talking about my husband here. No 'people.' Just him.*] I wanted to laugh too; it's a lot more fun to let the foibles of a silly species amuse you, than it is to be fearful of them. It took me a long time to understand people well enough to laugh, and even now the humor is tempered by sadness. [*Yeah, well not anymore. Lesson: a lot of time and continuing education make things funnier than you thought they could ever be. If my fun is tempered by anything, it's disgust.*]

Being an atheist in the United States is like being Neo, walking around inside the Matrix watching all the batteries living their lives believing they see reality. Or, it's like being Captain Kirk in "The Return of the Archons" episode of *Star Trek*, puzzling over the behavior of the "followers" of Landru and trying to avoid being absorbed into "the Body." Sometimes I want to shake the whole of humanity and scream, "Wake up!" But it wouldn't work because what they're doing is natural to them; it's a part of what makes them human. [*I don't agree with that—not exactly. I bet I only said it to be nice—to not offend believers, make them think I'm okay with it and I'm not going to scream at them later. I go into the reasons people believe stupid things somewhere below and the reasons they do are because of behaviors that are natural to humans. In that way, resistance to ideas that would shake them of their belief is natural. But it's not a necessary behavior and they should stop it. Really. Just stop.*] The methods used to untangle the web of theism and loosen its grip on each person differ. For some, nothing will work because they are so entwined both with the illusion and the love of it, that no matter what you show them, they will not see it as it is.

Believers have been defending "The Faith" against nonbelievers from the very beginning. As soon as followers of the Christ cult [*Oh, snap, I got the cult dig in early.*] started spreading the "Good News" that the majority of humanity was doomed to eternal torment, there were naysayers. The disagreement is nothing new. Believers think they have a truth that others don't have; they call those others all sorts of names like heretic, infidel, and heathen. The heretics and infidels think the believers have been duped into mistaking a lie for truth. [*Uh, yeah.*] But no matter how much debate is engaged in, nothing changes. Well, that's not entirely true...the theology evolves. With each new attack from science and rationalism, Christianity heals its wounds, shifts its paradigm [*You won't hear me admitting that I pronounced it 'para-dij-m' for ever so long until I heard someone smarter say it.*] to accommodate, and moves on. Christianity, as do all types of cultural beliefs, adjusts.

It is wildly apparent that nothing anyone can say will make someone who believes in God simply stop believing in God and there is no amount of persuasion a believer can engage in to force a nonbeliever to start believing. [*Really? Are you sure?*] The only reason a person will change is because something within him changes; he, for some reason, starts seeing things a different way. [*Maybe that reason is something somebody said.*] It can't be coerced. In fact, the more you try to induce someone to change his beliefs, the more fervently [*I said fervently. What a word.*] he will cling to them. When a person is devoted to his beliefs, showing him that he is in error won't make him stop believing; logic doesn't work. [*Egad. Showing him he is in error? I'm going to get a stomach ache from laughing at this stuff.*] The believer may adjust his beliefs to accommodate new information, but he will rarely abandon them. A person will only change his mind when he is open to doing so.

I've heard stories of Christian deconversions. Most claim the process was painful and disturbing. Abandoning a cherished belief can be traumatic, but still they did it. A complicated process of doubt and reason led them away from something they were certain was truth into skepticism. These particular people are lucky–they have seen the world from two places, two sides. Sometimes I wish I could force that process on believers so they could see the world from my perspective, even for just a few moments. We might then finally understand each other. [*Now, hold on there, bubbette. How is that understanding going to be possible when I've never been a real, honest to gawd, Bible believing Christian? I mean sure, there was that time I carried the book around and acted all pious until my mom told me to cut it out. And I read the nativity stories once or twice at Christmas time. But did I ever really believe it? I mean like these really into it Christians do? No. So, I'd have to see the world from their perspective, too. I'd have to get freaky and really believe it. Maybe stop showing my cleavage and go to church and hold my hands up in the air with my fingers all close together the way they do and sing praises to God. No thanks. Just forget that whole part about*

9

understanding each other. It's not going to happen and it's no big deal. We'll manage.]

In my experience, few believers (Christians, to be specific) understand atheism at all and the human propensity is, it seems, to demonize and hate that which we don't understand. I have felt the frustration of being misunderstood and denigrated for choosing the atheist label. People try to tell me what I think, what I believe, and who I am, as if they know me—when they have just met me. Believers attempt to explain atheism and atheists to me—they've told me what a depressing, hopeless life I lead, that I am wicked and willful. If I protest that I am not what they say I am, they simply smile that Collective [*ooh, another cult dig*] smile and explain that, though I don't realize it because Satan has blinded me to the Truth, I am, in fact, wicked, desperate, and hopeless.

If I do manage to clear up a few misconceptions with one member of the Collective, it does no good—along comes another with the same incorrect assumptions. I suffer under the delusion that if I share with believers what I think and why I think it, what I believe and don't believe and why, some might come to a better understanding of atheism and at the very least, not feel threatened by it. [*Delusion? Technically, if I'm aware of it, it's not a delusion.*] While I would like to explain why I don't believe the Christian message, I know I won't convince anyone that my view is correct. People have their good reasons for believing what they do—but very few Christians seem to understand why atheists don't believe the same things. I'd really like to change that but I wonder if it's possible—I wonder if there isn't some code in the

Collective that says members must adhere to a dogmatic definition of atheism and atheists. Or perhaps seeing atheism for what it really is would be a threat to the belief.

I can't speak for all atheists—we're all different—[*Isn't that the truth?*] I only speak for myself. And I can't speak to or about all Christians. I know that all Christians are not alike, don't believe the same things, or hold the same views—atheists are the same way. There, the labels atheist and Christian have something in common. The terms cover various types of people, uniting them under one common definition while allowing for their differences. Atheists are even more varied than Christians because there is no atheist dogma for us to accept. We all share only one thing in common: no god belief.

[*Okay, right here I'm going to explain which Christians I'm talking to and about when I get all pissy and sarcastic and start mocking and using words like dumb, stupid, and idiotic. I'm not talking about or to nice people who happen to be Christians. (Okay, when I talk about* beliefs *being dumb, stupid, or idiotic, yes, I suppose even nice people have those beliefs and they'll just have to accept that some of us think those* beliefs *are dumb, stupid, and idiotic even when they themselves might not be.) I'm not talking about people who care about others whether they're straight, gay, Muslim, Wiccan, atheist, or whatever. There are a lot of really good people who are Christians and they just don't think about it much. That might get harder and harder as our culture becomes more and more diverse, but there it is. And sure, in this book I talk about why I'm* not a Christian and originally I guess I hoped any kind of Christian could read it and get something from it, even though it was just a tad bit offensive. Well, now it's really offensive. But I'm not aiming that offense at those really good people.

No. I'm mocking and getting pissy about conservative Christians who think the Bible is literally true, the earth is 4,000 years old, evolutionary theories are false, atheism is a religion, and their children are being indoctrinated into it in the public schools. They think that homosexuality is evil and if we allow gays their right to marry the next thing you know people will be marrying horses (that is just stupid). Christians who think school teachers and administrators ought to be able to pray Christian prayers with other people's children and anytime a student and her parents protest, they shove her into the lockers, stick crosses all over their yards all over town to intimidate the family, tell them they should leave the country (as if only their kind are real Americans), and threaten them with physical violence. Those who believe that religious freedom means the freedom for Christians only to pray before government meetings, protest funerals, pray over loud speakers at high school football games, pass out their literature to public school students, and put their Bible clubs in public schools to lure and convert other people's children to their religion.

People who actually believe this is and was always intended to be a Christian country. People who believe our laws are based on the Bible. People who think that when gays, humanists, a-theists, and smart empathetic people start en-

*forcing a strict separation of religion and gov-
ernment, they'll act like conservative Christians
did when* they *were a majority and deny them
their rights.*

*Those are the kinds of Christians (and Mus-
lims while we're at it, and frankly anyone who
thinks he ought to be able to enforce his own
brand of morality on others because he thinks his
interpretation of his old religious book is more
important than my personal rights) I'm talking
about.*]

I don't expect Christians to accept atheists as
friends, although there are many who do. I hope
that we can at least allow that not everyone
believes the things we do and it's important to
learn about those who are different—to try to
understand them as best we can so that we can live
together.

[*I thought that if theists understood atheism,
they could accept it, and in doing that they'd
realize that having a strong separation between
religion and government was a good thing and
they would stop trying to make everyone live the
way they thought everyone should. The fact that
Americans United for Separation of Church and
State is not an atheist organization means that it's
possible. But the idea that I could do it by writing
a book is ridiculous.*]

What is an atheist?
Everybody seems to think he knows what
atheism is and what atheists believe but there is
the first clue that something is amiss. The term
atheist doesn't tell you anything about what a person believes...only one thing that he doesn't.

Atheism, in its basic sense, is lack of belief in deity. When someone says he is atheist, that's the only thing you can be sure of: he does not believe in deity–he has no such belief. Some people make a distinction between strong and weak atheism. A strong atheist would assert that gods do not exist or even that they can't possibly exist; a weak atheist only claims he has no belief in any god. The difference is fuzzy, but it is also profound. Strong atheism is a position with respect to gods' existence–deity does not exist or I don't believe (or think) it does. Weak atheism is the barest definition of the term and is a description of a person's nonbelief: I don't *believe in* gods.

Many atheists waver between strong and weak atheism. We must, for instance, take the strong position (that gods do not exist) when arguing the matter. It would be pointless to enter a debate on the existence of God with the attitude that God may exist but we simply don't believe it. We can't always live with the certainty we desire in a debate, however. Sometimes in normal conversation or thought, I am a strong atheist, feeling that the idea of deity is nonsensical or impossible. At other times I'm a weak atheist, imagining that deity is possible but acknowledging that I simply do not believe in it.

The theist rebuttal to the strong atheist position is typically to claim that there are, in actuality, no atheists. Imagine my surprise upon hearing that! [*I am so prissy!*] In order to know that gods do not exist, they say, you would have to know everything...and you can't know everything so the most you can be is agnostic. This is not acceptable reasoning. [*My god, I was a snot, wasn't*

I? I was really much snottier. I can feel myself trying to be as non-offensive as possible.] Do Christians accept the existence of every possible entity because they can't be sure that such an entity does not exist? Can we never make a claim that something doesn't exist?

A favorite example among many atheists is the Invisible Pink Unicorn. Do you believe in the Invisible Pink Unicorn? Does she exist? Is it at all possible for her to exist? You don't know everything, so you can't say she doesn't exist. How about fire-breathing dragons? Are you an agnostic with regard to fire-breathing dragons? You must be—you must claim that you do not know whether they exist or not. This leaves a person in a constant state of "maybe" with regard to all possible entities. Atheists might claim that theists, not having proof of the existence of deity and having to rely on faith, should honestly proclaim agnosticism as well. Because certainty of the existence of gods is impossible, by theistic reasoning we must all be agnostics.

When deciding the question of the existence of gods, the strong atheist weighs the evidence and decides against the proposition: gods are not evident, therefore, the probability of their existence is minute so, for all intents and purposes, gods do not exist. I know that gods don't exist in the same manner that I know fairies, gnomes, and unicorns don't exist. I have no evidence for their existence. There is no need to form a belief about them. I, in the same manner, have no need to build a belief around a deity for whom I have no evidence.

Theists claim there is adequate evidence for a

15

creator; I have studied all that has been presented to me, but have found it lacking. Therefore, it is quite reasonable for me to claim strong atheism: gods do not exist–at least until such time as evidence might prove otherwise. [*Quite reasonable. Quite. Maybe I'd been listening to a lot of Dawkins and my British was showing. Not that I have any British, really. I use to like to talk with a British accent. I went on a trip once with some girls (I know, weird) and we went to a night club where I talked to this guy with my British accent and he thought I was really British. I was going to tell him the truth, but I'd never see him again, so why bother? Then, another time, I did tell this guy the truth and started talking American and he didn't believe me. He thought my American accent was fake. And then I went to London and my mother told me to talk British to the hotel clerk. 'Really she sounds exactly like you people.' So I did my accent and he tried to smile politely, but said...no. Yeah, so, not British.*] With regard to the Christian god of the Bible, not only do I find no evidence of its existence, but I find it logically inconsistent and contradictory. I am, therefore, more certain of the nonexistence of that particular god than of any other. [*Please. I'm pretty sure they're all fake.*]

An atheist, though, is not someone who steadfastly denies the existence of deity as if it is proven fact; atheists know they can't prove gods' nonexistence, but, we may reasonably deny the existence of deity because there is no evidence that such exists. There is no reason to be continually on the lookout for deity any more than one must continually lookout for elves. There is even less reason to create a belief about deity in light of the lack of evidence.

Agnostic is supposed to mean "without knowledge." An agnostic might claim that we can't know if gods exist. They would be more likely to say they don't know if a god exists or not, as to say, as many atheists do, that no gods are evident therefore they do not exist. Agnostics generally have no *belief* in deity, so to me they are atheists–they don't believe in gods. [*Oh, they're atheists all right.*] I suppose it can be said that the agnostic, while claiming no knowledge of deity, is free to believe in deity and still remain agnostic. He would say, "I don't know if it exists for certain, but I believe in it." I've never met such agnostics, but I'm sure they're out there.

On *The Secular Web* at *infidels.org* [*which surprisingly still exists*] I have had the pleasure of reading debates on the atheist versus agnostic positions, their meanings, their uses as labels, and their relationship. [*My god, the time I wasted there. Let's just say I don't get along with agnostics. If you can't answer the question, 'Do you believe in gods?' with a simple yes or no, you've got issues. You either believe in a god or you don't. You either believe there is a supernatural realm, or you don't. It's that simple. And for those of you who have no idea what I'm talking about, yes, there are people who refuse to answer that question–claim it's meaningless. They'll go on and on with some funked up reasons but the actual reason is that they're just above that sort of thing. They're...philosophers!*] The best I can say about them is that you can never assume to know what a person means when applying the labels atheist or agnostic to himself. It is always best to find out from the individual just what form his nonbelief takes. [*Yeah, and then tell him how he's wrong.*]

If you want to play the semantics game, you could say that everyone is an atheist. The deists believe that there was a god that started everything, set the universe in motion, then left or sat back to watch. It isn't a personal god and certainly isn't the one in the Bible. That makes deists without belief in any number of gods and therefore atheist with respect to them.

Pantheists too are atheist. They believe that the universe itself is god. They certainly are atheist with respect to all the myriad gods of history, especially the traditional Western god. Those who practice nature religions don't believe in gods, but rather spirits and other supernatural entities, therefore, they are atheist.

Christians and Jews, too, are atheist with respect to all other gods but their own. In other cultures, it is Christians who are atheists. Stephen Roberts, a widely-quoted atheist on the Internet, [*Seriously. That was all the information I could find out about that guy at the time.*] said, "I contend that we are both atheists. I just believe in one fewer god than you do. When you understand why you dismiss all the other possible gods, you will understand why I dismiss yours."* It is important to understand the distinct difference between atheists and Christians. Atheists don't believe in any gods while Christians don't believe in all gods save one. Very simply, when you understand why you don't believe in Zeus or Vishnu, you will understand why I don't believe in your god. [*Well, that's it then; mission accom-*

plished! We can wrap this whole thing up and be done with it. But no, let's go on. Besides, it gets really snarky soon.]

I don't consider everyone atheist simply because there are some gods in which they don't believe. To me, an atheist is someone who doesn't believe that any gods exist or has no god belief. When I meet someone, I let them define themselves. [*Sure I do.*] I wish that others would grant me the same ability: to describe myself and my label as I use it. Instead, I am *told* what atheism is by someone who is not one himself and what they tell me I am is rarely the truth about me.

Where did this misunderstanding of atheism originate? It isn't all the fault of theists, though they define atheism on their own terms by claiming they know that God is real and atheists deny his obvious existence. Atheists too, have claimed different meanings for the word.

As quoted in *Bertrand Russell on God and Religion* (Prometheus, 1986), in an article published in *Look* magazine in 1953, Bertrand Russell said that:

> An atheist, like a Christian, holds that we can know whether or not there is a God. The Christian holds that we can know there is a God; the atheist, that we can know there is not. The agnostic suspends judgment, saying that there are not sufficient grounds either for affirmation or for denial. At the same time, an agnostic may hold that the existence of God, though not impossible, is very improbable; he may even hold it so improbable that it is not worth considering

in practice. In that case, he is not far removed from atheism.

Did you get that? Russell said that atheists think they can know there is not a god. Many atheists would not accept this definition. I do think that the lack of evidence for deity is sufficient to accept its nonexistence; but I also believe that it cannot be known with absolute certainty. It is so close to certain, however, that I reasonably claim strong atheism. I am not so sure that all agnostics suspend judgment. I have little doubt that agnostics call themselves agnostic for all manner of reasons. [*It's fancy to be an agnostic. Cue: Iggy Azalea, "Fancy."*]

Agnosticism was first coined as a label by Thomas Henry Huxley in 1869. [*In the original, I said it was Aldous Huxley, his grandson. I had it fixed later. But I'd bought, like, fifty copies by then. What the hell did I think I was going to do with fifty copies?*] George Smith, in *Atheism: The Case Against God* (Prometheus, 1989), writes:

It seems that Huxley originally meant this term as somewhat of a joke. [*How apropos. Ooh, look. I said apropos. I bet I won't get to use that word again anytime soon. And yes, I totally just dissed the agnostics. Sorry agnostics. I'm just playing with you.*] He selected the early religious sect known as "Gnostics" as a prime example of men who claim knowledge of the supernatural without justification; and he distinguished himself as an "a-gnostic" by stipulating that the supernatural, even if it exists, lies beyond the scope of human knowledge. We cannot say if it does or does not exist, so we must suspend judgment.

[*Gnostic is pronounced without the g, like 'nostic,' so, how come we don't say ay-nostic instead of ag-nostic? I really only just now that of that... Anyway, go ahead and suspend judgment all you want. You still ought to be able to say whether or not you believe any god or gods exist. And if you don't, you're an atheist. I'm really sorry about it. I mean, I get that you don't want to be one. But some things you just are and there's nothing you can do about it.*] Does the agnostic really suspend judgment? He doesn't act as if the supernatural and gods might exist, does he? [*Nope.*] I haven't met one yet who does. Sometimes the way we live our daily lives says one thing about us and our philosophical labeling says another. [*You mean like people who call themselves Christians and then lie or steal or send pictures of their penises to women who are not their wives on their phones? I'm willing to bet God doesn't even like you looking at your penis, much less photographing it.*] Philosophically a person could be an agnostic—when pressed on the matter he may claim that the answer to the god question is inherently unknowable. But he lives his life as if no god exists just as the atheist does. I can't say I am any different from an agnostic in that respect— if there is a supernatural entity out there, we don't know anything about it. But I don't suspend judgment entirely. If it's there but is unknowable, there is no difference between its existence and its non-existence therefore it may just as well not exist as exist; so as far as I'm concerned, it doesn't. But most importantly, I don't *believe* it does.

Why do the agnostics get better treatment from the Christian community? [*And they do. They really do.*] If you define agnosticism as mere doubt, the agnostic seems to say, "I don't know, you might have something there but I'll withhold judgment on it." If you define atheism as outright refutation, the atheist seems to say, "There is no god; I don't believe it." [*Right. It has nothing to do with those of us who are outspoken and enjoy a bit of mockery now and then...okay, every day. And then there's that whole ruining their public prayer time. 'Damn you atheists! We were doing just fine making all the people at our football games, graduations, and public meetings pray with us until you came along and ruined it. You've ruined Amurka!'*]

With the agnostic, then, the Christian might sense an honest questioning and with the atheist, an abrupt denial. [*With just a little bit of eye rolling and snorting added in.*] Because the Christian claims that in order to experience God you must be open to the possibility of his existence, he would naturally be antagonistic toward someone he thinks flatly denies that possibility. I don't feel these are adequate portrayals of agnosticism and atheism. They are both a lack of belief in deity for perhaps shades of different reasons. Many, if not most, atheists do not deny the possibility of deity but they claim the label atheist because they feel it best describes their position with respect to deity–they don't believe in it. [*I'm still giggling over my use of the word fervently earlier. Fervently. Snark.*]

How are people atheists?

[*Whenever I read this, I want to say, "They just are!"*]

There are a few ways people find themselves to be atheist. You could be taught to accept atheism uncritically, you could fail to or refuse to consider the question of deity, or you could arrive at the conclusion rationally. The best pathway to atheism, in my opinion, is through rationalism. Any other approach is not well-grounded.

Indoctrination and atheist parenting

To be atheist only because you were taught to be without examining the question of gods' existence critically would be a sad state of being. [*So sad.*] Claiming that gods do not exist, that you don't believe in any, only because someone you consider an authority has told you so is not acceptable, in the same way that believing in a god because someone else has told you it exists is not acceptable. [*Not acceptable to whom exactly? I mean, just who did I think I was, anyway?*] Atheist parents must be careful not to indoctrinate their children with atheism. But what is indoctrination?

There are no gods; that is apparent to me as I have not seen, heard from, nor experienced any. I have no problem discussing the prospect of gods with my children. It can be fun to imagine the possibilities of what life is all about, where it came from, what the universe is, etc.. But, after thoroughly studying Christianity, through the Bible and history, I am fairly certain the Christian god doesn't exist. [*I think I meant pretty damn certain.*] I can't tell my children that perhaps it does,

23

any more than I can tell my children that perhaps fire-breathing dragons or monsters exist. If I should tell my child that, yes, it's *possible* that the Christian god exists and if he doesn't believe in him and worship him properly a terrible punishment awaits him after death, how then am I to deny that it is *possible* that an invisible monster is indeed under his bed at night and may take him away and torture him? How can I deny one and not the other when, in my view, the evidence for both is equal–they are both characters from stories in books? Let me say that again for proper effect– [*Oh, lah ti dah, proper effect.*] the evidence for monsters under the bed and for the existence of the Christian god is equal. For the same reasons I reject monsters, I reject the existence of Jehovah.

I have heard of parents who spray water around the bedroom pretending to ward off ogres or spend several minutes exposing all possible hiding places proving them free of imaginary creatures. I don't do these things because I will not tell my child that his fears are reasonable when they are not. I tell my children that it is understandable to be afraid, but that monsters are fictional characters in books. Fictional characters aren't real. There's no need to spray the room with monster repellent; there's no need to check the corners. Monsters could not possibly be in the room because they do not exist.

Telling my child that monsters do not exist is not indoctrinating him against monsters. Telling him that fairies, gnomes, and elves do not exist is not indoctrination. Telling him that dinosaurs, no matter how real they are made to look in movies, are extinct and no longer roam the earth is not indoctrination. Teaching my children that fantastic things they read about in books and see in movies are fiction, is not indoctrination. And telling my child that gods do not exist is also not indoctrination.

Indoctrination would mean instilling in my child a *doctrine* of belief. It is telling my child: this is what you must believe; you must accept this and not that. How then, does an atheist parent keep from indoctrinating his children? Simply by not ever telling him what he *must* believe. [*Or what he must not believe, for that matter.*] Children should be taught to think rationally and be skeptical of all claims, and they should be taught to use critical thinking skills in determining what is true and what is not.

The question of gods, when it comes up–and it will–can be discussed and examined as is any other claim. Your child must be allowed to discover possibilities and explore beliefs but certainly he must always be expected to exercise critical thinking at his age level. My children, each in turn, expressed a belief in a god of some sort at different times in their youths. I never discouraged them– never told them they were wrong, or silly. I accepted their belief. I also never lied. When they asked me–and they always did–if I believed, I said no. When they asked me why, I was as honest as I could be. That is not indoctrination; it's honest parenting.

However, it must be noted that we live in a world where god belief is the norm. It would be inadequate for me to simply tell my children that as far as I can tell there are no gods, without also explaining to them that most people believe there are. As an atheist parent, I consider it part of my job to teach my children about all the world's religions from Christianity, Judaism, and Islam, to ancient paganism, Wicca, and Native American spirituality. I have read African and Asian creation myths to my children; we explored Bible stories; we compared and discussed religions. I never told my children they must believe one of them over another and I certainly never told my children they must not believe in any of them.

I hear a little Christian voice in the back of my head, saying, "But you presented the Christian God as myth to your children; you controlled their ability to accept him as real." That's right. I read the Christian story of creation alongside other cultural stories of creation and my children never batted an eyelid. Not once did they say, "Boy, the Christian story sounds so true, so possible, so different from those other stories!" Not once–because the Christian story reads the same as the other myths. There is no reason other than cultural programming and parental indoctrination to believe that the Christian myth is anything more than all the other myths of history. In other words, and this is very important, I didn't have to tell my children the Christian story was a myth–they were able to discern that for themselves. [*And yes, they've all turned out to be snarky atheists just like their mother.*]

Atheism without much thought
Traveling through life never considering the idea of deity is acceptable. [*I'm sure the people who do that appreciated my letting them know I approved.*] For some of us, the concept is never

brought to the fore, the question never arises. However, once you consider the proposal seriously you have a decision to make: will you accept that gods do not exist because someone tells you they do not? Will you accept that one or another god does exist because someone tells you it does? Will you read one of the holy books and believe in one of the deities told of in it because the author of the book says it exists? Or will you weigh the evidence for yourself and use your reason to determine your stance?

Many people might say that the question of gods is nonsensical and a stance is not necessary. This is certainly acceptable [*Once again, they thanked me, I'm sure.*] and is, actually, grounded in reason. Such a person, in declaring the term god meaningless, has used his knowledge of the world to make that determination. [*Maybe he's just stupid and doesn't know what the word means?*] As long as the person who finds it unnecessary to take a position is not simply deferring the question because he is uncomfortable with it or finds it confusing, he isn't open to attack by theists bent on absorbing him into the Collective. [*I'm laughing. Really, the image that came to mind...Christians attacking the poor unsuspecting guy who doesn't know what the word god means...then absorbing him. Like slurping him up. Thwooop.*] Claiming that a stance is meaningless because god is meaningless is different from ignoring the idea altogether.

There are all sorts of atheists around who have never really examined the question of gods' existence. They are everywhere; in all economic and educational levels—in all ethnic and age groups.

There are atheists teaching your children, running your government, flipping your burgers, guiding corporations. There are atheists in the churches, the synagogues, and mosques. But they don't all know that they're atheist because they haven't actually considered the matter of the existence of gods. [*Well, somebody should tell them, don't you think?*]

It is part of human nature that we go along with our society and community or that we continue to do what we were taught to do as children. We do what is comfortable. If going to church is comfortable, or gives us some reward such as a sense of community or business contacts or a feeling of peace and goodness, we continue to go. If not, we quit going; but we may still call ourselves Christian because everyone else we know says they are and we are social animals who crave a feeling of belonging to a group.

From what I can tell through observation and experience, much of the church affair is akin to a weekly self-help workshop as much as it is a gathering to praise and worship a deity. In that respect, I can see the appeal. But even those people who might secretly suspect they don't agree with the god part of the religious matter seem to be repelled by the idea of atheism.

Taking on the label

The word atheist really bothers people, especially Christians. It is the complete opposite of what believers claim to be, a denial of what they believe, an affront to their belief. I can understand that. If you believe in something and feel that everyone else ought to also, someone blatantly saying you're wrong could be a problem. Even people who don't believe in gods will back away from the label of atheist because of the reaction other atheists have received or because they have fallen for the negative definitions proffered by theists. [*Help, I've fallen for a definition!*]

"Atheists are rude," one Humanist told me, after confessing he was one himself but wouldn't use the label. [*Oh, go on and say it. He was a Humanist minister at a Unitarian Universalist church where I live. And I shit** you not. There I was, visiting his church, and because of that he makes an effort to chat with me. I tell him I'm an atheist and that's the first friggin' thing out of his mouth. Sheesh. Some people.*] I have no doubt that there are rude atheists. There are rude people of every sort. It may be that this man had only met rude atheists because it takes some nerve to go about in this country actually admitting you are atheist. [*This was in 2003. I hear atheism's all the rage now.*] It might be good for atheism if all atheists were kind and considerate...it might be good for Christianity if all Christians were kind and considerate, too [*Oh, snap!*]–but, that's not the way people work. I'll try not to judge all Christians by the worst I've seen, if others try not to judge all atheists the same way.

There are two kinds of people who are likely to make the bold claim that they are in fact, atheists: those who have thought carefully about their lack of belief and have chosen the label as the best description of that nonbelief, and those who want to piss people off. The teenager who rebels against his family and his religion and spends a few years pretending to disbelieve in his god's existence is not an atheist.

There are Christians who claim they were former atheists. Few of them, upon careful questioning, turn out to have truly been. Atheists do not believe that gods exist. Anyone who believes a god exists but denies that god's authority over his life is not an atheist–he is a rebellious believer. Someone who believes there must be a creator, a supreme being of some kind, but doesn't call that being the Christian God and doesn't believe that Jesus was the son of a god, is not an atheist except in that semantics game we played earlier.

Letters From a Skeptic (SP Publications, 1994) by Gregory A. Boyd was presented to me as a book in which a son converts his atheist father to Christianity through a series of letters between them. Was Mr. Boyd Sr. an atheist? In his preface, Mr. Boyd claims: "Exceptionally intelligent, intensely skeptical, very strong-willed, and seventy years old–could a more *unlikely* candidate for conversion be found than my father?" Yes, a more unlikely candidate could certainly have been found. From the start of their letters, his father admits he believes in a supreme being. His father wasn't an atheist; he was simply a non-Christian theist. Once a person is willing to accept the supernatural, converting him to one's particular brand of supernaturalism isn't such a great feat. It was an achievement–I don't want to discount Mr. Boyd's proselytizing skills; and his father was indeed skeptical of Christianity. But Mr. Boyd did misrepresent his father as the "most unlikely candidate for conversion" to be had! I don't recommend anyone approach an atheist with that book in mind. You must first persuade the atheist that there is a god before you can even begin to convince him he had a son.

Is "god" meaningless?

Some atheists and agnostics will answer the question, "Do you believe in God?" with the statement, "Define god." What is god? God is different things to different people.

I watched a talk show once on the topic of god. One of the audience members stood to tell the host that she didn't believe in god. The host countered with, "Do you believe in love?" The woman answered, "Yes." "Then you believe in god," said the host. [*It was Oprah. Okay? Oprah. I couldn't get hold of the transcript and didn't want to get into any trouble. But it was Oprah.*] How odd. What is it to *believe in* love? The host never bothered to find out in what manner her audience member believed in love, what she meant by believing in it, or what she meant by love. She simply enlarged her circle enough so that the audience member fit in. Why? Because if everyone believes, it's okay for her to believe too!

What does it mean to say god is love? Love is an emotion–a feeling of empathy, adoration, caring, and compassion. It moves us to behave in various ways, not all attractive. Christians like to say that their god *is* love but that is meaningless. In order for their god to be love itself, love must first be considered not an emotion, but an existing force...an entity. Then god becomes some sort of energy-in-motion for good only. Not only does this alter the definition of the emotion love, but it reduces the concept of god to an impersonal force.

Yet, the Christian god is said to be a personal god, not an impersonal force—and I've never heard of anyone praying to love.

I must assume they mean that God is all-loving. How one can accept the concept of Hell and an all-loving deity seems an exercise in mental gymnastics [*And honestly, isn't it fun to watch them do their flips and spins on that subject?*]; but, that's beside the point. Yes, some people believe that god is, in fact, love itself. If you believe in love you believe in god. That is nonsensical. What is it to believe in love? How does one believe in it? What do you believe about it? How can you pray to love? How does a person worship it?

Some say god is energy. They tend to believe this energy is purposeful and can be used for good, or can be communed with. Some people say the universe is god which reduces the concept to complete nothingness by enlarging it to encompass everything. Why not just talk about the universe? Why bother renaming it, making it more than it is? [*I think it's because they believe that the universe thinks and acts and we're a part of it. Like ants to a colony. Freaky isn't it?*] Why do we have this need to anthropomorphize everything?

Gods are supernatural beings—superior to humans. The Christian god is supposed to be supreme in the universe—a being that supposedly *created* the universe. The term "god" is not meaningless to me, but the being it represents is unknowable and undefined. If there is a being or entity that created the universe and/or the world, we don't know anything about it—neither you nor I—none of us do.

A brief note on the capitalization of the word god: Throughout history, man has worshiped many gods with many names. God is a common noun, and therefore should not be capitalized in normal usage. The Christian god has different names, probably because it's a combination of several deities. He is called Jehovah and Yahweh; but, because they think he is the only one, Christians most often call him, simply, God. [*I know I'm an arrogant cuss, especially in this book, but this is truly the most arrogant thing ever—your god is the only one so he's just God. Take that pagans!*] I try to refrain from capitalizing the term unless I am referring specifically to the Christian god, called God. God as a common noun, idea, or concept, remains in lower case.

[*You can find more writings by Stephen F. Roberts at Freelinks here: freelink.wildlink.com. And while you're out there on the Tubes, take a look at C Michael Patton's essay titled, "Why I reject other Gods, an answer to Stephen F. Roberts." Oh, why bother? I'll just tell you about it. Patton says that it's totally different with the Christian God. For one thing, those other gods weren't really gods, while Christians worship the god, you know...the one who created the universe. Those other gods were worshiped in a more faddish way. I mean, come on, people didn't really think Caesar was a god, right? Those other gods were "founded on social convention not philosophical, rational, and historic necessity as is the case with Christianity. Christianity exists not because of rural pragmatism, but because of historic events." And there you have it, folks. We reject those other gods because they aren't real like ours. Ours is real. Really real. Honest. Look, have some of what we like to call...evidence... bwahahaha.*]

[**The major curse words were going to come into it eventually. It couldn't be helped.*]

Chapter Two

My Life

> My father says that almost the whole world is asleep—everybody you know—everybody you see—everybody you talk to. He says that only a few people are awake and they live in a state of constant, total amazement.
>
> —Patricia Graynamore,
> *Joe Versus the Volcano**

I am an atheist. [*Uh, yeah. I think they figured that out already.*] I don't believe that gods exist. I also don't believe there is a supernatural realm. I didn't realize I was an atheist until I was in my mid-thirties. Up until that time I thought I was pretty much like everyone else I knew. I believed in god; I talked about god. But there was always the knowledge, deep down, that I was different. One day, that knowledge came to the fore. [*Came to the fore? So pretentious.*]

It started with a little click in my brain [*No,*

seriously. I clicked. Cue: Saliva, "Click Click Boom."] that told me I was tired of being something I was not. All my life I've claimed to be a deep and introspective person, probably because it sounded so wonderful. But while I was thoughtful, as in always daydreaming, I was rarely thoughtful, as in *thinking*. One day, with a little click in my head, I started thinking...and discovered myself.

We humans like to describe ourselves as thinking beings–that's what separates us from the animals, we claim. I have come to accept that most humans spend very little time really thinking; conscious, purposeful thinking isn't something most of us are accustomed to doing. What we do, more often, is go along with the crowd, believing what we're told; we get through life more than truly living it.

Several years ago, I was sitting on a bench at my children's preschool having a conversation with the mother of my oldest son's classmate. She was (and is) a friendly, outgoing woman with whom I enjoyed conversation. While usually in a fairly good mood, that morning she said she was depressed. I can't remember exactly what her reasons were, but I do recall her saying that she tried and tried to understand God's will for her life but couldn't–she felt lost and confused.

When she said that, I started in with my usual manner of responding to godly talk among acquaintances. First, I reworked *their* version of god into *my* version of god, which at that time was the "god is love" or "god is the energy back of all creation" idea. After translating god, I'd come up with my response such as "love guides us gently" or "we must use the energy in a positive way and let all negativity fall by the wayside in order to feel fulfilled." Then I'd have to rephrase that response into terms that my acquaintance would understand before actually putting the words in my mouth. For instance, I would say, "God is speaking to you through your heart and you need to put away all your anxieties to hear him." I believe I did that when my friend expressed her frustration with learning God's will on that morning so many years ago; but distinctly I remember that after I responded, I stopped listening to her.

Something had happened in my mind and in my emotional self. Something clicked. I can still recall the feeling I had that my face had frozen, that my eyes had clouded–I wasn't looking at my friend anymore. I was somewhere else. I was thinking, as if realizing it for the first time, "I don't believe in god the way she does."

I found that I didn't want to interpret anymore. I was tired of trying to fit my ideas about deity into the typical Biblical Christian idea of deity. Not only did I feel I couldn't filter my beliefs through the sieve of traditional Christianity anymore, I felt I wasn't completely sure of what I believed at all. I drove home from the preschool that day asking myself if I really believed that there was an energy that was love. Did I really believe that there was a particular force that directs the universe? In one of the first completely honest moments of my life, I accepted that I did not believe those things.

For a few days after that, I examined the rest of my beliefs. At that time I subscribed, casually, to what was called Science of Mind originated by Ernest Holmes, who wrote the book with that title. In the Science of Mind that I knew, there was a purposeful energy that could be used in our lives. That energy was love. If you filled your mind with thoughts of love, prosperity, peace, and joy, those things would come into your life. If you filled your mind with negativity, hate, envy, and greed, only bad things would come to you.

I believed that reincarnation was probable and that creatures evolved progressively with each life to a degree dependent on what was learned in that lifetime. You could not, therefore, be reborn as an animal because animals are not as consciously aware—as evolved in the spiritual sense—as humans. We begin our human period as rather dumb and progress toward total awareness of god. Of course, in that belief, humans are the top of the line and whatever else comes beyond that is supernatural.

I believed there were levels of awareness and that people who believed in the traditional religions such as Biblical Christianity were simply not as evolved as those of us who'd reached a higher level of awareness. Those who were below you on this spiritual grading scale were not to be looked down on though, because we were "all on the same path." However, I never believed in the idea that all paths lead to god, but just travel different routes; I always believed that Christianity and other salvation religions were not the correct path, but that they were the best that *that level* of spirituality could do in that particular lifetime.

I believed that the earth was created as a place for our spirits to be born and reborn to learn and to play. I believed that "what you think upon grows." And I believed that there was a benevolent nature to the universe.

I no longer believe any of those things. From that moment of realization that I didn't believe anything I thought I did, I found myself on a journey of learning and understanding that, while some spots were difficult and upsetting, was very much like rolling uphill toward self-enlightenment–I couldn't stop the progress, I couldn't stop the momentum, and I certainly couldn't go back to where I'd been. I once thought of the journey as much like peeling away the layers of an onion until my spirit was free to rise out of the empty center...and the tears along the way were the result of the fumes of the useless, bothersome beliefs that had hindered my life up until each significant layer had been shed. Once I started thinking about it like that, the tears weren't so important anymore. [*I'm tearing up right now. That was just so beautiful. Sniff.*]

My parents were without religion, but spiritual. [*Operative word: were.*] They were ships afloat on a sea of hope and imagination–anything could be true if you believed it. In my house, growing up, religion in the traditional sense was a nonissue. Jesus was presumed to have been an extraordinary man–a great teacher. We were all the children of god–all had the capability of being as enlightened as Jesus. Jesus told us that the kingdom of god was within, which clearly meant within each of us– we *are* god, each one of us, like pieces of a pie. God equaled Mind. Because of this, if we could only channel the power of Mind through ourselves, anything was possible (as in: with god, all things are possible).

I remember once my father saying that one day humans would be able to fly...like birds! Because we had it in our minds to fly, built craft to make flying possible, one day, through the power of Mind, we would fly as birds. It seems ridiculous to me now, but back then, I could believe it.

My mother's family was Southern Baptist and her experiences with Christianity in childhood were less than ideal which no doubt helped her to release it and accept New Age philosophies. She didn't abhor traditional religion, however, and for a time when I was about eight years old, she took me to the local Episcopalian church. [*Ooh, I'll have to remember to tell the story of the Episcopalian church mouse in my memoir! Suffice it to say I called the minister dude a murderer.*] I was also allowed to visit the churches of my friends.

When I look back on my life, my most honest moments were shrouded in shame. When I stood up and spoke out, I was shamed. When I behaved in the way I honestly wanted to, I was shamed. Is honesty so shameful? Perhaps. Honesty–total, conscious honesty–can get you into trouble. People don't really want you to be honest. They want you to go along with them, with their crowd. You *must* have a crowd. It's best if you are in the *right* crowd, but if you're in another crowd, one that's just a little bit different, that's okay. Even if you're in a crowd that's very different...it's still pretty much okay. Your crowd might be looked down upon by another crowd and vice versa...but at least you are in a crowd. You have to be in some crowd. If you're not, you're *the fringe*. [*Cue: Red Rider, "Lunatic Fringe."*] The fringe is dangerous– the fringe thinks, asks, acts. The fringe is honest.

I wasn't in the fringe–I hadn't yet begun to think for myself. I knew I was different, but not so different as to be incompatible with the majority. I felt I was part of a generation at least. We all moved together through elementary, junior high, and high school, the same familiar faces year after year. I hovered on the outskirts of various cliques pretending to fit in; I created relationships out of acquaintances. Looking back, I can see that my problem was not that I was odd so much as that I didn't know who I was. No one had taught me that all-important life skill: know thyself. [*Really? I actually wrote that? Cue: Gilligan, on Gilligan's Island, as Hamlet singing, "To be or not to be."*]

At some point as a pre-teen, my parents got involved in the religion I mentioned earlier called Science of Mind. Just like any other religion, Science of Mind had some good and some bad in it. What I got out of Science of Mind is simply that the mind controls the being. If you fill your mind with hateful, sad, miserable, bad thoughts, hateful, sad, miserable, bad things will come into your life. What you think on grows. It worked for me as a pre-teen and teenager, when I used it. It helped me to find some happiness, some success, some friendship, but I couldn't use it consistently be-cause I was human and couldn't live in a constant state of positive thought. Maybe it wasn't that I was human so much as that I wasn't stupid. I mean, to a point I can agree with the theory that when you hold onto happy thoughts you will be a happier person but no amount of positive thinking is going to save you if a drunk driver careens your way–positive thinking on your part cannot and does not alter events in your favor–it is not a shield. [*Hm. I thought I used the example of a piano falling out a window. No, I mean, you know how they lift pianos into upper level apartments with pulleys? Like that. It's a much better image than the drunk driver.*]

By about age twelve, I began to succumb to what I can only describe as extreme PMS. My hormones were in charge, not me. I vacillated between dark, bleak depression, mild weepiness, melancholy, and uncontrollable joy. No, I wasn't manic-depressive–I was going through puberty. I had little control of my emotions, my mind, my body–I was losing it. I managed to muddle through, as most teenagers do but I never turned toward religion and Jesus, as many did.

My mother eventually left the Science of Mind Church, which is nowadays called the Church of Religious Science, over an ideological conflict. Apparently, the leaders of her study group were adamant that any negative thought, no matter how fleeting, would bring a bad result into your life and that you must purge your mind of all negativity. My mother believed that positive thoughts over-came negative thoughts, so you could undo any negativity before it manifested itself in your life. This wasn't party-line, I guess. My mother couldn't accept that positive thinking would become a strict dogma one must adhere to; she also had a degree in psychology and probably knew the limits of the human animal's mind much better than the old ladies in her study group.

In my early teen years, my mother began attending a local Unity church. It was at Unity that I learned the idea of god as the pie and people as individual slices. That is where I was given a copy of a book called *The Big Me and the Little Me*. It was a Cinderella story in which Cinderella learns that the Big Me is the giving, loving part of herself and the Little Me is the part that people use when they are selfish and stingy...like her stepsisters. The Big Me got the prince and the castle. Believe it or not, that book greatly impacted me and taught me to be more positive. I was still an emotional wreck until puberty was under control [*I think I meant until I was thirty.*] but I began to have moments of positive joy and enthusiasm that only grew and grew.

In my early years, belief was not an issue. As an adult, Christianity and faith surrounded me, suffocated me, oppressed me—it was everywhere I looked. I heard about it from everyone I met. I read about it every time I opened the newspaper. But as a youth, it was rarely mentioned. It hardly existed.

I lived on a busy through street, with a huge neighborhood behind me. I played with a group of kids mostly of my older brother's age. One family was Southern Baptist and went to the First Baptist Church in town. I went with them once to see their youngest daughter baptized. I remember she told me that each person had crowns in Heaven—one crown for every good deed. I don't remember believing anything she said but I don't remember not believing it either. Her vision of god, it seemed, was a man in a white robe with a white beard. He sat in a throne in Heaven...a king.

I do remember one discussion in particular about death. We all argued about whether or not a person could come back from the dead and tell about it. There were stories, just as there are now, of near-death experiences. My brother and I, and perhaps some others, were of the mind that if you came back to life, you weren't dead to begin with. The others argued that if your heart stops beating for a certain length of time, you're dead. Then, if you're revived, you "came back from the dead."

I don't remember how or if the argument was resolved but it did nothing to interfere with the friendships enjoyed by the entire group. We could disagree without problem and the fact that only those Southern Baptists went to church didn't seem to matter. It was with at least one of those Southern Baptists that we all sat around while one of us read from *The Happy Hooker*. Childhood is different. Childhood is cleaner, more honest, less influenced by the fears that enshroud adulthood.

I never really broached the subject of god, religion, or Christianity seriously as a child. Later, in high school, I had a few boyfriends whose parents were Christian, but they were open to honest and curious dialogue. One of my more steady boyfriends and I used to get drunk and ponder the big questions of life, the universe, and existence. What was there before there was any-thing? What is *nothing*? Isn't *nothing* something? That's not easy to think on when you're drunk–it's hard enough to think on when you're sober.

One of my favorite acquaintances in high school was Sally (not her real name, of course). Sally was the friendliest girl I have ever known. She always had a smile on her face and never said a bad word to or about anyone–the girl was a saint. But alas, she succumbed. She and I attended a play performed by the youth group of a church in town. The plot was pretty silly, looking back on it, but it wasn't badly acted. It took place on an airplane where there was some discussion about

Christ and God and all that. Someone got saved and then the plane crashed. It wasn't enough to show the saved being swept up into the arms of God with a lovely blue light embracing them, they had to go on with the damned being burned by fire for all eternity (thank goodness the play didn't last that long) with a red light blazing down on them.

When the damned were getting their just deserts, Sally's hand slipped into mine and squeezed it tight. I was embarrassed for her; I was shamed for her, that she allowed such maudlin nonsense to stir her. It was pure fiction, in my opinion. Then the worst came. The lights went up and the sheep were called to the altar to be saved. It was all so contrived! First they scared you with the disease and then voila, here's the cure! But Sally got up and got her salvation. She was never quite the same again. While she was still the sweetest girl I knew, there were just the tiniest hints of both fear and elitism in her attitude after that. She had found the Truth and she really wished that everyone else would too.

The big church in town was Park Avenue Baptist. Everyone who was anyone, and not Catholic, went to Park Avenue Baptist. They had what they called Joy Explosions on Wednesday nights for the teenagers. I think they were a combination of parties and prayer meetings, on a teenage level. Sally went to them often. She became nervous—she was always concerned with God's will and what God wanted. One day, I came upon her crying in the band room. She'd just come from P.E. where God had told her to announce to all the kids waiting for the bell to ring that the Joy Explosion was that night and they were all welcome to attend. But she didn't do it. She was too afraid to speak up and God would punish her for that, she was sure.

My Science of Mind and Unity teaching came into play and I told her that god would not punish her for being human or for being afraid. God urges us to do right but god is gentle and fair and loving. God forgives. I think I made her feel better...but honestly, I don't remember.

I was lucky enough to belong to a sorority in school. [*I'm not sure lucky is the right word.*] I tried to fit in there as best as I could. It turned out to be a Christian club, something I didn't know when I applied for membership (not that it would have made any difference to me). We were supposed to go together to a different local church each month. One of the members was the daughter of a minister and one month we visited her church—I think it was Methodist. At the service we attended, her father the minister told us quite frankly that it wasn't enough for us to be saved and Christian to get into Heaven; if we didn't also go out and claim at least one soul for Christ ourselves, we got Hell! I recall being appalled at such a horrific idea and looking down the row at the other girls as if to say, "Did I hear that right?" But nobody else seemed to notice or care.

These brushes with fundamentalism were rare. For the most part, religion meant nothing to me. I did, however, call myself a Christian. Everyone I knew was Christian and they seemed little different from me, if at all. I included myself in that religious bracket without really thinking about what it meant.

That is how my religious life progressed from

then until a few years ago. Whenever god was mentioned, I translated. I took the way they meant god and changed it into what I meant by god. God wasn't a *being*. God *was* being. God wasn't a king, a ruler, a despot who controls, orders, and punishes. God was love. God was energy. God was existence itself. I spoke about god to people from my beliefs but always careful to phrase my words so that they would understand them from within their beliefs. [*I make it sound like I did this as a favor to people, or because I was kind and compassionate, when it was really about fitting in and not being laughed at.*] At first it was easy. I could comprehend little difference between god as a being and god as *Being*. But as I grew and matured, as my life changed, so did my ability to and my willingness to translate from their beliefs into mine and back again.

Then that something clicked and I started rolling uphill, shedding those layers of belief until I reached the core of total, pure honesty that had only occasionally bubbled to the surface in my life up to then. The journey was not without its bumps and pains, but overall, it was exhilarating and educational beyond belief—no pun intended, of course. [*Ah ha. So funny.*]

The first thing I did, after realizing that I didn't believe in the same things that others seemed to, was to look around me at the religious. They were all Christian. Christianity was everywhere—on every corner, down every street, on the backs of cars, in the ads in the telephone book—everywhere people proclaimed their belief in Christianity. I figured it must have some merit. I imagined that what was lacking was my knowledge of the Bible.

Christians read it, no doubt, and not only understood it, but believed it. I had never read it. I did experience a few months in my early young adult years when I read parts of the New Testament and carried the Bible around like a child carries a doll, for comfort. I called myself Christian then as I had done all my life, but with more understanding of what it meant to be one; I prayed fervently [*I said fervently again!*] for Christ to save me. Nothing happened; nothing changed in me. I eventually felt silly and stopped.

Now I read the Bible with keen interest. What was it about this book that caused people to believe in the god told of in it? In the Bible, I thought, I would find the answer–but I didn't. As I read the book, several things became apparent to me. First, it was obviously an ancient history– inaccurate and biased–and contained a great amount of mythology. Second, the god portrayed in the book was not as he was presented to me throughout my life. He was neither good nor loving, nor kind, just, forgiving, or merciful. Nothing about him resembled the god I thought of as the pinnacle of the Christian faith. I read the entire Old Testament and didn't find a good god anywhere in it.

Reading the Old Testament convinced me that I was an atheist, at least with regard to anthro- pomorphized gods such as Yahweh. It was in reading that book that I understood what humans do–they create gods and religions and phil- osophies to ease their fears of the unknown, to explain what they don't understand, to make themselves seem special and elite, and to set themselves apart from other tribes and cultures. I decided then that I wanted no part of any of that. I wanted only truth where I could find it. I would not believe something when there was no evidence backing it up. I didn't realize then how long it would take to achieve such a goal. I thought it would happen instantly–in a flash, I would rid myself of erroneous beliefs. Instead, they had to be shed like layers, one after the other over a period of time.

I stopped calling myself a Christian and became a Christian atheist. Seriously. I held onto the Christian label because to disown it was a frightening prospect–not that I understood that consciously at the time. Certainly there could be nothing wrong with following such a great man as Jesus–a man so revered that millions of people thought he was no less than a god! But I hadn't yet finished the Bible–I still had the New Testament to read.

The New Testament was unfortunately jaded by the Old. I found nothing in it but a few snippets of kind words from a man who seemed to me to be rather arrogant and rude. I was disappointed to find that, again, I'd been lied to. Jesus wasn't the great spiritual leader I'd been told he was. While he did say some beautiful and noble things, he also said some ugly and cruel things. He didn't behave the way a loving teacher would–he was no Socrates.

I realized then that I couldn't call myself Christian anymore. I was a spiritual atheist because, though I didn't believe in the traditional idea of gods, I still believed that there could be something else, something greater than we are, and something more to life after our physical bodies die.

Everyone around me believed in something–reincarnation, angels, a power greater than we are, and most importantly, some kind of eternal life. Though I could feel my beliefs slipping away, I wasn't ready to admit it; thinking consciously was something I learned gradually.

I closed the book that first summer of my unbelief without finding Christianity to be of any merit. I began to ask myself then, why do Christians believe what they do? Why do they see the Bible as something worthy of study? I felt a bit isolated and unsure of myself. I knew I didn't believe there was any spiritual truth behind the Bible but I wasn't sure that there wasn't something else to consider about Christianity.

I was on America Online at the time [*Is that still around?*] and was surprised and fascinated to find an atheist forum. It was wonderful to find that I wasn't alone, but I still had a need to understand why so many other people did believe in God. In the atheist forum, Christians infested the woodwork, darting out to damn us to Hell (most often in all capital letters) or ridicule our lack of understanding, only to scurry back into hiding–they never stayed around to hear our rebuttals.

I learned that there were other forums on the Internet where Christians actually engaged in debate with atheists and I was excited to find them and join in the arguing. For a year or two, I debated and found links to other sites and was recommended books on both atheism and Christian apologetics. A new world was opened up to me where I could begin to understand on what grounds Christians maintain their faith and on what grounds atheists reject it.

The first book I read on nonbelief was Dan Barker's *Losing Faith in Faith*. Next I read George Smith's *Atheism: The Case Against God*. Through these and many other books, I was finally guided toward rationalism and to an understanding of my own fears and bouts of illogic. Not everyone is born to think critically, that much is clear. I had to teach myself proper skepticism–how do I question, what do I question, what is logical, what is evidence? In the end, I found myself finally free of superstitious thinking and was proud to consider myself a rationalist.

I went through a pattern of phases with atheism–a generalized path that many other atheists may follow upon the realization of their nonbelief. First I experienced a period of confusion and sorting out of what exactly I believed or didn't believe. That was followed by a time of euphoria when a freedom overwhelmed me. This feeling wasn't like freedom from bondage–I wasn't celebrating the casting off of religion because I'd never really had it to begin with. It was a feeling of knowing myself, of the ability to be totally honest about who I was, at least with myself at first and then later, with others as well. This was, unfortunately, followed by a feeling of despair and loneliness when I found there weren't many others around like me. That was easy to overcome with the Internet sources available to me. A period of feeling angry and oppressed followed when I realized that Christians don't take too well to atheism. Eventually, I came out of it mellowed and settled happily into nonbelief. [*Oh, please. I was still a grumpy fart for a long, long time.*]

I imagine that a second or third generation

atheist wouldn't experience these problems. I can't say my parents are atheists; I can only say they aren't Christians. I wasn't indoctrinated with any theology as a child. Even when I believed in certain ideas, there was always the possibility in the back of my mind that I was wrong. I feel that I was most likely an atheist all along, but simply never had the opportunity or the gumption to address my assumptive beliefs sincerely until I gained enough self-esteem to handle it. I wasn't fully awake to myself and who I was. So, while I consider myself to have been an atheist all my life, it wasn't something I realized until adulthood. That reali-zation caused me to be thrown into a pattern of withdrawal. For Christians who find themselves atheists, the pattern may be even more traumatic as an entire social group must be left behind or at least dealt with and years of indoctrination must be overcome.

It must be said that not all atheists make it through all the stages. I've met a couple who are still quite angry about their situations; I don't blame them. I've questioned many atheists. Some have expressed the same feelings I experienced but many others said they had no problem at all in realizing atheism; it was a natural step for them.

I believe it is a matter of self-esteem that determines how easily or difficult a person's transition will be. I lacked self-esteem and came to my realization of atheism as a part of gaining it. The two growth areas in my life were either entwined or parallel. As I became happier and more content in life and with my own being—as I became a friend to myself, trusted myself—I was able to question myself about the erroneous beliefs

I maintained without reason.

Because of earlier bouts with low self-esteem, self-doubt crept in and caused this pattern of problems upon realizing atheism. If I had been a stronger person, I wouldn't have had the problems I had. But then, if I'd been a stronger person, I would have known all along I was atheist.

Attributing the atheist label to oneself can be a bit traumatic, especially for the weak-hearted, like me. It's no wonder to me why so few actually do it. There must be thousands of people out there calling themselves agnostic, Humanist, rationalist, deist, pantheist, pagan, etc. who are, in actuality and when you get down to the core of their philosophies, atheists. But some would rather call themselves liberal Christians than atheists!

The term atheist represents, for a very vocal minority in this country, immorality, at best and at worst, Satanism (although I am referring to Satanism as defined by Biblical Christians). Atheism is despised by fundamentalist and conservative Christians. They fear it, I suppose. Looking at atheism is, after all, looking at the possibility that they are wrong. They must demonize atheism, because if they allow it some acceptance, it is liable to interfere with their faith. Without their faith they would be lost, hopeless, desperate, and according to those I've spoken with, immoral. It appears that they project their own fears onto those whose ideas frighten them. Because they would feel lost, hopeless, desperate, and immoral without their beliefs, they assume that those who don't believe are, in fact, lost, desperate, hopeless, and immoral.

It is, to many Christians, inconceivable that

people can be happy, moral, and well-adjusted without belief in deity. They seem to fear a society and a universe without the thought of some controlling force behind it. Everything must be directed by a power greater than they are because without that, they are merely tiny, insignificant creatures in a vast and impossible-to-understand universe. That frightens them—it scares them so much they are unwilling to even acknowledge the possibility that such a control doesn't exist. I can, honestly, understand that fear. It is perfectly natural as a human to fear the vast unknown, this world and universe that are so much larger than we are...and that feeling that we are on our own. The thought of such fear, in fact, helps us to understand why people created deity to begin with.

Not all Christians think atheists are unhappy and immoral. I've spoken with many who know that atheists are capable of happiness and morality just as Christians are. They may believe, though, that the happiness they have as Christians is deeper, more profound, and that their acts of morality glorify and please their god while the nonbeliever's conscience is just a happenstance of having been created with an infused sense of morality...by their god, of course.

Calling oneself atheist may be setting oneself up for hatred, intolerance, demonization, mis-understanding, and no small number of aston-ished looks from most of Christian society. Some-times this isn't a problem. For the natural non-conformist, it's a normal day but for the average American, like me, it can be a difficult experience.

I always wanted to be liked. I wanted, more

than anything as a youth, to be with the *in* group, the popular kids, the kids who socialized easily. They knew how to deal with people. I either never learned that, or I wasn't built that way. I spent my young adulthood and early married life trying to find a niche, a crowd to be *in*. When I peeled back the layers of myself to find the person at the center, I was at the same time proud and horrified at my discovery. Here I was, at the source of my self-ness, the real me. How many people traveled the road I did to find out who they really are? How many people were awake enough to do it? It was exhilarating, freeing, wondrous, and awesome. Suddenly the world was a magical place again, the universe open to all my questions.

Then it hit me—I'm the shunned. I'm the hated. [*Cue: Korn, "Freak on a Leash."*] One of my country's presidents (one I voted for!) said he didn't even consider me a citizen. [*When campaigning for president, George Bush, Sr., during a press conference, said: "No, I don't know that atheists should be considered as citizens, nor should they be considered patriots. This is one nation under God." Don't believe me? Google it.*]

I'm the one they talk about in the Bible as wicked and always lumped in with those who visit prostitutes for some reason. Damn, I thought, here I am again, and this time I'm farther toward the outer rim of society than ever! In school I could at least talk to the in-group. Now I was suddenly Satan. What is a rational girl to do? [*Go all bitch on their asses!*]

My first goal was to learn why people believe that the Bible is anything more than historical fiction and why people believe that a man named

Jesus really lived and rose from the dead. I wanted to understand why people seem religious by nature. When I learned enough to satisfy myself that Jesus probably never existed, I began a search to understand how a myth became thought of as historical fact. By what process did the story of Jesus, whether based on a real human or not, begin to be believed as if it were a historical event? When I finally had the answer to that question, Christianity began to make sense to me.

I've learned that there is no such thing as a true Christian or true Christianity. I've learned that religion fulfills certain basic human desires. Christians in particular and religious people in general have a different way of looking at the world than rationalists. Jesus was most likely a Jewish version of the popular pagan gods of that time. Christianity in its original form was quite pagan and mystical. Most important to me, I learned why I don't believe in, or even like, the Christian religion of today.

I am not a Satanist—I do not believe Satan exists. There are rational grounds for dismissing Christianity and a person needn't be in denial to do so. In order for me to freely accept others and their beliefs and allow that I have no power over what they believe, they must concede the same for me. [*Huh? I don't think I meant that. I can do it without the return favor.*] Rationalists and religionists can coexist peacefully without having to belittle or demonize one another. [*No. I don't think they can.*] The most important thing lacking in the relationship between the two is education. I have educated myself to a great extent about Christianity, its history, its philosophies, its dogma, and its adherents. This is my attempt to educate others, a little, about atheism. [*Right. Because religious people have just been waiting all this time for someone to teach them about atheism.*]

[*Joe Versus the Volcano
*Amblin Entertainment/Warner Brothers, 1990
Excellent film with Tom Hanks and Meg Ryan
(Cue: Eric Burdon, "Sixteen Tons.")*]

Chapter Three

You Don't Say?

What do Christians think of atheism?
I've talked with many Christians, read their debates and arguments with others, shared letters with them via email and while I can't say that I know how every Christian thinks, I can offer you a sampling of what I have come to understand from the Christian teachers I've had the pleasure of interacting with.

[*Ugh. First, every single Christian who approached me acted as if he was the wise teacher imparting his vast and irrefutable "knowledge" to this lowly, ignorant atheist. Second, it was not a pleasurable experience. I was insulted; comments about what an awful mother I must be were often made; insinuations about my emotional and mental health were tossed around; assumptions were made about my life experiences and what bad things must have happened to turn me away from their god and their religion; I was told many times that I simply wanted to live an indecent, licentious life and that's why I needed their help. I think it was grand of me to toss them a bone here, but now I take it back. What I should have said was, "Here's what I learned from having to deal with Christians."]*

"There aren't any atheists"

Some Christians don't believe there are any real atheists. They say that atheists know, deep down, that there is a god. God, they say, is evident in all creation. They quote Paul in Romans 1:18-23, which says,

> The wrath of God is indeed being revealed from Heaven against every impiety and wickedness of those who suppress the truth by their wickedness. For what can be known about God is evident to them because God made it evident to them. Ever since the creation of the world, his invisible attributes of eternal power and divinity have been able to be understood and perceived in what he has made. As a result, they have no excuse; for although they knew God they did not accord him glory as God or give him thanks. Instead, they became vain in their reasoning, and their senseless minds were darkened. While claiming to be wise, they became fools and exchanged the glory of the immortal God for the likeness of an image of mortal man or of birds or of four-legged animals or of snakes.

Obviously, many people very early on didn't believe in the Christian message and Paul felt it necessary to defend his faith. According to Paul, everything that we need to know to know God exists has been made evident to us and we suppress this truth because of our wickedness. While the verses are specific to paganism, I can see how they can be applied to nonbelief as well. One might question in what manner the wrath of God is being revealed against the wickedness of us nonbelievers—I haven't noticed anything. One might also question the worship of the mortal man Jesus in light of Paul's words. Most importantly, one should recognize that all the writings of Paul and others defending their religious views are propaganda for the faith—men often make false accusations regarding the "enemy" to bolster their own positions.

Christians say atheists know as well as they do that God exists; we just deny him because we're evil. This, as you can guess, is not a very good way to approach an atheist. The odd thing is that once an atheist is offered this rather cruel opinion and dares to exhibit anger, the Christian is likely to point the finger at him and cry, "Aha! You're angry at God!" [*Or they'll say atheists are just angry people.*]

"Atheists are angry at God"

The "angry at God" accusation usually takes the form of "something bad must have happened to you to cause you to turn away from God." Anything unfavorable that may have befallen the atheist [*Befallen? Really?*] is brought up as a possibility for the poor soul's rash decision to turn from God: the loss of a parent, child, or loved one; poverty or loss of income; legal problems; poor health, or disease. It has even been suggested that because God does not answer my prayers in the manner I would wish, I am angry at him.

No matter how the atheist protests that he simply doesn't believe and that he can't be angry with an entity that doesn't exist, the Christian continues to claim it is merely anger at God or at his own life circumstance that causes the atheist's disbelief. It can be quite maddening. [*I dare say, old chap, that's quite maddening. Where did I get these words?*]

"Atheists hate God"

Related to the "angry at God" accusation is the claim that the atheist hates God. The atheist, for whatever reason whether it be the actions of God as described in the Old Testament, the death of a loved one, evil on earth, or simply a hardened heart, has a deep hatred for the loving Christian god.

Why, beyond Paul's assumption, do you suppose that Christians must continue to claim that everyone knows God exists and anyone who denies it must be troubled? If I tried to put myself in Christian shoes, I might be able to understand. Christians believe in something...they believe it with all their hearts and minds; at least they try to. This god of theirs is not clearly evident; he is subtle, works in mysterious ways, they experience him subjectively. When someone comes along and claims they believe in something that isn't there...I can imagine it doesn't feel good to hear it. But, it is wrong to turn our own discomfort onto others by assuming we know what they think, feel, and believe better than they do.

Christians must accept that atheists simply *do not believe it.* [*Look at me making demands of the Christians. You must accept this! Or else...what?*] I have found that the more secure a Christian is in his own belief, the easier it is for him to accept simple nonbelief. People who are angry at or hate God can't be atheists because atheists don't believe a god exists.

"Atheism is a choice"

Some Christians claim that atheists are such because they want to be–they choose to disbelieve in God because they do not want to live their lives according to his will. We want to be our own gods, they say; we want no authority over our lives save our own. Many will go so far as to claim that we want to live immoral lives. The immorality is almost always sexual–at least, no one has yet accused me of wanting to steal or murder...just sleep around. Although, it has been argued that without a god, there is nothing to stop me from murdering...but we'll get to morality later.

Perhaps it is a desire for agreement from others that causes believers to say these things about nonbelievers. Or perhaps they believe that the only reason they themselves are moral people is because they worship a god; so anyone who doesn't couldn't possibly be good. Atheists are normal people just like Christians. We aren't thieves, murderers, or rapists, at least, no more often than are Christians comparatively speaking.

I've been accused of wanting to be my own god–that atheists worship themselves–but, gods are supernatural beings, so that would be absurd. However, the Christian attempts to get around this by claiming that anything that a person worships is like a god. But, "like a god" and "actually a god" are different. The point in the assertion is that atheists worship something other than God. "Everyone worships *something*," I've been told. This is mere projection; an insistence that because they worship something, everyone else does also. [*Just like liars say everybody lies and tax cheats say everybody cheats on their taxes.*] I do not worship *anything*. I do not bow down to any idol, being, emotion, physical object, or monetary unit and praise it. I don't worship myself; I don't live my life as a hedonist by any means. I am a normal person just like most Christians...except that they believe in a god and I do not.

The point also is to claim that atheists resist authority. Yet, atheists are law abiding citizens as often as are Christians. We recognize and respect the authorities we have elected to govern our society. Atheists simply don't believe that there is a god exercising authority over mankind. In fact, it's rather clear to us that there is not because God's supposed authority only comes into play after we die. Here on earth, so-called free will reigns. God, if he has authority, doesn't exercise it. He doesn't punish the thief, the murderer, or the rapist...we do. Apparently, he won't punish the criminal even after death if he repents and turns his life over to Jesus before he expires. Atheists don't want to resist a god's authority; we don't believe that a god exists.

We don't choose our beliefs. We either believe something or we don't. People can't choose to believe God exists any more than they can choose to believe he doesn't. Atheism isn't a choice; it's a label.

"Atheists deny God"

Christians often make the claim that atheists deny their god. They do this because it is a subtle reinforcement of their own beliefs. God is real, to the Christian, and anyone who claims otherwise is simply denying God and God's will. [*Like Holocaust deniers. Calling someone a denier is getting to be ridiculous. When believers can call me a Bigfoot denier, we've got problems. Skeptics and thinking people should stop calling people who won't listen to reason and accept valid evidence deniers. Just call them what they are: credulous.*]

A person can't deny someone who, or something that, doesn't exist. Gilligan, the one on the island, does not exist. My saying he does not exist is in no way denying Gilligan. My father, on the other hand, exists—if I claim he doesn't, I am denying my father. There is a difference. I can very much understand the Christian claim that atheists deny God because they believe it is a point of fact that their god exists. In order for them to understand atheists, however, and to be able to engage in discourse with them, Christians must accept that for the atheist, the question of a god's existence is not decided. It is debatable. [*Is it, really? I don't think so. There's no debate. No evidence means nothing to debate.*] There is no evidence beyond the subjective experiences, feelings, and desires of other humans to offer on the pro side. The atheist is well within the realm of logic in his rejection of the claim of a god's existence and the Christian should kindly respect the atheist's lack of belief. Atheists do not deny God because, until proven otherwise, God is a fictional character.

"Atheists worship Satan"

There's no arguing with a person who believes that atheists worship Satan. [*Believe me, I've tried.*] Naturally, the atheist response is that we can't worship an entity we don't believe exists; but the problem is that the Christian who believes we worship Satan will claim that we don't know we're doing it. Satan has blinded us to the truth of Christianity and to the truth of his own existence as well. [*Clever fellow.*] We worship him because he controls us and we do his bidding, presumably by turning innocent Christians into atheists or insulting God, without realizing we're doing it. We wouldn't be susceptible to Satan if we'd turn to God.

There's just no arguing with that. [*And yet, for some reason, atheists still do it.*] But, I suppose one might ask...how do you know? How do you know when Satan has control over you and when God does? How do you know that Christianity isn't Satan's ploy to lure Jews away from the truth of God? You don't.

If I can be blinded by Satan so much that I am convinced that I don't believe something I supposedly really do, or even that Satan himself doesn't exist, then how could God be more powerful than Satan? How can God allow Satan to blind people so? The Christian tells me that it is my sinful human state that allows it. In other words, I allow Satan to convince me that neither Satan nor

God exists. This seems silly to me. [*Seems silly? Seems? Hell, it's hilarious. Why am I so serious? This book is no fun at all.*] Why would God create me without the ability to resist Satan? Why would he allow Satan to continue with such a ruse?

If it is possible for Satan to so convince me of a lie, then it is equally possible that Satan is deceiving Christians. Maybe Satan has turned Christians away from the true nature of God. Maybe Satan inspired the Bible and not God. Or maybe, as is possible to believe after a good reading of the Old Testament, God is the bad guy and Satan is the good guy. [*I once asked about this possibility on a Christian-run debating email list and was nearly booted off. Blasphemy!*]

It really doesn't matter to me—I don't believe either of them exists.

"Atheists have no purpose in their lives"

Christians sometimes think that atheists have no purpose in their lives because they don't believe in an eternal life or in a creator. I can understand this difficulty. [*No I can't.*] To some, the thought that this life is all we have is frightening and sad but, it isn't for all of us. I can't explain why that is; perhaps it's genetic. [*That's right, it's your genes. Snark.*] I do know, however, that I am not bothered by a finite lifetime. In fact, I have considered the idea of eternal life and I am not thrilled by it. I don't find the idea at all appealing. I wouldn't mind living for a few thousand years I suppose, but not much beyond that. As Susan Ertz said, "Millions long for immortality who don't know what to do on a rainy Sunday afternoon." (From BrainyQuote.com) [*I don't know. I've got-*

ten myself addicted to jigsaw puzzles on my iPad and believe me, I can imagine an eternity doing that...as long as there is an endless supply of puzzles and I don't see why there shouldn't be.]

Christians have told me that their purpose is to glorify their god. Without that purpose, the human has no reason for being. Naturally an atheist wouldn't accept this claim. That kind of purpose is meaningless to me. I don't see any design for human life in general. We are a highly evolved species, [*I don't think I'd go with 'highly.'*] here, not because of the guiding hand of a deity-creator, but through the evolutionary processes that resulted in life on this planet. Life is, in essence, without purpose; but not having an ultimate reason for being doesn't affect the everyday lives of humans.

Atheists have purpose in their lives in the same way believers do. We find meaning in daily living, joy in our hobbies, satisfaction in doing a job well, or enjoyment of spending the money our jobs earn. Atheist parents experience the same joy in raising their children as Christians do. Our hearts fill with love and pride at our children's first smiles and steps in the same way theirs do. Purpose in life for atheists is very much the same as for Christians. The atheist even goes beyond that to a grander, larger purpose: that of our descendants. Atheists are part of those who work for a better tomorrow, a cleaner, healthier earth, for scientific and medical research to improve the lives of those who will come after us. But atheists don't go further than that to a supernatural, or eternal, purpose. We don't need one.

"Atheists are depressed and hopeless"

Ah, Nietzsche, the anvil you've laid on our backs! Nietzsche was a great philosopher and thinker; his works are still influential today. But yes, he went mad from syphilis and died insane. Whenever anyone wants to claim that atheists are depressed and bound to end up crazy, they point to poor Nietzsche as if he was the epitome of atheism. He is not. Why do you suppose they are always pointing to Nietzsche? Because he's an easy target. [*Does anyone point to Nietzsche anymore?*]

I've been told that atheists are depressed, hopeless people. I have found that to be untrue. I've been fortunate enough to meet many atheists, mostly on the Internet. [*Because meeting people on the Internet is no different than meeting them in real life.*] I was lucky enough to join hundreds at a convention of American Atheists in 2001. I joined thousands in the first Godless Americans March on Washington on November 2, 2002. I attended an awe-inspiring convention hosted by Atheist Alliance International in 2003 and will continue to enjoy such meetings in the future. [*No I won't. That's a big fat piece of self-delusion right there. But how could I have known I'd grow tired of the whole atheism thing?*] There are local groups of atheists in all communities, just as there are in mine. So far, all the atheists I've met have been normal, joyful, intelligent people. [*Now, that's just bullshit, right there. All of them? Hardly. Most of them, sure.*] Atheists suffer no more from depression than do Christians. [*That much is true.*]

I can understand the fear and sadness many

may feel when they contemplate the fact that this life must end, but I don't believe that Christians think about death every minute of the day. I don't think they think about it any more often than atheists...and that isn't very often. Why would the atheist be overpowered with sadness simply by occasionally considering the fact that he will cease to exist? It's a fact of life, it comes across my mind sometimes; I don't fear it–it doesn't overwhelm me.

Atheists grow and learn, just like Christians do. They forge bonds with families and friends, fall in love, marry, and raise–even homeschool–well-adjusted children. [*This is too rosy. Here, let me fix it: They get divorced, stalk their exes, visit their children in jail, shoot each other, and become alcoholics, too. We're no different, we believers and nons.*] They teach others, help others, and care for others, [*ignore beggars in the medians, break hearts, and cheat on their spouses*] just as much as Christians do. The only difference is that for some reason, maybe Christians have a deeper need to feel safe and secure than atheists. Or maybe atheists have that need also, but we are just able to accept what we perceive as our reality regardless of our feelings about it.

"Atheism is a religion"

Religion is a belief in or reverence for supernatural powers, like gods. The word also refers to particular systems of belief. Does that sound like atheism at all? Atheism is lack of belief in deity. Deities are supernatural entities. The atheist does not believe in such, have reverence for, nor worship such. Atheism is not a religion. It's a descripttion. [*You know what sucks? A few atheists now claim atheism is a religion. They do it because they think it will help in the fight for equality, or a secular government, or something. It's not helping.*]

The only definition that might be construed in such a way as to make atheism into a religion is that of religious passion–a cause, principle, or activity pursued with zeal. This still doesn't speak of atheism, however, because atheism isn't a cause, principle, or activity. Separation of church and state is a cause. A lack of belief in something is not a cause. "Do only good" could be a principle. Lack of belief in something is not. Speaking out against prayer in school is an activity–lack of belief in something is not.

The best you can say is that some atheists have philosophies of life that they pursue with a passion–call it religious, if you like. You could say that some atheists protest government intrusion into our lives with religious zeal. But you can't say that atheism itself is a religion. [*Well, apparently you can. But that doesn't make it one.*] Atheism does not speak to the individual atheist's beliefs, only to his lack of belief in deity.

Why try to call atheism a religion? Theists are always trying to make atheism into something it is not in order to attack it more easily. The assertion that atheism is a religion is an attempt to make atheism into a positive claim, instead of a lack of belief. That way, the Christian can try to force the atheist to support his supposed positive claim that there is no god. But atheism is not a religion, it is not a belief. There is no positive claim. It is, clearly, the theists who claim that something not evident exists and they have the burden of proof on their shoulders. Until they admit this fact, there will be problems between our two camps, because trying to make atheism into something it is not to avoid the fact that there is no proof or valid evidence to offer for god is disingenuous.

Even strong atheists who claim that god does not exist do not have the burden of proof. Claiming god does not exist is not a positive claim; it is a denial of the theists' positive claim. Look at it this way: I believe that *Gone with the Wind* is historyically factual and Scarlett O'Hara existed as a real person. You say: Scarlett O'Hara is a fictional character; she does not exist. Who has the burden of proof? I do. This is no different than the theist/atheist debate in which believers point to a book of stories, the Bible, claim it is historically factual and that Yahweh, a character in the stories, exists as a real entity. I say: Yahweh is a fictional character; he does not exist. Who has the burden of proof? Believers do.

I am not asking Christians to admit that atheism is correct, or that Christianity is wrong. I only ask that they accept atheism for what it is: simple nonbelief in gods–and allow that the atheist and the theist have different ideas about what constitutes evidence. [*Askin' ain't gettin'*.]

"Atheists are closed-minded"

This, above all, is the most perplexing comment hurled at me in discussions with Christians. What does it mean to be closed-minded? It sometimes seems as if, to the Christian, a closed-minded person is anyone who disagrees with his dogma. I admit that isn't always the case with every Christian I have come across. One told me that I am closed-minded to the spiritual realm, to subjective experience as evidence for deity. This is still not true of me. I have had subjective experiences that have encouraged me to explore ideas beyond the reality that rationalism makes evident to me but, because I have no evidence that these experiences are anything beyond normal human phenomena, I do not give them any special weight in determining truth and reality.

As to the spiritual realm, I don't have any experience of such a realm. I have never interpreted any feeling of mine as communication from gods, demons, angels, or any other supernatural being; as far as I know, no otherworldly creature has interacted with me or possessed my body or that of anyone I know. When I believed in a Universal Mind, I often felt that profound "oneness" with existence on contemplating love or being. It was a tingly, filled-up sensation—I felt I was more than just my physical body. Many people experience this and interpret it in various ways. For the Christian it is being filled with a holy spirit. For me, it was being at one with existence. As a rationalist, I see it as a deep awareness of my reality. I experience the same thing I did before...I merely interpret it differently now. I am not closed-minded to subjective experience. Simply show me some evidence linking it to a god or a supernatural realm and I'll make a judgment.

What is closed-minded? A person is closed-minded when he refuses to examine evidence, accept facts, or consider an opposing view. Closed-mindedness is adhering to a dogma—a set of principles that must be believed. I am not that person.

I am willing to look at any evidence presented to me of views that I do not hold. [*Yeah, well, not anymore. If you have evidence that fairies exist in your garden, don't bother me. You're crazy, that's all there is to it.*] I have no dogma to adhere to that would prevent me from accepting facts and evidence at odds with it.

But, I am a rationalist and I use my reason first to determine truth. Reason tells me there are no gods, the Christian god cannot exist, and that Christianity is not true. I must filter any evidence you offer me for your beliefs through my reason. I am more than willing to do so...I have done so. I am still atheist–not because of a refusal to believe (that would be closed-minded) but because the evidence is lacking.

I have been told that atheism is just as dogmatic as Christianity. How so? There is no dogma attached to atheism. Atheism says nothing about what one must believe...only a description of one thing a person does not believe. Many Christians say that the atheist dogma insists atheists believe in or accept the following: evolution, reason and science above subjective experience, anti-religion, pro-abortion, and the Democratic Party. This is absurd. I have met Republican atheists–I was one. There are atheists on both sides and in between on the abortion issue; some atheists are very into the supernatural, not all are against religion by any means and not all atheists are convinced of the facts of evolutionary theories.

Assuming anything about atheists beyond their lack of belief in deity tells them that you aren't listening to them, that you haven't thought about the label or worse, that you are trying to make them into something they're not in order to attack them.

So, what do atheists "believe?"

I once visited a Church of Religious Science where I thought I would meet people who could at least understand atheism. After the service I was approached by a big-haired woman who wanted to know what brought me to her church that day. I told her a bit about myself and mentioned that I was an atheist. The first words out of her mouth were "everyone believes in something."

What does that mean exactly? Isn't that just another feel-good phrase that helps people feel secure? [*Yes.*] Everyone believes in something, so it's all right if I believe this thing, strange as it may seem to others. I was put off by her remark. I felt she was making a claim that I could not be atheist ...it wasn't acceptable to her. I don't believe that everyone has to believe in something.

[*I never went back to that church. I was worried for a long time that the minister–if that's what they call them–might have thought it was because of his sermon. He came out...or he outed his kid or something. But I was just exploring. I think I was looking for a place to fit in, even though I was an atheist. I never found such a place. I might have gone back once or twice, but big-haired woman turned me off. Let's just say it was her fault.*]

Christians tell me that everyone has faith in something. First, we'd have to define faith. Faith means different things. Faith in common usage means confidence in something, someone, or some idea. Faith in the religious sense can mean belief that doesn't rest on logical proof or physical evidence, the virtue of having faith, or a religion itself.

With the first definition in mind, yes, I as an atheist do have faith in some things like my husband and family–that is a confidence and trust in them. But that's not what Christians mean when they tell me I have faith in things in the same way they have faith in their god. I'm not saying they don't experience feelings of confidence and trust in their god; certainly they do. I'm saying that they are trying to equate that kind of faith with the faith that is belief without evidence. I don't have any belief without evidence...in anything.

I've been told that I must have faith or I couldn't live. Every morning, I have faith the sun will rise. Every time I dare to cross the street I exercise my faith that I won't be hit by a car. I am told that this is faith, indeed, and it is the same as having faith that Jesus rose from the dead. I don't agree. [*It's not a matter of agreeing or not agreeing. It's a matter of definitions and twisting them. So the better thing to say is: that's bullshit.*]

I don't know that the sun will rise tomorrow but, it has risen every morning of my life. I understand how the Earth works, how it spins around giving me the illusion that the sun rises and sets. I understand that one day far in the future the sun will burn out and about eight minutes later, the earth will be in darkness. My experience has taught me that the sun will rise tomorrow. I don't have faith in the sun's rising. I don't believe it will rise. I expect it to, based on evidence and experience.

I don't know that I won't be hit by a car crossing the street. I don't have faith when I cross. I don't say a little prayer before stepping off the curb. I use my knowledge of cars and speed to determine the best course of action. My experience with heavy objects and in reading about people being hit by cars and the fear that arises when I consider such stories brings me caution. I don't use faith to cross the street. If I used faith, I'd just step off the curb whenever and have a go, but instead, I use my knowledge and experience to cross the street and do my best to avoid harm.

Faith, in the religious sense, is harmful. Faith (belief that doesn't rest on logical proof or material evidence) can be dangerous. Believing in something without evidence leaves a person open to belief in all sorts of nonsense; it takes scientific, logical evaluation out of the equation; it allows humanity to continue to deny its reality and its finite nature; it hinders progress.

Faith is often tied to dogma and dogma is dangerous. Dogma allows some people to control or hate masses of others. Dogma closes the mind to inquiry and doubt–the things from which creativity, science, and discovery arise.

Granted, there are those who have faith in gods, nature spirits, and afterlife who have no dogma ruling their beliefs, but I think that a society rooted in rationalism would be a far better one than a society based in a supernatural realm for which there is no evidence.

But, what do atheists believe? That depends on the atheist. Some atheists believe in life on other planets, that life on Earth was purposefully spawned from life on another world, that aliens came to this earth long ago and ancient man drew pictures of them on cave walls, that crop circles are supernaturally or alien made, that the stars and their placement at the time of your birth can determine your personality and events in your future, or that after we die we are reborn as a more enlightened individual, or as an animal. There are all sorts of people in this world who don't believe in gods, but believe in other equally indefensible propositions.

The atheists I am acquainted with, however, tend to be rationalists. [*What a load of crap. I'd say very few I knew at the time would qualify.*] Rationalism, as a philosophy, [*I wouldn't call it a philosophy. It's more of a first principle from which a philosophy could be established. I think.*] asserts that reason, not subjective experience, authority of any sort–man or book–or spiritual revelation, is the *primary* basis for knowledge and should be used to determine reality. Rationalism leads to atheism. All rationalists are atheists (Thomas Paine notwithstanding–he claimed that rationalism leads to deism, an opinion I dispute). [*I dispute it because it's wrong.*] But, and this is very important, all atheists are not rationalists. Rationalists don't *believe in* anything.

Belief versus knowledge

Christians have often asked me how I can believe in nothing. It has been difficult to pin down their exact meaning. It is not true that I believe in nothing. *Nothing* is not something one can believe in, because it is...*nothing*. It is not that I *believe in* nothing but that I don't *believe in* anything. There is a difference.

What does it mean to believe in something? As

with faith, the term belief has a variety of meanings. When we believe in a proposition, we hold it to be true. Does truth require belief? Solipsism aside, [*Solipswhat?*] we must accept that there are many things we can hold to be true and factual. That we exist and our reality is as we objectively perceive it can be taken as fact (in other words, we can reasonably assume we aren't dreaming this existence nor are we just brains in jars, or batteries in tubs of goo as in *The Matrix*).

There is truth to be had and we don't have to believe in it. We believe in those things for which we can't know the facts or the truth. We believe in things we don't know for certain. Dan Barker illustrated this point humorously in his book, *Losing Faith in Faith* (FFRF, Inc. 1992):

> Truth does not have to be believed. Scientists do not join hands every Sunday, singing, "Yes, gravity is real! I will have faith! I will be strong! I believe in my heart that what goes up, up, up must come down, down, down. Amen!" If they did, we would think they were pretty insecure about it.

Truth doesn't require belief. Nor does it require defense—it can stand on its own. [*If only that were true. Humans are so stupid, and so easily fooled.*] Rationalists look for factual, objective evidence. If none can be had, we remain without an answer; we do not create a belief in order to have one. When you know something to be true, you don't have to believe in it. And that is why people must believe in God—they don't know that he is there. If they knew it, belief and faith would be unnecessary. If

God could be objectively perceived, making it possible for his existence to be known, we would all know it. In that respect, the mere fact that the debate over God's existence occurs is evidence that *he* does not.

I don't believe in anything because I don't want to create a belief where I can't have a truth. I am more comfortable without an answer than with a belief that could be false.

Chapter Four

There's No Such Thing as a True Christian

No man ever believes that the Bible means what it says: He is always convinced that it says what he means.

–George Bernard Shaw

What is a Christian?

I've learned a great deal by talking to and debating with Christians. One thing I learned is that they are all very different. I have had the opportunity of discussing faith with a variety of believers in many different forums. I've found that there are all sorts of Christians. [*Did I just repeat myself?*] There are Christians who believe that Jesus was a prophet, not the one and only son of God. There are those who do not believe the Bible is the word of God but writings of fallible men. There are those who believe that the Bible, when interpreted correctly, is a symbolic story of salvation, and Jesus is our savior only in that he was the only human in history to come as close to awareness of the god in all of us. Then, there are those Christians who believe that every word in the Bible is utter Truth (with a capital T).

Most of those who believe that the Bible is true and inerrant have probably never read it. Those who have, and have studied Biblical inerrancy, have very interesting methods of interpreting it so that it is not, for them, contradictory or error-prone at all. They call on all sorts of techniques from literary style, comparative understanding of words, to determining the nature of Jesus and then interpreting everything he said according to what he must have meant or what the text must mean according to what they claim to know regarding Jesus' intentions. [*That was a mouthful. All it means is that they decide what Jesus must have meant, so the text couldn't mean what it says.*] With those sorts of Christians, for example, hate doesn't mean hate; it must mean "to love less."

I agree that not all of the problems that skeptics point out in the Bible are indeed unexplainable. A few of them are understandable when read without the determination to find fault with the text. A small number of them are understandable when interpreted with literary style, cultural differences, and symbolism taken into account; but that doesn't leave the Bible free of contradiction and error–it hardly lessens the problems with the book at all. There *are* contradictions in the Bible–blatant ones that can't be argued away.

Did God create man before the animals (Gen

2:18-20) or after (Gen 1:25, 26)? Did God order a census (2Sam 24:1) or did Satan (1Chron 21:1)? Is wisdom good (Prov 4:7; Prov 3:13) or bad (1Cor 1:19)? Is the god of the Bible peaceful (Rom 15:33)? A god of love (1John 4:8)? Or is he a god of war (Exod 15:3)? And vengeful (Nah 1:2)?

Christians run the gamut from the inerrancy group to the most liberal quasi-Christians you may find in a Unity Church. They all adhere to the teachings of Jesus as they understand them. They all interpret the meaning of the word Christ as they see fit. They all interpret the Bible correctly according to themselves and they all lead their lives according to their own personal choices in the matter.

There really isn't any such thing as a true Christian. Every Christian I've talked to, from the screaming (typing in all-caps) lunatic on line to the friendly neighborhood church-goer, told me he was a true Christian–the real thing. Usually this statement was made to separate the true from the false who, they assured me, was the type I had run into in the past.

The more liberal or progressive the Christian, the less likely he is to claim that other Christians are false; that nonbelievers, followers of other faiths, and other Christians will suffer in a place called Hell after this life on Earth; that God prescribes a strict moral code for our lives; that theories of evolution are false and that there is only one true path to salvation, that being through Jesus Christ. The more liberal the Christian, the more tolerant and loving he tends to be.

Needless to say, many of the Christians I refer to in this book are not, by any means, the most liberal. I have little problem with Universalists who believe that we are all children of the divine and that when this life is over, we will rejoin that divine parent. I don't accept their theology, nor their assumptions and presuppositions, or their methods of determining truth. But while their beliefs contradict science and rationalism, they are, for the most part, leaving me alone.

What is Christianity anyway? If all Christians believe that they are true Christians and they all believe that they have it right–the right inter-pretation of scripture, the right viewpoint, the right moral code, the right church–then how do we know which are true and which aren't? If they're all correct, how can they be so different?

Some Christians tell me that all the Christian denominations aren't that much different. They all agree on certain basic principles. Most of the traditional Protestant churches agree on certain ideas like, Jesus is the son of God and he was crucified and rose again. That's pretty much a must that you have to believe if you want to be a Christian, right? Not according to what I've learned. Some believe that Jesus is God. Some believe he was a man. Some say he was both God and a man. Some churches believe that there are three gods in one: Father, Son, and Holy Spirit. [*Oh my god, it's so fun to listen to them try to explain how it can be three and one at the same time! Sometimes I miss those days.*] Others believe there is only one god. Some venerate Mary; others consider that a desperate sin. Some believe that salvation is gained by faith which leads to works; others by faith alone; others by works alone; others by works *and* faith. And some believe that neither will get you eternal life as only God can bestow it by grace. The problem is that Christians can easily claim that all true Christians think and believe pretty much the same by simply asserting that anyone who doesn't believe that way, isn't a true Christian.

The best answer I ever received about what a true Christian is was on an email list created for the express purpose of asking and answering questions about Christianity. A true Christian, the moderator told me, is a person who believes that Jesus Christ is his personal savior. At the very least, a Christian must be a follower of the teachings of Jesus, whether man or god. This is what I understand to be the case but when cornered, when pinned down to explain point by point what these teachings of Jesus are, for some strange reason, Christians end the conversation.

What did Jesus teach?

I would have said, long ago, when I thought Jesus was a great moral teacher as he is still purported to be, that "love one another" was one of Jesus' basic teachings. But was it? Jesus taught in parables, stories that have a deeper meaning. In his stories we can glean the ideas of caring for the poor and sick, living humbly, and forgiving others. Jesus said to the rich man that to get into Heaven he must: not kill, not commit adultery, not steal, not bear false witness, honor your father and mother, and love your neighbor as yourself. (Matt 19:16-19) These are all very good things to strive for (unless you've been abused by your parents, of course). It is easy to see why people would concentrate on these good teachings that Jesus supposedly gave us.

If we look closer at the gospels, however, we read that not everything Jesus told us to do was good and not every sentiment spoken by him was what I would expect from a loving god, his son, or even a wise prophet. Consider the parable of the ten gold coins. This is a fine story about God, or Jesus, entrusting his followers with spiritual gifts or talents, to be used to better the world, themselves, or God's kingdom. The servant who buries his talent, however, is punished–his talent is taken from him. This makes sense. Make the most of your gifts; if you hide your talents, they are worthless and you may lose them. It's what Jesus said in the end of the story that bothers me. Speaking as the one who gave his servants coins (that would be God or Jesus), he said, "Now for those enemies of mine who did not want me as their king, bring them here and slay them before me." (Luke 19:27) What did he mean by that except that the master (God or Jesus) would have those who don't worship him killed? That doesn't sound like the actions of a loving god to me. It isn't the sort of language befitting a great teacher. Would a loving god who desires a relationship with its creation use threats of death to gain it?

In Jesus' explanation of the parable of the weeds among the wheat in Matthew 13, he claimed that there are evil ones, those who cause others to sin and sin themselves, children of the devil. At some point in the future, harvest time, the angels "will throw them into the fiery furnace, where there will be wailing and grinding of teeth." I have a hard time understanding this theory of a loving god versus an evil god. In the end, the loving god will triumph by torturing the evil god and his followers in a fiery furnace. Not only does it sound magical and fictional, it is so obviously divisive that it has caused many to claim self-righteous superiority over others by simply labeling their enemies as children of the devil...exactly the way many Christians deal with atheists. This doesn't sound like a god of love to me.

Jesus said that spreading the gospel of God would cause problems for his disciples. The word of the loving, benevolent father/god will cause a lot of people to get very mean with Christians. This could be explained by the actions of sinful Adam damning all of us and making us so unworthy that hearing the good news about God will make most of us really pissed off.

Jesus admitted that he was divisive when he said:

> Do not think that I have come to bring peace upon the earth. I have come to bring not peace but the sword. For I have come to set a man against his father, a daughter against her mother and a daughter-in-law against her mother-in-law; and one's enemies will be those of his household. (Matt. 10:34-36)

I guess that I would have to first agree that man is inherently evil, sinful, and unworthy before I could accept this as good news. Jesus was saying that people are going to hate you for what you say and do. But hey, that's God's word and it's going to cause a lot of problems because it's so good and loving and merciful and kind. Only if humans are so ensconced in evil could goodness, love, mercy, and kindness cause division in households. I don't accept that view of humanity. The fact that Jesus did causes me some pause. [*Causes me some pause? Cue: Pitbull, "Pause."*] But Jesus' words are understandable; when you preach condemnation for others, you ought to expect some flack.

In what way is it good that a person can't follow Jesus unless he hates his mother and father, wife and children, brothers and sisters, and even his own life (Luke 14:26), especially considering that would be going against one of the commandments Jesus claimed in Matthew 19? I have heard only one explanation for that particular problem—Jesus didn't mean hate; he meant "love less than me." I appreciate the need to make things better but, frankly, if Jesus didn't mean hate, why is the word hate in the verse? The only way out of this predicament is to say that Jesus would not have said such a thing so it can't possibly mean what it says.

If the Bible, the word of the one and only God, doesn't mean what it says, how can we take any of it as truth? If we can reinterpret different parts of it and claim that the words themselves can't be defined by normal, daily usage, we are left with a book that can't be trusted. We are left at the mercy of others to tell us what it means. We are left in the hands of fallible men.

[*I once had a lively discussion with a couple of Jehovah's Witness ladies who came to my door. I told them that if the Bible was the word of God, and the instruction book for life, I should be able to read it and understand it and see the truth of it. They told me that the Bible was, indeed, all I needed to know and understand God. I told them* that I read it and it didn't do me any good–it was contradictory and not very nice. Oh, but you have to learn what it means at church to understand it all. But you just told me it had everything in it that I needed. If it's all anyone needs, then it should be understandable on its own. It is all you need, they said. But you said I had to go to your church to learn what it means. Yes, that's right. But you just said... It went on like that for a while. That's insanity, right there, folks.]

What Jesus didn't say is as important as what he did. He never spoke out against slavery; in fact he seemed to be okay with it. Jesus clarified a parable by describing the beating of servants as if it was of no consequence (Luke 12:47, 48). That hardly sounds loving, gentle, merciful, and kind.

Though Jesus said a few good things, he wasn't, when objectively viewed, a loving teacher. He treated his disciples with contempt for human failures, like their inability to understand the meaning behind his convoluted parables, and their inability to believe the impossible, like his walking on water. He also treated his mother and siblings with rudeness; he didn't follow his own commandment to respect his mother.

The worst thing Jesus did was to forever cause hatred, war, slaughter, burnings, and divisiveness among humanity when he said, "Whoever is not with me is against me..." (Matt 12:30). That must be true, considering he taught "whoever does not believe [in him] has already been condemned, because he has not believed in the name of the only son of God" (John 3:18). I suppose it's just me, but I don't see condemnation, hatred, and Hell being related in any way to an all-loving deity.

89

On the other hand, if we look at the possibility that Jesus didn't exist, that he was a construct of the Jewish pagans and the gospel stories were written during varying times of oppression of the Jews, the words attributed to Jesus begin to make more sense. When we look at them as written by the persecuted, as propaganda for a cause, they are more understandable.

Do Christians follow Jesus' teachings?

Christianity is clearly based on the person of Jesus Christ. As the Christ, Jesus is the savior of mankind and the world. His teachings are quoted in the gospels; we are to assume his words are correctly attributed to him and are true. Jesus' words then, above any other person's in the Bible, are sacred.

Jesus offered his followers precepts that seem rather tough to live by; and certainly many, if not most, of the Christians I meet aren't abiding by his words. There are some glaring differences between Jesus' teachings and the Christian churches' today.

The most important difference regards the Old Testament laws which Jesus said he didn't intend to abolish. He said if you didn't maintain the law better than the Scribes and Pharisees you were in danger of punishment (Matt 5:17-20). But no Christian today follows those old laws. Perhaps the problem is that in other parts of the gospels, Jesus contradicts himself by amending some of those older laws. If I were a Christian, I would accept amendments to the law only in those instances where Jesus said it was allowable and I would not consider any of the laws abolished.

According to Jesus, not only can't you kill, but

you can't even be angry. If you call someone a fool, you're in trouble. (Then of course, Jesus went on to call a few people fools in Matt. 23:17.) [*Well, he's Jesus; he doesn't have to follow the rules. We have a rule in our house that you can't leave dirty dishes in the sink. But I'm allowed to, of course. Not that it matters, really–they still leave dirty dishes in the sink.*]

Not only can you not commit adultery, but you can't even look at a woman with lust because when you do, you've committed adultery in your heart. If you are prone to leering, you must pluck out your eye. I don't know why Christians try to say Jesus didn't really mean for you to pluck out your eyes when he said it pretty clearly: pluck out the offending member to save your soul (Matt 5:29).

The Old Testament law said you could divorce your wife but Jesus said doing so would make her guilty of adultery. Anyone who marries a divorced woman is committing adultery. Any man who divorces his wife and marries another woman commits adultery. All divorced Christian women, all men who have married previously-married women, and all men married more than once are adulterers. The penalty for adultery is death (Lev. 20:10).

Jesus also said to "offer no resistance to one who is evil," then went on to talk about people hitting you and asking you to walk with them. You aren't supposed to resist mean people; you're supposed to let them have at you. Offer them your other cheek to slap. Walk not one mile with the slave driver but two. When someone asks you for something that belongs to you, hand it over. I don't know any Christians who live this way.

Jesus said to "be perfect, just as your Heavenly Father is perfect." (Matt 5:48) And yet, I always see bumper stickers that say, "Christians aren't perfect, just forgiven." [*Seriously, what's with that? Do they not even read the book?*] Jesus told his followers to be perfect; if they're not, then they're not very good Christians, are they?

Jesus said not to let people see you doing good deeds just so you get rewarded; I guess you're supposed to be modest. And he said not to pray like hypocrites pray, standing in synagogues and on the street. You're supposed to go to your inner room and close the door. Jesus also said not to babble when you pray like the pagans do because God already knows what you want before you open your mouth. Go to your closet and pray with your mouth shut. Funny, I hear all about the "see you at the pole" prayers at schools; our government representatives pray all the time in public meetings before they do their jobs. I've witnessed parishioners in churches praying out loud, their hands upraised, dancing and praising God; on television they really go at it. That doesn't seem to be what Jesus wants them to do.

You're not supposed to shore up treasures on earth. You shouldn't accumulate jewels and expensive collections and such. Jesus said that no one can serve two masters and that therefore you shouldn't worry about your life, what you'll eat, drink, or wear. God will fulfill your needs. Naturally Christians aren't going to follow this tenet. [*Is that really a 'tenet?' Was I just trying to avoid using the word rule?*] If they did, they'd be beggars and homeless people. God said he'd provide, but he doesn't really so they have to get jobs and accumulate some wealth. If Christians really just let God provide and he actually did, they might have some evidence for the validity of their religion. [*Isn't that the truth?*]

Christians are to stop judging others–that would include me, I suppose. In the manner that they judge others, they too will be judged. But so many Christians are so judgmental! They are so quick to tell us who is bad and who is good, who is a true Christian and who is not. I guess any Christian that passes judgment on anyone else isn't a true Christian.

Right after Jesus said not to judge people, he told Christians not to "give what is holy to dogs, or throw your pearls before swine, lest they trample them underfoot, and turn and tear you to pieces." (Matt 7:6) If he wasn't really talking about dogs and swine there, wasn't he making an awful judgment about certain people and calling Christians to do so as well?

I've been told that even though Jesus clearly said, "Do not judge," he didn't mean it–he actually taught how to *discern* between the good and bad people. That's a slippery evasion if I ever heard one. "Do not judge" actually means "here's how to judge." Sure, sure. Apparently the rules can be played with so that Christians can behave the way they want, regardless of what Jesus said, and still count themselves among the elect.

The most glaring denial of Jesus' teachings is about wealth. Jesus said to the rich man: "If you wish to be perfect (which according to his own words you are supposed to be), go, sell what you have and give to the poor." (Matt 19: 21) He told everyone that it is very difficult for rich people to get into Heaven. I do wonder how it is that so many Christians are so rich. When I think of all that money spent on big churches, houses, boats and cars, Ivy League college educations (and United States presidencies) for their children, and vacations to Europe, I have to wonder how much good it could be doing for the poor.

I am told that Jesus was talking just to that rich man, not all rich men. Of course, any rules that Christians want to follow, that are convenient and easy to abide by, are meant for everyone. Only those they don't particularly like are specific to persons long dead. [*Snap!*] I've also been told that Jesus didn't mean we couldn't be rich; he was just warning us about worshiping money above God. If only Jesus had said exactly that–but he didn't. He made it pretty clear to the rest of us that he meant for Christians to sell all they have and give the money to the poor. The poor are still waiting.

One of the strangest things that Jesus said is that people who believe in him and are saved will be able to drive out demons, speak new languages, pick up serpents, "and if they drink any deadly thing, it will not harm them. They will lay hands on the sick and they will recover." (Mark 16:17-18) There are some churches in which the believers handle snakes; some of them get bit and die. I guess they weren't true believers. I don't know of any Christian who can drink poison without being harmed–I don't even know any who will try. Most importantly, Christians lay hands on the sick all the time without healing them. If there are true Christians out there, they aren't giving us their signs.

The two greatest commandments, according to

Jesus, are that you should love God with all your heart, mind, and soul and you should love your neighbor as yourself. The way I see it, Biblical Christians only love the parts of God that are palatable to them and only follow his word where it suits them. They only seem to love neighbors who agree with them.

[I made some excellent points there, if I do say so myself. I could have ended the book right there. 'Nuf said. Christianity, consider yourself debunked. Next! But seriously, don't you think it's odd that, while everything I wrote there is true—the Bible really does have Jesus saying all of those things clear as day—none of it registers with people who believe that Jesus is their savior? People are pretty weird.]

Who reads the Bible, anyway?

It would be helpful to me if all people who determined to call themselves Christians would read their own holy book. *[Yes, and everyone is eager to be helpful to me, I'm sure.]* They should all be required to study, at the very least, the New Testament at length, not just the good parts, the quotable and palatable parts, but the whole of it.

I have had too many conversations in which I realized that the Christian I was speaking with knew less about his own Bible than I did. That is insupportable. If you're going to claim you believe in something, you ought to know full well what it is you are saying about yourself.

Most Christians go about their daily lives without considering their beliefs. They may sit in church on Sundays (though the majority forego church altogether) and hear snippets of the holy book that is supposed to be God's word—you'd think they'd want to memorize the entire thing—and then have satisfied themselves that they are indeed Christian.

I must say, I respect more the Biblical inerrantist who knows full well the ugliness of the Bible and calls it good than the Christian who claims the belief without having read the book at all. [*Really? I don't know...*] I have little doubt that if more Christians actually read the Bible, there would be fewer Christians.

Chapter Five

Religion Satisfies Certain Human Desires

[*Ooh, looks like I'm going to get all psychological now. That's cool. I took some psych classes in college.*]

A great deal of intelligence can be invested in ignorance when the need for illusion is deep.
—Saul Bellow

When I look at this world, when I see and experience no gods, demons, spirits, angels, or any supernatural entities whatsoever, I think that the most likely answer to gods is that humans made them up. [*I'm not sure if I ever really hammer this point home. If anyone really wants to know why atheists are atheists, this is it. Religion looks made up. It sounds made up. It feels made up. There is nothing (nothing at all—no matter what you say) that makes it any* less apparently made up. That's all there is to it, really.] There are many unanswered questions regarding existence but, until some god makes itself known to all of us objectively, I have no reason to accept that it is there at all.

The claim that a benevolent god exists and created me for a purpose is unbelievable to me.

So, why do people believe the unbelievable?

The fact that the Bible is loaded with supernatural imagery of things that no longer occur, if they ever did—animals that talk, magical fruit, God causing the earth to swallow people up—does nothing to deter the person who wants to believe that the Bible is literally true and inspired by a god. Tertullian, one of the earliest apologists, wrote in his *Adversus Marcionem* the following bit of illogic: "And the Son of God died, which is immediately credible because it is absurd. And buried he rose again, which is certain because it is impossible." [*Lawlz. Oh, come on! That's funny.*] Only a strong desire to believe would cause a person to declare that the more incredible a claim is, the more likely it is to be true.

Why would otherwise intelligent people turn away from reason to devote part of their lives to what others see as a myth? [*Wait, what? Did I just say 'turn away from reason?' As if people would normally be able to do it, but they've turned their backs on it? No. No, I don't think so. People simply do not reason. Period. It's hard. It's no fun. And you die in the end.*] Why do they see other stories of gods and miracles as myth...but claim their god and their miracles are true? There has to be something in it for them—and there is. The Christian theology fulfills certain basic human desires. [*All of the mythologies do that, right? Just imagine it. Fulfilling our human desires is so important, a person might blow himself up or behead someone on video to make it happen. That's whack.*] It offers people a sense of worth and specialness while at the same time reaffirming their feelings of self-loathing. It gives them a community in which they can feel understood and supported. It eases their fears about life and death, offers them hope for immortality. It also gives them a feeling of superiority, of having an edge over others.

We, as humans, have some basic desires; we want comfort and pleasure—we don't want lives filled with fear. There is nothing wrong with that and I don't mean to condemn Christianity or theism for fulfilling human needs. I'm not claiming there is or was some kind of conspiracy to do so in order to gain control over the masses. (While I do believe that people have used religion, Christianity in particular, to gain power, I don't think Christianity was specifically designed as a method of control.) I believe that fulfilling these needs is the role of religion. It's what we developed religion for.

In *The Dogma of Christ and Other Essays on Religion, Psychology and Culture* (Holt, Rinehart, & Winston, 1963) [*Obviously not believers in the Oxford comma.*], Erich Fromm explains the supportive nature of shared fantasies:

> The common fantasy satisfactions have an essential advantage over individual daydreams: by virtue of their universality, the

fantasies are perceived by the conscious mind as if they were real. An illusion shared by everyone becomes a reality. The oldest of these collective fantasy satisfactions is religion.

[*An illusion shared by everyone becomes a reality. I love that! Does that make me a psych nerd?*]

People believe in the supernatural, gods, and Christianity so fervently partly because such belief is reinforced in the community. When everyone else believes, it makes belief not merely acceptable but preferable; more problematic, however, is that communal fantasy becomes a reality so ingrained in society that turning oneself from the illusion may be difficult, if not impossible, for the majority. [*And yet, despite claiming to understand all this, I still chastised Christians who approached me if they didn't do it nicely enough to suit my snobbish sensibilities. It's almost as if I wasn't paying enough attention to the things I learned. Then again, I suppose it's true that I wrote this book at the end of all of that sniping and arguing. Still, I'm sure I read Fromm in the middle of it. I'm not proud. Not ashamed exactly. Just not proud.*] Not all people succumb to the illusion. Many don't buy into it in the first place; others grow out of it; still others fall out of it only after a difficult period of transformation.

Michael Shermer, in his book *Why People Believe Weird Things: Pseudoscience, Superstition, and Other Confusions of Our Time* (WH Freeman, 1997) [*Yay! Shermer totally gets the importance of the Oxford comma.*], outlines twenty-five fallacies that lead to errors in thought and allow people to accept invalid ideas as truth. Among these fallacies are the belief that bold and forceful statements and the use of scientific language make a claim true; problems with placement of the burden proof; reasoning after the fact; rationalization of failures; and an inability to distinguish truth from false analogies, coincidence, and appeals to ignorance.

All the problems Shermer points out could be corrected among the majority if our education in critical thinking skills and science was improved. [*Yeah, no, I don't think so. I think humans just aren't into it. My mother, who I probably shouldn't talk about in print, but I'm doing it anyway, once went with me to an atheist convention. Yes, atheists get together. And no, they don't just talk about how they don't believe in gods. Sheesh. There's a whole lot of stuff to talk about–science and evolution, education, separation of church and state, activism, outreach, on and on. Oh, okay. Back to the story. So, I'm there with my mom and we're sitting at a round table with a bunch of people and there's this nice, good-looking, older man talking her up. Unfortunately, she tells him she's not an atheist; she's just there with me. She says she believes in a lot of neat things. I don't remember what she said, but let's say it was the equivalent of astrology and crop circles. And she says to this guy that she believes in this stuff because it's fun. Oh. My. God. Way to go, Mom. Yeah, so my point: most people just aren't into the boring stuff that you get with reason and critical thinking.*]

As more and more people not only stop believing, but also make their nonbelief known, nonbelief, at least in the traditional salvation religions like Christianity, will become acceptable. Already we see a growing trend throughout the world toward more liberalized salvation religions as well as growing bases of ancient religions such as Wicca and paganism. Though traditional religions fulfill many people's needs; one needn't find a religion in order to have one's needs met. [*Needs, needn't, needs. That's poor editing right there.*]

The feeling of being special

Christianity tells humans that they were created special, by a god. Humans are the end result of God's yearning. He wanted a creature that would worship him and praise him. [*Jeez, what a guy. Probably wears a wife beater. That's, like, a white tank top that's too tight, right? I can hear God now. Stella! Stellaaaaa! Cue: Green Day, "The Time of Your Life."*] The Earth is merely the home he created for us. I haven't figured out what the rest of the universe is for yet but Earth was definitely created for human habitation and all the other animals were put here for man's pleasure and use. [*Some Christians take that a bit too far, don't they? Oh, come on! You're not going to try to tell me those nuts are atheists, are you, because you know they're in church on Sundays after using the sheep on Saturday nights.*] But, as some would say, due to Satan's interference or the fall of man, some things in the world are irritating to man, if not horrific...from cold germs and viruses, to earthquakes and floods.

From an objective standpoint, the world appears to be under no supernatural influence. Good things and bad happen to believers and atheists alike. Still, feeling that you, either as an individual or as a species, were created special by an omnipotent, omnibenevolent (except for that Hell thing) god makes most of us feel good. It gives us the impression we are remarkable.

Christianity also explains the feelings that we all have from time to time that we are not so special. Most, if not all, humans suffer periodic bouts of self-loathing and the Christian theology explains this as our sinful nature. We are filled with lust, envy, greed, etc. because of our fall from grace. So humans are, at the same time, special to God and unworthy of his love and attention. [*Hard to imagine such a perfect guy creating such imperfect beings. He probably did it on purpose so he'd have something to kick around.*] It's a perfect psychological dichotomy, addressing both the need of worth and the explanation of self-loathing. It's quite an impressive theology, I'll admit, but merely addressing human nature insightfully is not enough to make the claim of deity true. [*Let me say that in a less snooty way: Just because it works for you doesn't mean the god exists.*]

As an atheist, I don't feel that humans are special in any superior sense to other life on this planet. [*Hon, please. I'm not fond of the species at all.*] Certainly, we are the most intelligent species [*That would depend on how you define intelligence.*] and the most creative, if not also the most adaptable (though I have to give roaches a good score on that final point). We are special in that way but, outside of that, I don't feel that humanity has a distinct place in the cosmos. We're just the highest rung on the ladder of intelligence at this point on this planet. [*My god, that's sad, isn't it?*] When I think of the vastness of the universe, I imagine how comparably tiny we are.

Where do I turn to feel special? Humans can experience a sense of specialness in each individual's unique abilities and talents. We also are made to feel special by those we love and who love us. That is all the specialness I need. [*Well, lah ti dah.*]

A sense of meaning and purpose

Very much like the feeling of being special, is the sense of having some greater purpose–a feeling that one's life has a meaning beyond the few years we have here on Earth. I've been told by a few Christians that if there was no god, it would mean, for them, that this life had no meaning and purpose and they couldn't bear to live. I can understand that feeling, especially in view of the ugliness evident in our world. Many see life as a trial, as trudging from one problem to the next. They need to believe that there is a reason for the misery and pain of existence. I can appreciate that. It might make suffering easier if you believe that you will be greater blessed in an afterlife because of it. It may make it easier to endure if you sincerely believe there is a lesson to be learned from it, or that some good will come of it.

I don't believe there is a reason or purpose for life on Earth. I've met some Humanists, agnostics, and atheists who believe that humans are here for a reason. They don't necessarily claim to know what that reason is, but they believe there is one just the same. I don't. I have no cause to believe there is a reason. I see no evidence of a reason or purpose to existence. I only know that I exist and I must make the most of it. That is my purpose.

Life is meaningless in the sense that one day I will not exist as I do now—and of course, the Sun will eventually burn out and all life on Earth will cease. [*Cheery much?*] Who thinks that far in advance? Who travels through life constantly at odds with the end of it, with the end of time? Atheists have the same kind of meaning in their lives as Christians. [*Well, what? What meaning? Why didn't I elaborate? What I was trying to say is that, in day to day living, we're no different. We find meaning in our jobs and families and talents and hobbies. We find meaning in just living. In appreciating the sunrises and sunsets. Enjoying nature and art and entertainment. That gives our lives meaning.*] Atheists, for some reason, don't have a need for any greater meaning than is apparent.

The feeling of security

Belief in a god allays fears of the unknown. It is a comforting thought that your spiritual father is there to take care of you and that death isn't really death. Death scares most people. I'm not sure why [*Seriously?*] but it no doubt has a lot to do with instinct and survival. Death only scares me a little and only because I like living and want to keep doing it for a while longer. I realize, when I think about it, that when I'm dead, I won't exist any longer and therefore, neither will any fear or sorrow that I associate with death. It won't matter once it's over. I think about the time before I was born—I didn't exist then and it didn't bother me. I imagine death will be little different. [*Uh, I mean no different. No difference whatsoever.*] That gives me comfort.

Christians also take solace from knowing that their lives are guided and protected by their god. In reality, Christians are no more untouched by the horrors of living than the rest of us. They die in hurricanes and floods, they are murdered, they are killed in car crashes and plane crashes, drowned, burned to death, ravaged by disease just like the rest of us. Their god is not doing anything for them except giving them a pretense of protection through it all. [*It's a little vulgar when you think about it.*]

When they are saved, when they survive the flood, crash, attempted murder, etc., God or an angel was watching over them or their prayers were answered. When they don't, their loved ones agree it was God's will. If this gives them comfort, so be it–it wouldn't give me any. I am rather a-mused by the bumper stickers that proclaim "God is my co-pilot" as if this god will actually protect the driver from the horrors of this world. If that were true, if Christians never suffered the evils that other men did, it might be considered some evidence for the truth of their beliefs. [*Exactly!*] Unfortunately, belief in God makes little difference in when and in what manner death finds you. If I knew that a god was watching over me while a man with a knife attacked me, stabbing me to death, I'd hardly consider myself blessed for his lack of attention just because he considered it my time to go or because he decided that I should die in such a terrifying way, or worse, because he won't interfere with the free will he gave the murderer. I find no comfort in that idea—I'd rather more likely feel as if I were entertainment—in the manner of Job, perhaps. [*Yeah, see, to me, that's sick. Really sick.*]

I do, however, take great comfort in many things about this life, as unpleasant as it may seem at times. I'm consoled in knowing that many of us are striving to love one another and to make peace. Some of us are lunatics and go about murdering others or abusing children, it is true. Some of us are really filled with hate. But I can look past those few (and yes, considering how many of us there are on this planet, they are few) to the majority of us who, I believe, want to be kind and loving and peaceful.

I take comfort in knowing that this life is temporary and that each day of it counts greatly. I take comfort in that because it is my excuse, if you will, to take time out to read, write, play with my children, watch television and movies, to enjoy this precious time I have. I have little doubt that many Christians treat life in the same manner.

I take comfort in knowing that the stuff I am made of has existed since the beginning of time as we know it. The stuff of the universe is not only all around us—we are it. The same particles of matter in me, that *are* me, will exist forever, as far as I can tell. In a sense, what I am made of is immortal. No, I don't believe that I, myself, my mind, will exist beyond my lifetime. While I do take comfort in the hope that my progeny will continue for as long as humans do, I realize that the only constant is change and that at some point, humanity will evolve so far beyond its present state that I will be too insignificant to count as ancestor, or it will die out. But that won't matter because that substance that is *me*, is the stuff of the universe and will go on—not that I'll notice...I'll be dead.

[*When you really think about the finality of death, a lot of the stuff you see going on in the world makes no sense. People blowing themselves up or flying planes into buildings for a cause seems really stupid on its own. But add to it the fact that, so far as we can tell, that's it for those schmucks. There is no afterlife, no Heaven, no reward. That life was all they got and that's what they did with it. It makes it all the more sad and stupid.*]

A sense of community

Religion also gives people an important sense of community. Having a church social outlet must be very helpful to the human animal. I appreciate people's attachments to their church families, if they get a sense of support and community from them. I can imagine that would be difficult to let go of once you are a part of it. Of course, I also imagine that there are some people who become part of a church social group for reasons other than genuine belief and sincere social intercourse. [*Oh, man. I said 'social intercourse.' What was I thinking?*] I'm thinking of savvy business people who might join the wealthiest and largest churches in town for contacts.

Nonetheless, it can't be argued that the human animal is not social and doesn't need social outlets. When I first realized atheism, I felt as if I were alone in the world. Luckily, the Internet has changed the social landscape, allowing us to find each other more easily and congregate in our own way. [*Yeah, that worked out so well for me. See my essay, "Why I Quit Atheism," also known as Chapter Sixteen.*]

A sense of superiority

I don't know what it is about humans, not being a social psychologist myself, but they generally seem to have a need to feel superior to others. Throughout human history we can witness humans trying to prove their superiority through their gods, wars, racism, sexism, and any other method they could find. Mankind is a fearful species–fearful of death; fearful of the unknown; fearful of change and fearful of people who are different from themselves. Humans try to conquer that fear by demolishing those who are different in order to prove that their own way is the right way.

Religions, especially the traditional faiths like Christianity, do this for a lot of people, most especially fundamentalists. The fundamentalist knows he's right. He's got the right deity, the right religion, the right church, and the right interpretation of his holy book. He is saved and the next guy probably isn't. Definitely those Catholics aren't saved–unless you ask *them*. For sure those Jehovah's Witnesses aren't–unless you ask *them*. We know the Mormons are lost souls–unless you ask one of *them*. But this guy, the fundamentalist Christian, he is definitely one of the elect. When the rapture comes, he'll be gone and all you'll find left of him are his clothes...if you believe the movie.

The point is people like that have to feel that they are better than somebody, preferably a lot of somebodies. The smaller the group of chosen, the more powerful and special they feel. There is a word for that–elitism. The elitist Christian doesn't have to be a fundamentalist; but a fundamentalist is always an elitist.

While I can agree that the experience of being right is a good one [*I should know. Snork.*], I haven't found satisfaction in a feeling of superiority over others. [*I wouldn't say I don't get any satisfaction. But it's definitely more of a resigned acceptance. And am I saying that I'm superior to some people? Yep. That's what I'm saying. Superior in what way? Smarts mostly. I'm smarter than a lot of people and I'm not ashamed to admit it. Of course, I'm sure really stupid people think they're smart, so there you go.*] It more often than not causes me to feel sad. It's not something I practice. [*I don't know what this sentence means by 'practice.'*] If I am smarter than one person on a certain subject, I keep in mind that there are others who are smarter than me.

I think that many Christians feel the same way but there are those who feel superiority over others not because of anything they know or can do, but simply because they believe they have found a truth that others have not. Unfortunately, I have met some that continue in their superior attitude while seeming to temper it with an expression of pity for the unsaved. This type of person is always sweet, almost apologetic, about being one of the elect and claims to be truly sorrowful for the fate of the lost souls, knowing what they will endure in their eternal torment. It saddens them deeply and gives them a good excuse to try to save them. This attitude may convince the Christian that he isn't elitist, because he expresses pity instead of scorn, but his mannerisms betray him. [*His mannerisms betray him? Sheesh, what a writer snob. Let's just say he's a poser. An 'oh my god you are so going to burn in Hell but look how nice I'm being to you' poser. Atheists do the same thing. We're the 'jesus h. christ could anyone be more stupid but look at how condescending I am' posers.*]

I don't think anything can be done to end the elitism of Christianity as long as the concepts of Hell and salvation are a part of it. If mankind needs to be saved and the only way to do it is through their god Jesus, there is nothing but elitism in the cards. They can't escape it. Only a Universalist Christian can. [*More posers.*]

Some atheists may consider their intellect a source of superiority; but honestly, a person doesn't have to be an atheist to be an intellectual. And of course, not all atheists are intellectuals, or even very smart. I don't have a comparable feeling of elitism. I don't feel that I belong to a special group or am better than any group of people. [*That is such a lie. Of course I'm better than some groups. I'm way better than Westboro Baptist Church and anyone in it—in all kinds of ways! I'm better looking for one thing. I have much better sign-making capabilities. I have more of a charming personality. In fact, if you met me in person you wouldn't even know I'm a rabid*, crazy, meme-dismantling atheist! And I know that protesting a society that refuses to acknowledge how right I am about everything is cool so long as you don't cross certain lines and picketing funerals is one of those lines. Oh, you can do it. I'll stand up for your right to do it. But I contend that I'm better than you for having the compassion* not *to do* *it. I'm still a poser, though. I'm one of those 'look at me I'm so special I don't fit in anywhere and that means I'm superior' posers.*]

Power

The only way the person in the pew can have a feeling of power is via his elitism, no matter how subtle, but the person on the altar has power; the church hierarchy has power. Power and control are major motivators for many people in the business of god.

I have no equivalent feeling with atheism. Atheists, as far as I can tell, have no political power. I think a lot of Christians would disagree. For many, the attempts to maintain a secular public school system and a secular government are driven by an atheist or Humanist conspiracy to force people to give up their religion. To me, these are simply the results of having a basic idea of separation of church and state. The secularist has no desire to keep people from worshiping a god– that is a personal choice we all may make. The secularist simply wants to protect the minority from the majority.

Not all people in this country believe a god exists. It is wrong for the majority to force the minority to act as if it believes in a god when it doesn't. The phrase "In God We Trust" should not be on our money, or displayed in government buildings. The phrase "...under God" should not have been allowed to be inserted into our Pledge of Allegiance in 1954 during the shameful McCarthy era. It's frustrating to hear people say that the majority should be allowed to place its religious view into our government and force others to claim a god exists when pledging loyalty to their country. We are the majority, they say, and atheists should just ignore it, go along with it, or worse, leave the country if they don't like it. It's so easy to overlook oppression when you are in the majority. Atheists are just as much citizens of this country as theists. We should not be put into positions in which we have to ignore or tolerate god belief. Theists claim we are trying to force them to hide their worship, but that is not true. They are free to build churches and congregate within them. They are free to utter prayers at any time they wish, as long as they are not forcing other people to do so as well. Freedom and justice for all is not possible if this is "one nation, under God." [*Hear, hear! Or is it, here, here? I'll look it up. Cue Final Jeopardy theme. Da da, da da, da da daaa... It's definitely hear, hear–apparently as in 'hear him!'*]

Christians claim that atheists made praying in school illegal; they say we took God out of school, but that is not true. [*Right. Because it wasn't atheists, plural. It was one atheist (actually a handful...and one main one in the end, but who cares about Engel when you've got O'Hair to kick around (easy target). The point being, we're not a cabal, but we have rights just the same.*] Students and faculty can utter silent prayers at any time they wish. What is not legal (nor moral) is a person standing before a class or assembly and calling for prayer. Why is that so difficult to understand? Why is it considered such a restriction? Why must Christians insist on praying publicly and calling others to pray with them, knowing full well that such an audience may consist of non-Christians? [*I could have sworn I already answered that question somewhere up above: because if everybody believes in this thing you can't see or hear or even define, then it's okay for them to believe in it and not feel weird. And if everybody gets together, closes their eyes, bows their heads, and starts begging this unseeable, unhearable, undefinable thing to not kill them or to help them fix the iPhone they just scooped out of the toilet, they're not creepy at all–they're normal. Perfectly normal. Nothing freaky going on here! That's how humans work.*]

Non-Christian students can opt out, they say. But why should non-Christians and atheists feel forced to leave a classroom or assembly just so Christians can pray? Christians can pray in church, at home, and silently to themselves at any time. [*Any freakin' time! Except on an airplane. That will get you in big trouble.*] Why must they insist on everyone joining them? Why must those who do not wish to pray be singled out? [*Why does it seem like I keep asking the same question over and over?*]

I think the crux of the matter is that Christians believe that anyone who doesn't believe the way they do is not only wrong, but immoral, and therefore, tolerance of that position is out of the question. There is a movement in the United States toward a theocratic government. It is insidious and sly, but becoming more and more apparent. I am awed by the technique the religious right has employed, infiltrating government positions, altering their language so as to appear less fanatical than they actually are. They are doing a great job; most people are being lulled into believing they are harmless; most people don't bother to research before they vote; most people don't care.

This leads to the kind of power and control I'm talking about, akin to the Taliban in Afghanistan. [*No, no. The Taliban is so yesterday. ISIS is all the rage now.*] There are Christians in the United States who would like to establish a theocracy here. They want political power so that they can instill their version of morality, of god, and of government on all the people. That is very frightening to an atheist—as it most likely is also to a pagan or Wiccan or any other non-traditional believer. Fighting against such power and control is the cause of liberty, rather than another form of control. It is the opposite: it's standing up for the minority, so they aren't trampled by a self-righteous, elitist majority.

A sense of justice

The world is a frightening and dangerous place for some people. [*Oh, it's a frightening and dangerous place for everybody—they just don't all see it. It's a wonder to me that we're not all running screaming down the streets during normal business hours. I really should give humanity more credit than I do. There are some things we're good at, after all. Blinding ourselves to anything we don't want to see is one of them.*] There is evil everywhere [*Everywhere, I tell you!*] and the bad people don't always get their just deserts. People are getting away with murder. [*Well, now, I shouldn't make it sound like that happens all the time. I bet most murders are solved.*] People are bilking others out of their hard-earned savings and walking away free. People are causing pain and torment in others' lives and never face prosecution. People break promises, seduce young girls, divorce their wives, cheat on their husbands, betray their friends and are never punished. If you are a victim of any sort of violence, betrayal, or discrimination, it can be upsetting to know that the person or group of people who hurt you continues to live their lives as if they've done nothing wrong; some even prosper. Christianity, in particular, provides a nice sense of justice. You can believe that, even though your enemies aren't punished here on Earth, in the afterlife, they will be. [*Do you suppose some really sick people miss the 'good old days' when they could get together for a good lynching or witch burning? <shudder> People suck.*]

There is some justice. We have laws, and courts to deal with those who break them. We have some laws governing treatment of people but not all injuries are covered by law. There are many instances when you are hurt and nothing can be done about it. It may appear that there is no justice.

Part of justice is in your attitude–what you will make of the events in your life, what you will learn from them, how you will handle them and how you will treat the person who hurt you. Your attitude affects your outlook–it *is* your outlook. People who can forgive more easily are happier; people who hold grudges are miserable. I can appreciate wanting to know that there is some ultimate justice that will balance everything at some point...but I have to wonder how much is the desire truly for justice, and how much is it for revenge?

Immortality

The desire for immortality is, perhaps, the strongest desire among humans. [*Really? Stronger than the desire for sex or brownies?*] Most of us are terrified of death. Religion promises immortality. You can't get any more comforting than that. [*Uh, yes you can...brownies!*] You won't die–you will live on perhaps in a different form. [*Will you be able to eat and enjoy brownies? Because if not, I'm not interested.*] Better yet, all those people who believe exactly like you do (so you don't have to hate or fear them) will join you in a paradise and all those people who didn't believe what you believed (so you hated and feared them) or the ones who did very bad things to you will suffer an eternal torment in Hell. You can't get any more elitist than that.

I don't want immortality. [*This is still true.*] The desire for eternity and the promise of it given by religions throughout time is evidence that gods and religion are manmade. We need comfort, we need justice, we need to suppress our fear of death, so we eagerly believe whatever would satisfy our needs; and we teach this salve to our children and to anyone else who will listen. I suppose I can understand this fear, and the hope that religion offers. But I don't want it–I don't want a comforting lie. I don't want comfort for comfort's sake. I am much more concerned with honesty, truthfulness, and what is real. [*So, I'm kind of like a philosophical masochist? Ooh, baby, give me some more of those hard, cold, facts. Yeah, that's it. Just like that. Ouch.*]

What Do I Desire?

I as a rationalist desire truth above all. I do not want to be swayed by my fears, my feelings of self-righteousness, or my emotions. I want the truth. Even if it's depressing, discomforting, or ugly–I prefer the truth. [*I like it like that!*]

I don't fault any person for believing in comforting ideas but, once those ideas become dogma, once the claim of superiority or the threat of punishment is made–once the attempt is made to control my life and force me to accept a particular religion as reality, then I will stand against it. I have no choice. If others are to be truly free to believe, I must be free to not believe. [*It's more than that. I must be free from a government that would impose its will on me based on other people's religious beliefs. I don't care what your god says about abortion or marriage or drugs. It's not your right to impose your morality on other people.*]

[**You'll find the rest of this one later. Yes, I can do that. I'm the author; I can do whatever I want.*]

Chapter Six

The Differences between Us

People like to think that most others are just like they are–it validates them. Some people are worse about it than others. I've known people to insist I would behave exactly as they had if I'd been in their situation, no matter how I might deny that I would. People have a hard time understanding that, while we are all human and pretty much wired the same, we do differ, in some cases extraordinarily. Difficult as it may seem to theists, I truly do not believe in deity and find no evidence for the existence of such. It may be hard for some to accept because they think that I am very much like them and experience the same things in the same way they do, think the same, and am persuaded by the same things they are. Because they might think that, they have to believe that what keeps me from accepting that god is obvious must be some sort of unwillingness or blindness on my part.

The differences that separate theists from atheists lie on a scale, something like a number line. At one end is rationalism and at the other is emotionalism. Rational does not mean smart and emotional doesn't mean stupid.

Rationalism is a philosophy whose adherents rely on reason to determine reality. Certainly, we are humans and can't entirely separate ourselves from intuition and emotion. The extreme end of rationalism is impossible, as well as unattractive. At the other end, emotionalism in the extreme is insanity. All sane humans utilize their reason to some extent. Most humans, in my estimation (a nonscientific one, I grant you) lie just to the right of center, leaning more toward emotionalism than rationalism. [*No, no. Not just to the right of center. Pretty far to the right of center.*] They allow their feelings, hopes, aspirations, and intuition to guide them. They want reality to be a certain way and are willing to accept, or deny, evidence to bolster that view. They may also feel that science can't explain everything and that it is quite possible for another realm to exist which can't be studied objectively so we must rely on our senses and "spirit" to explore it.

Some people, most notably the majority of scientists, are on the left, more rational in their approach to reality. They rely less on their emotions to guide them in the pursuit of truth. The farther toward rationalism a person is, the more likely he is to think that what we can know, we only know through objective study. All else— revelation, authoritarian discourse, hope, and subjective experience—yields untestable, unprovable results and therefore cannot be relied upon to offer us any truth.

I am a rationalist. There is no objective evidence for a realm beyond the reality we know to exist and I refuse to create a belief about any such place. I do not trust the subjective experiences of others as necessarily truthful; nor do I consider ancient, unverifiable texts a valuable tool in the search for truth. Rationalism may well be called my world view. I view the world as the reality that can be objectively experienced. Any other phenomenon, being that it emanates from either my own subjective experience or is related to me by someone else who claims to have had the subjective experience, is *without objective reality*. [*That means it is not real. Just to clarify.*] It can't be demonstrated, reproduced, tested, evaluated, or measured–therefore, it can't be said to factually exist. [*Like I said: not real.*]

I suppose one could accept that it *might* exist. Anything might exist. Unicorns might. Garblesnooks on a planet billions of miles from here might and, yes, gods might exist. But they do not interact with the world and humans in an objective, measurable way so their existence can't be verified. You wouldn't believe in the garblesnooks, if I asked you to, would you? It doesn't really matter to you one way or another if they do or don't exist so you lose nothing by ignoring my insane belief. And you recognize that I am insane when I claim they exist and communicate with me.

Yet, millions of people accept that various versions of a god exist, that at least one of these actually made himself into one of us and had himself killed for our salvation only to rise again from the dead. Millions of people believe this unverifiable, untestable, unprovable story and claim it is perfectly sane to do so, perfectly rational even. Why? Because their world view is opposite mine. Millions of people are either brought up with, or accept at a later age, the idea that a supernatural realm exists. Of those who are brought up with the idea, it is easy to understand the strength with which they hold to that view. For those who weren't instilled with the idea as children, society offers them plenty of reason as young people and adults to accept the world view, mostly in the form of community support and acceptance—everyone else believes, and they really want you to believe too.

Humans, not to be too hard on them, are rather stupid creatures. [*Stupid as mud.**] Look at the things some of us believe. Some believe that the stars and planets and their alignment at the time of our births will determine our personalities and even the events of our lives. [*Snork.*] Biblical Christians believe astrology is witchcraft and a sin. [*Burn the astrologists!*] Some believe that aliens from other worlds visit the earth regularly and often take humans aboard their spaceships and perform experiments on them. [*Aren't they special?*] I can't begin to imagine the Biblical Christian view on that, but no doubt it has something to do with Satan. [*Did Satan...probe you?*] How many millions of people call psychic hotlines and pay untold sums of money to hear someone finagle information from them and feed it back to them calling it ESP? [*Step into my parlor, Madam President.*] People believe ridiculous things for two reasons: they lack solid critical thinking skills, leaving them gullible, and they have already accepted that there is another realm beyond the objective reality of the world.

Once the idea of supernaturalism is accepted, any number of beliefs can be had regarding it. There are all sorts of religious beliefs in the world. In the United States alone you'll find paganism, Voodoo, Wicca, and Native American spiritualism, just to name a few. There are millions of people who don't subscribe to any particular dogma but simply believe whatever strikes their fancy: reincarnation, karma, chakras, or auras. [*I should add homeopathy, chiropractic, cupping, acupuncture, aromatherapy, feng shui, those pads you stick on your feet at night, the list just goes on and on.*] Once you've accepted a hidden, subjectively experienced realm, anything goes.

For the dogmatists in the U.S., who tend to be rather controlling people, the most popular is, of course, Christianity. [*The anti-vax movement is close second.*] Its story is no more believable than is astrology's or astral projection's, but it is more acceptable because it is the more popular belief. Popularity doesn't equal truth by any means. For how many hundreds of years did European culture claim that the Sun revolved around the Earth? It wasn't true and the thing that showed us it was a lie was skepticism. Someone had to doubt the popular belief and dare to check it out.

The supernaturalist and rationalist world views are opposite and there is no middle ground between them. Once a person finds himself on one side or the other he cannot reconcile the two. The problem is not that the rationalist hasn't experienced what the supernaturalist has; he simply doesn't interpret the experience in the same manner and doesn't give as much weight to his feelings in the matter. We have the same sensations, emotions, fears, and desires but what a theist may claim as a holy spirit within him, may be to the atheist no more than great joy.

I do not believe that there is anything a theist can say to a rationalist to convince him that a supernatural realm exists. Some might claim this is closed-minded, but I don't agree. I am open to the possibility but I am not so open as to accept *any* notion. I'm certainly not going to accept something just because someone tells me it's true. That's called skepticism and there's not a thing wrong with it. We should all be skeptical. You can't just tell me there's a supernatural realm; you have to give me evidence. Unfortunately, the evidence I've been given thus far is woefully inadequate. I'm told, "You won't accept my evidence because you just don't want to believe." Well, that is correct. I don't want to *believe* something that I don't think is true. Any notion that has to be *believed in* is obviously lacking material evidence. Believing in things is not rational. [*Snap!*]

Evidence for God

For hundreds of years now, atheists have raised objections to the belief in the existence of gods. Christians have responded with answers to those objections. It's a "yes, but..." sort of conversation we've had going for so long that, when looking at it from the perspective of the long haul, it looks as if believers and atheists are just talking past each other. It doesn't matter what the atheist says, the Christian has an answer for it. The explanation is enough for the Christian to maintain his belief but not enough to convince the atheist of the existence of a god.

What I offer here is not an objection to belief in god. [*Not that I don't object.*] Theists believe that a god exists and nothing I say is going to change their minds. Instead, I'd like to outline the arguments I have heard on both sides, briefly, to make known the positions of most atheists and Christian apologists on the issues.

As far as I'm concerned, it's a draw. [*No, it's not. Not really. The rationalists win.*] All the evidence has been laid out on the table. The atheist, and rationalist, accepts this evidence as all that Christianity has to offer and finds it unconvincing. The believer accepts it as proof. That's all there is to the problem and all there ever will be. Atheists and believers are divided over one crucial difference: our opinions differ greatly on what constitutes evidence.

The only real objection to the existence of God on the atheist side is lack of evidence. There is no evidence that a god exists. The theist's response to this objection is that there is ample evidence for God's existence. The evidence is as follows:

- You can't get something from nothing
- Life exists
- Miracles
- The Bible and prophecy
- Answered prayer
- Subjective experience
- The effects of belief
- The spread of Christianity

I will briefly explain why none of these constitute evidence for a rationalist.

You can't get something from nothing

Theists say that nothing comes from nothing so something had to exist before the universe existed. They say that everything has a cause so there must be a First Cause. This is known as the Cosmological Argument for the existence of God. It may be an argument, but it's not evidence for a god. We haven't established as fact that everything must have a cause, and if everything does need a cause, God would also need one. If God could have existed forever, why couldn't the universe, or something else that led to it? You can't just slap God at the beginning and give it special status and expect the rationalist to go along. We don't know what, if anything, existed before the universe came about. People much smarter than you and I are studying it right now. I don't know how the universe came to be, what existed before it, if it's eternal, or if there was a god that created it and *neither do you*. We don't know. That isn't evidence for God—it's only evidence of our limited knowledge.

[*Entire books have been written on this subject. All the yakking and hand-waving and obfuscation and for what? So people can call themselves great thinkers! Philosophers! So they can believe what they need to believe and still maintain a sense of reason. Yeah, well, it's a 'sense' of reason—like the smell of chocolate. It's not the real thing, but just enough to make you think it's okay to believe you've got some in your top desk drawer.*]

Life exists

As we've seen, evidence for God usually begins

with statements of incredulity. The believer says things like, "All this could not have happened just by chance. The odds are astronomical that mankind would emerge from lower forms of existence." [*One time at a meeting of atheists, a Christian woman sat in with us and afterward, she took my brother aside over at the window and pretty much said, "But look at the leaves! The leaves! No two alike! Therefore: Christianity!" This is one reason why I don't go to meetings anymore.*] The problem with these remarks is that, because you don't know how something came to be doesn't leave you to invent an answer with the expectation that the rest of us must accept it as correct. [*Okay, I get it. The Christians of today didn't invent the answer. No one did, really. The answers just evolve over time. They show up in the psyche because, by god, we've got to have an answer! We can't go on without knowing! Here, take this answer–it's way cool, people will love it. Just keep saying it over and over until they finally accept it as complete truth.*]

Theists say that because life exists against insurmountable odds, there must be a supernatural force behind the universe; but the fact that something exists is not proof of anything except that something exists. [*I hope I repeat that sentence a few times in this section. It's got to be the simplest, most important thing to remember about evidence.*] It has nothing to do with whether or not a god or gods exist. There is no reason to apply a god concept to everything that we don't understand or that seems highly unlikely to us.

Theistic claims regarding odds are misleading. They assume mankind was the necessary result, that there was a process at work that had to result in humans and they assume astronomical odds after the fact, which is nonsense. The universe exists; mankind exists. The die is cast–the odds are: one. Odds are expressed as numbers between zero and one. Something that is absolutely certain not to occur has odds of zero. An outcome that is absolutely certain to occur has odds of one. Once an event has occurred, the odds for its occurrence are one.

Take a deck of cards, for example. Let's say I ask you to lay all the cards out in a line across the room. When you lay them out they will be in a particular order. After you lay them out do you marvel at the odds against them being in that order? Do you claim the odds against them being in that order are so against that supernatural powers must have been at work? No, you simply laid them out in that order...they had to be in *some* order, right? The odds of them being in that order are one, because you are calculating the odds after the fact.

Let's suppose I list all the cards in the deck in any order I wish beforehand and then ask you to calculate the odds of laying them all out in exactly that order after shuffling to your heart's content. The odds are highly against your doing so but you notice that we've decided what the outcome will be before we've laid out the cards. Calculating the odds that life would arise on Earth is like going back in time and predicting that life (or humans specifically) would arise exactly as it already has and then claiming the odds are so ridiculously high that a god must exist. It's meaningless and non-sensical to do this.

128

Theists also claim extraordinary odds against creatures like us simply popping into existence. Life couldn't arise from non-life, they say, as if life came to exist fully formed–something like a tornado blowing through a junkyard resulting in a 747. [*Yeah, that one was really funny while it was going around. It's not still going around is it? Tell me they've got some new stories!*] Cells don't just pop into being. No one (but theists) has made the claim that cells, much less entire complex organisms such as humans, simply appeared. When you break the process down into tiny steps, one after another, each building on and adding to the former, the odds aren't so great anymore, nor the idea so incredible. But many theists have some sort of mental block in this regard. [*I think it's called an aversion to science. You know how, when you're reading a science article and your eyes start to glaze over? That. Science is hard, dang it. Why can't we just have fairies and gnomes in our gardens and forget the hard stuff?*]

Creationists ask how the eye could have possibly evolved as the complex, interwoven series of parts that it is, when the individual parts can't work without each other. What good is half an eye? They're not thinking in steps–small alterations, little by little over millions of years, each step adding to the one before it and allowing the organism in question to survive better than those that didn't get that tiny improvement.

One light-sensitive cell is better than none. Half an eye is more beneficial than no eye. Each step, each little mutation that benefitted the organism helped it to survive and reproduce. It's not odds that are the problem; it's letting incredulity, ignorance, and wishful thinking clog one's ability to grasp the real scientific explanation, and simply accepting without question the nonscientific attempts to refute it. [*But, but...the eye! The bumblebee can't fly! God flies the bumblebee! Just look at the leaves!*]

Creationists seem to think they can prove God by disproving evolution. They are stuck with a false dichotomy: we either evolved naturally, or the god of the Bible exists. There are plenty of other possibilities but because their real enemy is scientific intellectualism, they realize they must try to make evolutionary theories look as bad as possible. They do a good job of muddying the waters, confusing people with a lot of scientific-sounding jargon, lying, misquoting, and misrepresenting people and facts. [*Cue: Bee Gees, "Jive Talkin'"*] Species adapt among their own kind, they agree. [*Some agree. Some others are crazier than a box of rabid cats.*] The peppered moths certainly changed color with the tree bark over in England. Yes, we can watch the changes in bacteria in the laboratory. But one species will never change into another. Fish don't turn into amphibians. Reptiles don't turn into birds. If they had, you'd find missing links in the fossil record. Where are the fossils of half-bird, half-reptile creatures? They say you can't find them because speciation is a lie.

[*My youngest son, bless him, got attacked quite often at school in the early years before I started homeschooling him. It wasn't violent– although I still remember him telling me one kid would smack him on the head with a little New Testament, probably in an attempt to drive out*] *his atheist demon. Anyway, the same kid asked him at lunch once if he believed in evolution and my son said yes (I'd yet to teach him that 'believe in' isn't correct) so the little brat (who is no doubt in preacher school at this very moment) laughed and yelled out, "J---- thinks a fish crawled up on land and turned into an alligator!" Is that the stupidest thing you've ever heard or what? And you know the kid got it from his parents. The stupid is so bad it hurts. I wish stupid would stay with its host organism and not get spewed all over my kids.]*

Creationists do not think small enough. Species don't "turn into" others; they gradually change, step by step over millions of years, until what you have doesn't look at all like what you started with. Who decides what a reptile is, anyway? Who says when a creature is an amphibian or a reptile? What is a platypus? Humans make these distinctions—humans put life forms into groups. Plenty of animals are in between or don't fit well into one group.

There are fish that can breathe oxygen while on land. Not only do they utilize cutaneous air breathing (breathing through the skin) by remaining moist, but they've also adapted the ability to carry a bubble of air in their gills for long periods of time. These mudskippers use their fins to scoot from puddle to puddle during dry spells. Can't you imagine that after a few thousand more years their descendants will be able to breathe air all the time and their fins will have changed to something more like legs? Any changes in that species that make moving from puddle to puddle easier will enable it to survive and reproduce to make better mudskippers until finally, you've got something that's not a fish anymore.

Each and every fossil we find is another link between species. Each fossil is a transitional form. It's all transitional, constantly changing. There is no missing link.

When theists point to complex occurrences such as the human eye as proof of God, they are proffering a theory called Intelligent Design. ID Theory is the new Creationism. Pushing Creationism hasn't worked because intelligent people have trouble accepting the stories of creation in the Bible as true, when they blatantly contradict reality. [*As in: utter nonsense.*] Day and night could not have existed before the sun, for instance; neither could vegetation have survived. And yet, according to the Bible, the perfect, inerrant word of the almighty god of the universe, day and night have nothing to do with the sun, and plants don't utilize photosynthesis. We know that the sky is not solid and doesn't separate us from water. Rain isn't the "floodgates of the sky" being opened. We are sure that humans are not made of dust, that men have the same number of ribs as women, that serpents don't talk and magic trees bearing corrupting fruit don't exist except in mythology. Creationism is beyond silly.

So the movement stepped back and tried a new tactic: Intelligent Design. There is no mention of the Bible in ID theory; the god at the back of it is not identified. ID theory is all about science, or rather, pseudoscience. Complexity and design in nature are highlighted to explain that design implies a designer. When you find a watch on the ground, so the story goes, you reason that it had a designer. When you look at the human eye or the (seemingly) impossible flight capability of the bumblebee, you reason, as well, that such could not have been brought into existence (wholesale, they mean but never say) or made possible without a superior, intelligent force to direct it.

ID theorists like to talk about the Second Law of Thermodynamics. This law, they say, proves that evolution is impossible. If the universe is moving from order to chaos, how could complex life-forms have possibly arisen out of slime? I'm no scientist, mind you, but if the average person took just a small amount of time to read up on the basics they could [*We hope. I mean, they could just be that dumb.*] immediately recognize the failure of this argument. The only people who make the assertion are those who understand neither evolutionary theory nor the Second Law of Thermodynamics. The law relates to entropy in closed systems. The Earth is not a closed system; it receives energy from the Sun. If the Earth was subject to the Second Law, there would be no life here at all. Of course, Creationists simply invoke the supernatural powers of God to explain that.

Once the credulous agree on the points raised by Intelligent Design theorists, the claim is made for the Christian god, and because we live in a Christian-dominated society where almost everyone believes in and prays to this imagined creature, another soul is saved.

Intelligent Design is Creationism in disguise. No one is fooling the skeptics. Complexity is understandable if you stop thinking of it as arising complete in one fell swoop. If you learn to think in billions upon billions of years, thousands upon thousands of generations, one tiny change after another each building on and improving the survivability of an organism over those millennia, speciation isn't an impossible concept to embrace.

Abiogenesis is the next logical point of contention. Even if you can convince a Biblical literalist that theories of evolution best explain the fossil evidence, they will still claim the odds of life arising from non-life are astronomical. This is another argument from incredulity; they can't imagine it, so it couldn't be true.

Have you heard of the chimps with the typewriters? If an infinite number of chimpanzees sat typing, what are the odds that one of them would eventually type the Declaration of Independence? Pretty high? Not really. With an infinite number, and an eternity, eventually they would type out all possible letter sequences. But the Creationist isn't thinking this way. He's thinking: put a few monkeys in a room with typewriters and then what are the odds? Because the Creationist thinks in big steps, he's imagining the wholesale, one-time chance of a chimp clacking away on the keyboard and producing the Declaration complete.

That's not a proper model of abiogenesis. Chemicals didn't have to start from the beginning each time with nothing, attempting bonds over and over from scratch, until by some wild chance they formed into a bacteria. No one claims it happened with just one trial, done over and over again. Instead, billions of the available chemicals interacted over billions of years, producing combinations until some of those combinations led to what we call a life form.

Think of the chimps again. This time, imagine

just one chimp at a keyboard and let's say that "life" equals the phrase "When in the course of human events." Only combinations that match the phrase "work." Combinations that don't match are discarded because they don't "fit." The first round might match a few letters. Those letters aren't discarded–the chimp doesn't have to start all over again with a blank sheet. Those matches work; they "fit." They are advantageous because they link together; they form building blocks to which the next try can add. In the next round, more hits are produced that match the building blocks linked together so far. It won't take very many rounds before the chimp will succeed in typing out the phrase that we've decided equals "life."

Remember that we are the designators of labels. We choose what we will call life and what we call non-life. We know that ancient earth contained the necessary chemicals; we know that these chemicals bond; and we know that the earliest form of life was extremely elementary, nothing more than simple molecules.

It's that problem of not thinking small again. Creationists think big–things pop into existence fully formed in their world view. They imagine simple chemicals lumping together to form bacteria and marvel at the odds against. They can't seem to imagine tiny building blocks, linking to each other, adding more blocks, and more until something exists that is no longer merely chemical compound, but living. Then after more steps, over more time, something like bacteria evolved.

There are plenty of other problems with Creationist attacks on theories of evolution and abiogenesis. You can read about them on the Talk

Origins website at www.talkorigins.org. [*Which still exists!*]

Miracles

Christians point to miracles as evidence of God's existence but most of the miracles they point to are in the Bible. We can't use the Bible miracles as evidence of God because they are in the very book which God is claimed to have inspired. The Bible is not evidence because it's nothing more than a very old, inaccurate book until it is proven otherwise. The Bible is fiction until it can be shown to be factual.

Theists also point to modern-day miracles as evidence but none have been shown to be anything more than mass hysteria, wishful thinking or, at worst, fraud. Crying statues of Mary or Jesus' face baked into pancakes have never been shown to be the work of any supernatural entity. Jesus' face on the side of a building isn't a miracle, it's humans finding patterns in their environment. That's what humans do.

Have you ever noticed that only Catholics get Mary in their miracles? [*Well, that might not be true. I mean, even Baptists believe Mary was Jesus' mom, so they might think she's special enough to get baked into something, too. That makes me wonder...why is Mary's baby daddy never in miracle sightings? What ever happened to poor Joseph?*] How can a non-Catholic discount Mary miracles but accept gold fillings showing up in teeth at mass prayer-fests as evidence? Don't you think that Muslims have their miracle stories too? Are their miracles evidence that Allah is the one true god and Muhammad is his prophet?

Shouldn't everyone convert to Islam then?

Miraculous healings are reported but they are never documented by the medical profession, are never written up in medical journals, and never involve obviously impossible events like lost limbs suddenly reappearing, people losing their heads and then growing them back, or people coming back from the dead after embalming and burial. No, they're always unverifiable healings, like tumors disappearing, bones growing a few centimeters, legs lengthening, eyesight improving. After the healings take place, there's no follow up; nobody checks to see if the lady had a tumor in the first place, nor if it's gone. Nobody checks to see if the person puts her glasses back on later. If God exists and performs miracles, why aren't they better ones?

Miracle stories are almost always given to atheists second-hand. When asked for evidence of God's existence, the theist may say his best friend's cousin, or his friend's grandmother, or a group of kids he goes to school with had an experience. There's never any documentation and rarely any first-hand testimony.

I did hear first-hand testimony once. The miracle involved God, or a good spirit, fighting with Satan, or an evil spirit, for control of a radio. [*God says, "Cue: Pharrell Williams, 'Happy.'" And Satan says, "Oh, my God! Not again. I'm so sick of that song. Cue: Van Halen, 'Running with the Devil.'" And God's all like, "Fuck you, Lucy. You're so vain." And Satan says, "Cue: Carly Simon, 'You're so Vain.'" And God says, "Why does everything always have to be about you? Cue: R.E.M., 'Shiny Happy People.'" "You're sick, you know that?" Says Satan.*] My correspondent was a young man whose family had been in turmoil for some time. His mother was sure that she was possessed by a demon and that evil spirits were trying to take control of the family. They set their radio station to gospel music in an attempt to ward off the demons. The young man claimed that he witnessed the radio dial move, changing the station from gospel to something else. He believed that the evil spirits were changing the station. The dial moved, he was sure, because he saw it with his own eyes. Looking beyond the paltry nature of the miracle, it doesn't surprise me at all that this young man believed that he saw the radio dial move. His family obviously believed bizarre things and was in a high state of anxiety at the time. But I don't believe that the station changed, or that he saw the dial move. I believe he imagined the entire thing, possibly even in hindsight. [*Well, I can believe that the station changed. They do that all the time. But it's not gods. It's to do with the radio waves.*]

I have been asked what it would take to convince me a miracle had taken place. It's very simple, really. If people's severed limbs suddenly reappeared, and we had documented proof of it (including the remains of the severed limb), I'd be pretty convinced. If dead and embalmed bodies came back to life, and we had the medical documentation to prove it, that would convince me. If Christians really could ask anything in Jesus' name and get it, they would have some good evidence for Christ. If they really could handle venomous snakes and drink poison without being hurt, I'd think there was something there. If they really could just lay their hands on the sick and heal them, I'd start considering it. *But they can't.* Faith healers are frauds. There have been no documented miraculous healings–they are always obscure, unverifiable events. Nobody ever shows documented evidence. Let's see Benny Hinn [*Is that guy still around?*] make a severed leg reappear! That would be a miracle. But it never happens and it never will.

If there was a flood and only Christians survived it because the flood waters miraculously flowed around their homes, or better yet, over them leaving them in pockets of air space, then I'd be with you, thinking maybe there's something to this God thing. If Christians, or those who believe in the right god, anyway, always walked away from fiery plane crashes without a scratch on them, then I'd begin to wonder. All the above goes for Islam and Muslims or Judaism and Jews or any other god belief that says miracles prove it.

But things like that don't happen. There are no miracles. There are only humans believing in miracles. That's not evidence of anything except the human imagination and the power of belief.

The Bible and prophecy

Many Christians claim that God exists because the prophecies in the Bible came true. But believers only point out prophecies that were apparently fulfilled and either have no knowledge of or conveniently forget to mention all the prophecies that went unfulfilled. Any objective study of Biblical prophecy will uncover a sad history of failure. Some of the prophecies did apparently come true, but not all. The ones that did are suspect because the stories of them coming true are told about in the same book in which the prediction is made. We can't trust them. Just look at the New Testament stories about the actions of Jesus done for the express purpose of fulfilling supposed prophecy. Well, sure, if you get the book of prophecy out and start fulfilling...that's cheating.

Obviously the authors of the New Testament were familiar with the Old. Why should we assume the authors of the books of the Old Testament were not aware of books written before their own? They may have rewritten the older books to make it seem as if a prophecy had occurred. How do you know the books weren't written at the same time and some only made to seem as if some were written earlier and predicted events that the author witnessed himself? How do you know that the author didn't just write that a prophecy was fulfilled whether it was or not? There is also a chance that when you predict one hundred events, some of them may happen, so the fact that some of the prophecies were fulfilled means nothing beyond chance in action (if the stories are true to begin with).

Many of the verses that are claimed to be prophecies don't read like prophecy at all. A prophecy is an inspired revelation of divine will—a description of what the inspiring deity has planned for its people. Prophecy is prediction, inspired by a god. Much of what passes as prophecy simply *isn't*. If a prophet in the Bible makes a prediction, it is supposed to be inspired of God. If he turns out to have been wrong, he was a false prophet.

Ezekiel, in Chapter 13, receives God's feelings

regarding false prophets: "Their visions are false and their divinations a lie. They say, 'the Lord declares,' when the Lord has not sent them; yet they expect their words to be fulfilled. Have you not seen false visions and uttered lying divinations when you say, 'The Lord declares,' though I have not spoken? Therefore, this is what the Sovereign Lord says: Because of your false words and lying visions, I am against you..." (Ezekiel 13:6-8) If God inspired a prophet to make a prediction, we must assume that it would happen in the way the prediction is made. If God inspires the prophet, he can't be wrong. We can assume, then, that any prophet who predicted something and turned out to be wrong was a false prophet and God was against him.

Apologists like to pick out some predictions that worked, and then claim that all the prophecy in the Bible was accurate. They tend to leave out any verses that are inaccurate. Take Ezekiel, himself. The claim is made that Ezekiel predicted that Egypt would "never again exalt itself above other nations. I [God] will make it so weak that it will never again rule over the other nations." (Ezekiel 29:15) But the prophet also said that God would make Egypt a ruin and a desolate wasteland for forty years—that no man or animal would pass through it during that time. That never happened. Those other verses are conveniently glossed over as merely a prediction that Egypt would be ruined but would recover. But it reads just like the rest of the prophecy, distinct, clear and specific—and it was false. Ezekiel's prophecy also includes a dispersal of the Egyptian people and the drying up of the Nile, neither of which happened. But the apologists won't tell you about those. That is the pattern of prophecy in the Bible. Only those few verses that appear to have been correctly predicted are offered as proof of the truth of the book. All the others are left out.

Where are the prophecies of modern day occurrences in the Bible? Some televangelists illustrate them with charts on their walls explaining all the figurative language in the Bible and how it predicted what is happening today—but it's all shadow play. You can interpret those supposed prophecies to mean anything you want them to mean. We have proof of this when we study the history of modern-day prophetic interpretation—when we learn how numerous preachers convinced their flocks the end was near and nothing happened; they'd go back to the book and reinterpret everything. Next year, they'd say. I suppose it is best for the frauds that real facts are usually left out of prophecies—it makes them harder to show inaccurate for those persons unfamiliar with the previous generations' interpretations.

Those verses that Christians claim predict the coming of Christ don't look at all like prophecy. It's as if early apologists searched through the Bible looking for anything that might remotely be construed as telling of the coming of Jesus and slapped the prophecy label all over it. That, to me, is disingenuous [*by which I mean desperate*]; but it has been a tactic of the Christian community from the beginning to create evidence where none exists.

Isaiah 53, for instance, sounds eerily similar to the trials of Jesus. "Yet it was our infirmities that he bore, our sufferings that he endured...but he was pierced for our offenses, crushed for our sins...but the Lord laid upon him the guilt of us all...the will of the Lord shall be accomplished through him." Unfortunately, the scripture in question doesn't read like a prophecy–a prediction; it's written in past tense and is describing the nation of Israel, not one man. I have to wonder if some verses in the Old Testament weren't simply hinted at in the stories of Jesus to give them more credence. [*Duh.*]

Isaiah 7:14 says, "Therefore the Lord himself will give you this sign: the virgin shall be with child, and bear a son, and shall name him Immanuel." Unfortunately, this prophecy is fulfilled later in the same book. In Chapter 8:3-4, the prophetess "conceived and bore a son." There are other problems with this prophecy. The word *almah* is translated elsewhere in the Old Testament as maiden, not virgin. There is another word for virgin, *bethulah*; but it seems many translators preferred to make the maiden a definite virgin in this verse. And, of course, Jesus' mother never referred to her son as Immanuel.

Whenever you attempt to show a contradiction or error in the Bible, you're likely to be told that you've taken the verse out of context. Yet, every so-called prediction of Jesus in the Old Testament is gotten by taking the verses out of context. Nowhere is there a verse that specifically predicts anything about God becoming man, being called Jesus, dying for our sins on the cross, and rising again three days later. God's track record with prophecy is abysmal. If you're going to give him the same benefit of doubt as Madame Cricket and her 800 number, does that mean Madame Cricket is a god too? [*Snap!*]

Answered prayer

Theists claim that prayer works but it doesn't. Prayer has some physical and emotional benefits; it's like meditation—comforting, calming. That's a good thing but it isn't evidence that what you are praying to exists. Prayer can help sick people because it makes them feel better, that's all. It has nothing to do with the validity of their beliefs.

It says very clearly and plainly in the Bible that whatever you ask for in Jesus' name, you'll get—but it doesn't work so what happens? Apologists make excuses for why prayer doesn't work. It doesn't work because God is running the show not us. Sometimes the answer is no. But that's not what it says in the Bible. It says nothing about getting whatever you pray for unless God says no, or unless it's not the will of God. It says, "And whatever you ask in my name, I will do, so that the Father may be glorified in the Son. If you ask anything of me in my name, I will do it." (John 14: 13-14) Plain as day! But it's a lie, isn't it?

What about praying for a sick person to be healed? Theists do that all the time. It says in the Bible that if you pray over a sick person, God will heal him! No maybes, no "only if the answer is yes." It says, "Is anyone among you sick? He should summon the presbyters of the church, and they should pray over him and anoint him with oil in the name of the Lord, and the prayer of faith will save the sick person, and the Lord will raise him up." (James 5: 14-15) But it's a lie! Believers pray over sick people all the time and they die; so what do we get? We get apologists again saying the will of God takes precedent regardless of what it says in his book. God's will means sometimes the answer is no. In other words, prayer has no effect. If God wills you to be healed, you'll get better, if he doesn't, it was your time to go. If it's up to God to begin with, why did James tell people to pray? Why bother with the praying at all?

You can see why [*Ever the optimist.*] a rationalist won't accept that because someone prayed for something and got it a few times he has evidence for the existence of the god to whom he prayed.

Subjective experience

Humans are very strange; it's no wonder the practice of psychology exists. Figuring out the human psyche must be a daunting task indeed. [*Indeed? I sound like a snooty research librarian with those cats eye reading glasses hanging from her neck on a string of fake pearls.*] Take the human penchant for thinking that everyone else thinks just like we do. People tend to believe that everyone has the same feelings, beliefs, and experiences as they themselves and yes, in a way, it's true—we are all human. We all do weird things and we share much in common as a species. Of course we do, but that doesn't mean that your subjective experience must be interpreted by everyone else the same way you interpret it.

Humans, it seems, live in their own worlds; they are self-centered creatures, tending to assume that other people would believe what they do, if they only had the same subjective experiences. What is difficult for the believer to accept is that atheists do have the same experiences; they just interpret their origin and meaning differently. Being self-centered also means thinking that what you believe to be true *is* necessarily true and if others don't accept it as true it is their fault, somehow, or their denial of that truth. [*Déjà vu, man. Did I say all that already?*]

The believer experiences feelings of a presence, a loving energy, and he interprets them as emanating from whichever god he happens to believe in by upbringing or culture. The atheist has these feelings and interprets them naturally, as expected results of the chemical reactions in the human brain—as feelings of immense joy or peace while meditating, perhaps, on some particular beauty or wonder.

I think that if one god did exist and wanted his presence known, a subjective experience of him would be exactly the same for each individual and there would be an objective reality on which to base that experience—no incorrect interpretation would be possible. Deity, if it wanted to be known, would have an objective, real presence in this world, not just inside our hearts, souls, or minds.

Theists say that they just know that God is there—they experience him, feel his presence, commune with him. But a person's subjective experience isn't evidence of anything except that he is feeling a sensation that he attributes to the presence of a god. I accept the individual's story is true for him, but it isn't evidence. I believe that he is experiencing what he says he is—but I don't accept his interpretation of that experience. If I must accept the Christian experience of God as proof of God, he must not only accept the Muslim experience of Allah as proof of Allah, and the pagan experience of Goddess as proof of Goddess, but also my experience of no god as proof of no god. [*That's a good one. I agree. Naturally.*]

The effects of belief

Christians tell me that when you become a Christian, your life is changed. People have won battles against drugs, crime and, of course, sexual perversity [*There's always a sex thing.*] after turning their lives over to Christ. That's evidence, they say, that God is real. Well, not really. It's evidence that these people found something to believe in that gave them courage and hope and support. That's the power of belief...and the power of a supportive community. It isn't evidence of the validity of the belief itself. What about people who turn to paganism and Wicca, and their lives are better for it? You can't claim evidence for your god and deny the same evidence for others. What about those of us who turned our lives around without the help of any supernatural beliefs or spiritualism? Is that proof that there are no gods?

[*Of course not! Don't be silly. Christianity, you see, is true. So what Christians feel is evidence of its truth. But your lack of belief is false, so anything you experience is just your spastic gyrations and protestations against the truth. It's so obvious; I don't see the big deal. Just believe, okay? Just look at the leaves!*]

The numbers game

The believer generally assumes that because the vast majority of humanity believes in some kind of god, there must be some kind of god. They claim that humans are conscious of God because

God exists or that if no god existed, humans would not have an awareness (subjective experience) of or consciousness of God. Believers haven't shown that belief in God is inborn–that it isn't a learned behavior.

[*Hasn't there been some kind of new funky research about a god gene? Or something about a difference in brains in those who believe and those who don't–a difference in the way brains communicate between the various regions within them? Or some new research on Asperger's and atheism? From what I've read, the distinction between coincidence and causation hasn't been fully explored, at least in the first two ideas. You should go look into that.*]

Majority god-belief is not evidence. The fact that most people believe in a god only means that most humans believe in a god. It has nothing to do with whether or not there is a real entity toward which that the belief points.

The spread of Christianity

Finally, Christians tell me that the massive and quick spread of Christianity is evidence that it is the true religion [*No man-made idea could possibly spread so fast!*]; but that's only evidence that people adopted Christianity, not that Christianity is more valid than any other religion. If it were, the fact that Christianity isn't the only religion in the world, or that most people are not Christians, should then be evidence that it isn't true. [*Seriously, two-thirds of the world is not Christian. What does that say about the efficacy of the Christian god? Oh, why bother? They'll just switch to one of those free will arguments without*

skipping a beat on the cognitive dissonance train.
I think I just mixed a metaphor.]

The above evidence for God is not relevant to the rationalist. We have different standards for evidence. [*That's right. We think it ought to actually be evidence.*] I have been told that I can't see or experience the evidence in a manner that will allow me to accept it until I am filled with a holy spirit. That means that I can't believe it until I believe it and that you accept the evidence only because you believe it, while I can't accept it because I don't. That seems a bit silly to me. [*A bit?*]

I try to imagine what life would be like if a god did exist. If the god of the Bible existed, I imagine life would be just like it was in those stories. God would be evident everywhere, every day interacting with his creation in a real and objective way. But, God has disappeared; he is hidden. He exists only in the subjective experience of those who believe in him. No one has any real evidence for God. People who believe he exists are stuck with exactly that: belief. You have to just believe it, because you can never know for certain. That's just not good enough for me.

[*I think the implication here is that it shouldn't be good enough for anyone. Seriously, every human being should demand a high standard of evidence for everything, in every facet of his life. And it obviously still bugs me that I'm part of a species that refuses to do it—no, that's not right, nor is it generous. We don't refuse to do it—we are unable to do it. But it can be learned. I'm certain it can be learned. (Is this a belief? Maybe I should seek out more evidence before I decide on that.)*

I shouldn't be so snarky and mean when I write about this subject. And I would like to say that I don't expect religious people to not be upset when they read my thoughts about the stupidity of some beliefs and the dumbness I attribute to the people who hold on to them. And yes, I know that people can hold on to really stupid beliefs and still be relatively smart in other areas—emphasis on the word 'relatively.' And I get that it's not nice of me to act this way (please see more below almost contradicting this statement). But I still do it. Why? Because the beliefs are stupid. They are. And we really, really need to move past them as a society.

Do I think it's going to happen? I have some serious doubts about it even being possible. When I look at what people do in the name of religion— murdering women for the 'crime' of adultery; slaughtering each other over land; killing daughters for becoming too Western; screaming at women trying to get abortions; holding signs that say 'God hates fags' at funerals—I have little hope of progress.]

[*I said people are stupid as mud. You know what that means? It means some Christian somewhere is going to read that and say that people being stupid as mud is evidence of God. Why? Because God made Adam out of dirt. People are stupid as dirt. Therefore: God.]

Chapter Seven

The Making of a Christian

[*Well, that chapter title sounds ominous, doesn't it? Sounds like I'm going to get some real snark in here. Maybe I'll quote* Young Frankenstein. *You know, this part (condensed):*

Dr. Frederick Frankenstein *(to Igor—pronounced eye-gor): Now that brain you gave me. Was it Hans Delbruck's?*
Igor: *...No.*
Dr. Frankenstein: *Ah! Very good.*
Would you mind telling me whose brain I did *put in?*
Igor: *Abby someone.*
Dr. Frankenstein: *Abby someone? Abby who?*
Igor: *...Abby Normal.*
Dr. Frankenstein: *(chuckles) Are you saying I put an abnormal brain into a sev-*

en and a half foot long, fifty-four inch wide gorilla?

That's just perfect, isn't it? Talk about apropos. (I said apropos again! I like that word.)

This reminds me of The Big Bang Theory *episode where Leonard tells Penney it's not nice to mock people's beliefs. I totally disagree. You may have surmised this already. Look, it's like this. I'll grant you it's not nice to mock children for what they believe. And it's not nice to mock the developmentally or mentally disabled for what they believe. It's probably not really nice to mock what these groups of people believe without mocking them personally, if what they believe is original. Like, say a kid believes he has a fairy in his pocket. You don't tease the kid, right? That's not nice.*

But adults should know better. They really should know better. And frankly, mockery has a place—a noble, honest, effective (at least for the mocker), historically precedented place in public discourse. I think it's just fine to mock beliefs, when they deserve mockery. I wouldn't go up to someone at a party and start mocking her, however. I wouldn't even start mocking her beliefs at a party. *I'm not really rabid, you know. I was just joking before. But I have no qualms about mocking stupid beliefs in general in public. And I have no qualms about mocking certain people for their beliefs in public. County Commissioners, for example. Politicians, Popes, preachers, pundits, you get the idea. But it's not like I'm going mock Sally Citizen—earlier, now deleted, blog posts notwithstanding. (You do understand the differ-

ence between mocking beliefs and mocking a person for his beliefs, don't you? I hope so.) (And you don't get the chance to use a word like notwithstanding very often, do you? I really like that word: notwithstanding. It's like those German words that are a bunch of other words put together. Like lebensabschnittgefährter which ends in farter which is really funny even though it's probably not nice to mock other people's languages.)

I do not believe in tolerating stupid beliefs and I certainly don't believe in treating the people who hold them with special care lest we hurt their feelings. If you don't agree, that's okay with me. But if you don't agree, why are you reading this? Never mind, I get it.]

I don't have a problem with the idea of some unknown cause bringing about the universe. The deists are fine by me. [*No, they're not. Why believe something like that? Why? What purpose does it serve? Why isn't 'we don't know' good enough?*] I don't believe it; it doesn't seem plausible; but I suppose it's possible. [*But until we have some evidence, it's as good as nonexistent.*] I often wondered, however, how a person gets from "I don't know how it all began" to Christianity. Granted, many, if not most, Christians were indoctrinated with the belief from a very early age–reasoning their way to Christianity was unnecessary and only the opportunity to take a rational look at their beliefs would cause them to apply it. Once applied, however, what line of reasoning leads a person to Jesus? I can't pretend to know the path that all Christians took to arrive at their beliefs but I was honored to have one Christian of my acquaintance share his reasoning with me and I would like to outline it here. It begins with the question of the origin of the universe and ends with Jesus rising from the dead.

[*I really like the way I glossed over that part about being honored to have this guy tell me his story. The reality is that I asked, on a forum or email list, how a person gets from the starting point of 'there must be a creator' to Jesus. I said I honestly wanted to know. And this guy said he would to tell me how it worked for him. And when he did, I took apart his reasoning and pretty much told him he was an idiot. I didn't use that word, of course. I don't think I got that mean unless someone else went there first. I think the two words I kept using after each of his points were 'unsubstantiated assertion.' It's the intellectual's way of telling you you're stupid. (Well, okay, not you, but your reasoning.) It wasn't nice at all. And he let me know it. I feel bad about it now. I should have thanked him for sharing with me and left it at that. He wasn't just posting his thoughts in a place where he would expect to be torn apart, after all—he'd only responded to a query.*

There was a lot of nastiness back then, on both sides. There may still be; I'm just not a part of it anymore. Oh, I can still get nasty with the best of them, as this book is proof. I'm just no longer in the trenches. What was it I was trying to prove? And to whom?

I think I was testing my own reasoning, my own critical thinking skills. And honing them a-gainst the arguments made by apologists. (Isn't the word 'apologist' funny? It really is like they're apologizing for trying to make sense of the non-sensical. 'I'm really sorry I'm trying to force one plus one plus one to equal three. But I have to do it. It's my religion.') And, in my defense, I'd been treated very harshly by Christians. That's sort of like saying they started it, so I won't go there too deeply. I just wasn't mature enough at the time to handle myself better when talking to believers who were being dumb in public. If that doesn't sound like an apology, it's probably because it's not...not exactly. I'm sorry I was mean. I couldn't help it at the time. But that doesn't mean the beliefs and denials and nonsense being defended weren't dumb.]

First Cause deism

The First Cause argument states simply that the universe is not infinite, it had a beginning therefore it had a cause—that cause is God. The problem with this argument is immediately evident: if the universe had a cause, we don't know what that cause was—no one knows. When you call it God, you assume quite a bit and you assume it without any evidence. It is a mere assertion.

Theists look around the world and say, "I just can't believe all this came about by mere chance so there must be a guiding hand; there must be a god." But, this world operates on basic natural laws about which we are learning all the time. It wasn't mere chance. Most importantly, just because you can't imagine that the world came about naturally doesn't mean it didn't.

Some scientists theorize that time and space had no beginning—that the universe is cyclic, eternally expanding and retracting. The universe is, then, eternal. Theists say that is impossible, because an infinite amount of time could never be traversed to arrive at the present—in other words if the universe has an infinite past, you'd never get to now. At first glance that argument made a little bit of sense, but something nagged at me every time I heard it. When you talk about traversing a certain amount of time, aren't you presupposing a temporal starting point at which to begin traversing? If the universe is eternal, I don't think we can talk about traversing time—I don't think time would work in quite the way we humans consider it. The same argument, it seems to me, works against God. If God has an infinite past, how could he have gotten to the point at which he created the universe? But, for some reason, arguments used against nonbelief are never considered valid by theists when they are used against God. [*See my 'because Christianity is true therefore I have evidence and atheism is false therefore your evidence isn't' argument somewhere above.*]

Many scientists theorize that there was a moment before which time did not exist and after this singularity, time began and the universe existed. This does not answer the question of what may have existed, if anything, prior to that singularity. Theists want to say God, but that is just a guess.

Let's agree for the sake of argument that the universe had a beginning. Christians tell me that everything has a cause. If you regress through the causes of everything you eventually come to the First Cause which, strangely enough, need not have a cause. Why can this First Cause be uncaused? The answer is obvious: evasion. The problem Christians have been plagued with is the question: If everything has a cause, what caused God? This will not do. So, they claim that the First Cause had no cause—an assertion with no reasoning behind it. If gods can be uncaused, why can't the universe?

A clever ruse to get around the problem is to claim that everything that *begins to exist* has a cause. [*Seriously. The twists and turns the human brain can come up with boggle me.*] God did not begin to exist therefore, God needn't have a cause. This is nonsense. [*To put it mildly.*] If you put everything that begins to exist in one basket and everything that is eternal in another, what have you got in that eternal basket? Only God. All the theist has done with this argument is create a special case for his god and then act as if it proves something.

Some Christians claim that only a created universe makes sense. They say that man has questions such as, "How did humans get here? Why am I here? What is my purpose?" Only if there is a god, they say, do those questions have answers. I don't agree. If there is no god, here are the answers: We evolved. Probably no reason in particular. [*Uh, no. The answer is: There is no reason why you are here.*] And, you probably don't have one. [*You don't have one, until you give yourself one.*] What the Christian is looking for is not an answer, but an answer that he likes. The Christian who uses this argument is really just saying that he likes the thought of the universe being created because it answers certain questions in the manner he prefers.

[I don't really think it's a matter of liking it. It's a matter of needing it. Some people need to believe there is something more than this life. They need to believe there is a reason for their existence and a purpose to their lives. They don't want to contemplate death and nonexistence. They don't want to think about a world without order and without some ultimate judgment. It scares them. So they don't do it. And it's easy not to do it. There's a handy mythology all around us that will help them set all that aside if it ever gets too close to their consciousness. And it comes with a handy answer book—never mind that the book really doesn't have any answers.]

That's fine, really but, it doesn't mean that there is a creator. Claiming that the universe is created simply because man has questions is putting man at the center of it—saying that supporting mankind is the purpose of the universe. Pretty egotistical, don't you think?

The Christian asserts that the universe had a cause and we call that cause God. So far, he's a deist and he has made a leap of faith to get there; he has no evidence that there was a First Cause and no evidence that it was a god. He merely asserts these things and believes them to be true.

God's plan

The next step is the assumption that God had a plan. If there is a god and he created the universe, he must have had a reason. Again, this is just an assertion, just an idea that people have. People don't do things without reason, they say, so why would God? Except, of course, that people do things all the time without thinking and without real cause [*or reason*] and why should a god be anything like a person anyway? We've taken another leap of faith in assuming that our god had a reason for creating the universe and a plan for mankind.

God's revelation

Now we assume that if God had a plan and a reason for creating humans, he would want to let us know what that plan is. Not only is this another mere assertion without any evidence to back it up, but the Christian assumes that the Bible is that revelation. All other holy books and revelations of gods past and present are false, only their book and their god is the real one.

The only reason I have been given for preference of the Bible over the revelations of other gods is that the Bible and Christianity are the best explanation of the world and human nature. That isn't true, of course, except in the mind of the person who prefers the Bible, and it's highly unlikely that Christians have studied all of the ancient pagan religions as well as Judaism, Islam, Hinduism, Shinto, and Buddhism. It is more likely that most Christians believe the Bible is the only word of the only god because they've been taught that and live in a society that supports it. These are not good reasons for accepting it as true.

The son of God

Then of course we arrive at Christianity after our long line of assertions. If the universe had a beginning, if there is a god, if he had a plan, if he revealed that plan, if that plan is the Bible, then Jesus is the son of God and rose from the dead.

159

That's it. That's what makes a Christian a Christian as far as I have learned; but it's all quicksand. It's based on nothing but assertion after assertion. Is there any evidence for any of it? No. I have heard Christians make lots of claims for the validity of their religion. There are two reasons for this. For most, they have not investigated the claims for themselves. That is the reason why the vast majority of Christians accept the Bible as the word of God and believe that Jesus existed and did and said what the Bible says he did. They've been taught that it is true and have no reason to question it. For those who have investigated and still believe, it is because their standard of evidence is different from the skeptics'. They accept the supernatural world view, subjective experience, feelings, other people's testimony, and errant views of history as evidence for what they believe.

What makes an atheist? At what point do atheists and believers part ways? At the very first assertion the rationalist balks. We don't know how the universe and our existence came to be. *No one knows.* Rationalists are not willing to accept an assertion—that there must be a creator—without adequate evidence. Theists and non-theists part ways as soon as theists start creating the world view that suits them.

Evidence for Jesus

Most Christians, and even many non-Christians, agree that Jesus was a historical figure. I accepted it too, for much of my life, until I began investigating the facts for myself. I am no longer convinced that such a person ever existed. [*Well, I wasn't ever 'convinced.' I just assumed it was true.*] I imagine most Christians believe that Jesus really existed because it says so in the Bible—and they have been taught to value the Bible as truth—and they've been told he existed by their families, churches, and culture. There is no reason for them to doubt it. Even those Christians who accept that much of the Bible is allegory and symbolism, utilizes literary device, and is error-prone because it was penned by men, still believe that the stories of Jesus are generally true.

I find it amusing that Paul stated explicitly that "every human being is a liar," (Romans 3:4) and then went on to teach us about Jesus. The entire Bible was put to paper by men. If all men are liars, how can you believe any of it? For people who are more skeptical of the Bible, its benefit as evidence for anything is doubtful. While the New Testament stories can be considered sources of information regarding the existence of Jesus, we must determine how valid they are as evidence. And we must look outside the Bible for unbiased corroboration.

Contemporary extra-Biblical evidence for Jesus is nonexistent. The way I see it is this: here is the son of the one and only god come to earth to tell us the good news, that if we only believe in him, we are forgiven of our sin and can go to Heaven after we die. Surely this is a most wondrous event, the most miraculous, fabulous, awe-inspiring, loving event in our world's history! So, why are there no mentions of it in any historical writings of the period? Why didn't anyone notice until a few years later when the writings of Paul circulated and a few years after that when the gospels were written? God became man and died for our salvation and *nobody noticed.* The reason is clear: incarnating, resurrecting, miracle-performing gods, saviors, Christs, and Messiahs ran rampant at the time. Nobody noticed because the story wasn't special.

Christians will attempt to prove it happened by pointing to several historians of the time for verification, but they all fall short. The most often cited is Josephus, a Jewish historian who was born in 37 CE and died about 100 CE. Immediately Josephus can be discounted as a contemporary of Jesus–he was born after Jesus was supposedly killed. Anything he wrote would be nothing more than hearsay from followers of the new Christian religion.

Josephus is cited in two places in *The Jewish Antiquities*. The first is the Testimony of Flavius, most often cited and most obviously fraudulent. The second is a reference to James as the brother of Jesus which is generally considered legitimate. I challenge everyone to read the Testimony of Flavius–not just the paragraph in question, but the entire sections before and after it. The paragraph about Jesus abruptly interrupts the discourse–it is so obviously a later insertion that has nothing to do with the original text that I fail to understand the passion with which Christians claim it as proof.

I understand that Christians would appreciate confirmation of their beliefs, but it's just not there. No scholar worth his merit would claim the passage in *Antiquities* is anything beyond forgery. The only difference is that some believe the entire paragraph to be interpolation while others claim that only the words about Jesus as Christ, miracle worker, and resurrected were. The fact that Eusebius (about 260 to before 341 CE), an early apologist, didn't mention the passage in *Antiq-*

uities at all is further evidence of its lack of authenticity. Regardless, both passages cited in *Antiquities* as evidence were written too late to be anything beyond hearsay.

All other writings offered as evidence for the historicity of Jesus are too vague to be considered evidence and are written too late to be considered confirmation of anything beyond people's belief in his existence.

Tacitus (55-120 CE) wrote a passage in his *Annals* some eighty years after the supposed death of Jesus. In it, he explained that the belief that Christians were responsible for the great fire at Rome in 64 CE could not be dispelled. He called the founder of the religion Christus and claimed he was put to death by Pontius Pilate. This proves nothing beyond the fact that Christianity existed and its founder was believed to have been a historical person.

A snippet written by Suetonius (75-150 CE), in *The Deified Claudius*, written too late to be evidence, merely mentions a Chrestus expelled, with his followers, by Rome. There is no confirmation that this Chrestus is Jesus. If Chrestus does mean Christus, that still would only mean one of the many Messiahs running around Rome at the time was expelled. Christus, in Latin, simply means Messiah and there were plenty of them handy in those days.

Pliny the Younger (62-113 CE) wrote a letter to the Emperor Trajan in Rome in 113 CE in which he discusses Christians, and Emperor Hadrian (117-138 CE) wrote a letter to the Asian proconsul about Christians–both too late to mean anything except that Christians existed at that time.

Thallus is often claimed to have been a witness to the "darkness" that occurred when Jesus was killed. Solar eclipses were a common claim at the deaths of kings or other historic events in the Mediterranean. The only citations of darkness at the time of Jesus' death in the New Testament can be found in Mark 15:33, Luke 23:44, and Matthew 27:45. No other New Testament authors, including Paul, make the claim. According to the Gospels, the darkness occurred during a full moon (impossible for a solar eclipse) and lasted three hours, covering the whole Earth. It is very telling that the only witness outside Biblical testimony to mention this incredible event is a pagan historian for whom the only information we have comes exclusively from early Christian apologists. His name and what he wrote come from the apologists beginning in the second century. We can't be sure when Thallus wrote. Thallus was first mentioned by Theophilus in about 180 CE. It is most likely that Thallus wrote sometime in the second century and was not a witness to the crucifixion.

In the year 221 CE the Christian apologist Julius Africanus claimed that Thallus explained the darkness at the time of Jesus' death as an eclipse, an opinion with which Africanus disagreed. That is all we know! To what eclipse did Thallus refer? Did he, himself, ascribe it to Jesus' death or was that assumption made by Africanus? We don't know because none of Thallus' writings exist. [*This section on Thallus is not very clear. The point is that Thallus was apparently a Pagan historian, but none of his writings exist. All we know about him concerning Christianity was a citation by apologists, and so we have no way of knowing if he really wrote it or when.*]

What about Phlegon, the Greek freedman of the emperor Hadrian? A few modern apologists still trot him out as evidence of the darkness at Jesus' death. But just as with Thallus, the writings cited by apologists no longer exist; they are merely quoted by early Christians Julius Africanus and Origen. Phlegon was born too late, no surprise there, in about 80 CE and he wrote in the second century. He could not have been a witness even had we his own words to make the claim.

But, more interesting are the fragments of Phlegon's writings that *were* preserved. Phlegon, it seems, loved tales of the fantastic. From his *Olympiads*, a sixteen volume work, one chapter that survives is called *On Marvels*. It's all about ghosts, prophecies, and monstrous births–an accounting of ancient superstitions. His credulous claims include a dismembered head that tells the future, a man who changes to a woman and back, and men giving birth. This is the "historian" apologists turn to for verification of the existence of Jesus?

The thing about Thallus and Phlegon and the darkness is that both of them are quoted as calling the darkness an eclipse–a three-hour long eclipse. This eclipse happened during the lifetimes of Seneca and the elder Pliny. Seneca was a philosopher and writer who lived from 4 BCE until 65 CE, the perfect time frame in which to remark about a historical Jesus and a three-hour eclipse. Pliny the Elder (23-79 CE) wrote, among other things, a 37-book compilation called *The Natural History* which he completed in 77 CE. His *Natural History* covered a great number of subjects, including astronomy. Neither of these Roman intellectuals mentions Jesus, Christianity, or a three-hour eclipse.

Another source offered by Christians for the historicity of Jesus is the *Talmud*, compiled between 70 and 200 CE. But this mention only says a Yeshua was hanged on the eve of Passover. The reference is too vague and too late to mean anything.

Mara Bar-Serapion is sometimes referred to as evidence for Jesus, but as usual, he wrote too late (between 70 and 200 CE) to mean anything beyond the existence of the cult. Bar-Serapion wrote from prison to his son persuading him to emulate great teachers of the past, of whom Jesus was one.

And finally, Lucian, a second-century Greek satirist poked some fun at Christianity, stating that the Christian law-giver was crucified. Lucian was born about 120 CE and enjoyed ratting out the numerous pagan sects for their gullibility. Therefore, say Christians, the fact that Lucian said, even in satire, that Jesus was crucified must mean he really was. If Lucian knew Jesus was not a historical figure killed under Pilate, he'd have said so. Possibly, but, there was no way for Lucian to have known such a thing as he was born in the second century and his knowledge of Christianity would come primarily from its sects. It's also possible that Lucian didn't doubt Jesus as historical because he wouldn't have been the only real man going about the countryside supposedly casting out demons, healing people, and claiming a connection with the spiritual world.

There are more serious problems with these supposed references to Jesus besides having been written too late to confirm his existence but, because they are so easily made unacceptable as evidence for the historicity of Jesus, I needn't elaborate on their other issues.

There is no outside corroborating evidence for the existence of Jesus. Even the stories told of him in the Bible and the Gnostic gospels found at Nag Hammadi were written years after Jesus' supposed death. Christians say that there is little evidence that people questioned the historicity of Jesus or what the New Testament writers claimed of him. There is some, but I agree there is little evidence of detractors at the time just as there is little evidence of historicity. But one thing we know about the history of Christianity is that once it gained power, its leaders began a systematic cleansing of all opposition, including the various sects of its own religion that didn't agree with the orthodoxy. It is not a mystery to me that little anti-Christian documentation exists today.

If we take all we have regarding Jesus, we might assume he did exist, but was just another charlatan or a misunderstood philosopher. I believed for a long time that Jesus was a wise man, a great teacher. After reading the Bible I thought differently. Some study of the history of the time period in question helped me to understand that Jesus was not the only god incarnate, nor the only person (if he existed) making the kind of claims he supposedly did. After I read about the correlations between the pagan mystery religions and the Gnostics, suddenly Christianity made sense to me. When taken literally it is a confusing mesh of contradiction and absurdity; when looked at through paganism, it has meaning. If Jesus existed as a man, the religion built around him was absorbed from the various pagan myths abundant in his lifetime.

It is not a foregone conclusion that there is a god, that he had a plan, that he revealed that plan, that the Christian Bible is that plan, nor that Jesus actually existed and was the son of God. In fact, the evidence is nonexistent for all of those claims. They are all suspect, doubtful, mere assertions–the nonbeliever's position is not without merit. [*Hah! To put it mildly.*]

When Christians accept the assumptions necessary to reach their conclusion they do so by faith. I am willing to accept that as their reason for believing. In my opinion, they should admit that they believe by faith alone and leave the attempts at reasonable justification aside. In order to claim that belief in Christianity is reasonable and based on evidence, it is necessary for the Christian to defend the indefensible and to, as a result, make derogatory claims regarding the opposing side– atheists. In order to continue to assert they have objective evidence to support their belief (which if true would render belief unnecessary) they must try to put atheists into the position of denial of their supposedly obvious truth. If they had evidence to support their beliefs, the debate would be over–but because they have none, they eventually turn to demonizing the enemy. As soon as the disparaging claims are made–atheists are willful, blind, immoral–it is apparent that Christianity has no solid base on which to stand.

So, why don't Christians admit theirs is a faith that can't be defended? Because when they do that, they will have to concede that nonbelief is reasonable and acceptable. They will be forced to tolerate it, to admit they could be wrong, and to allow that atheists are just as moral and decent as they are. They will have no excuse not to separate religion and government completely, to cease the posting of religious symbols and phrases on government property, to stop trying to get everyone else's children to pray to their god in public schools, and to stop trying to have their creation myth taught as if it were factual.

Christians cannot do those things, at least not yet. Too many of them are grounded in self-righteous bigotry and the rest are simply going along for the ride, secure in the belief that they are right and there is nothing wrong with forcing their religion on others. I hear there are more tolerant Christians out there–Christians who do acknowledge the rights of nonbelievers. If that's true, perhaps a more liberal Christianity will one day grow out of the ashes of fundamentalism. We can only hope. [*There already is a liberal Christianity. And there is a liberal Islam. The existence of ISIS and the Taliban make it clear that it does us no good at all to have a liberal faction of a violent, bigoted, elitist religion running around. We need reason, not religion.*]

Chapter Eight

The Making of a Religion

Once I realized I was atheist, I looked at the Christian theology with a skeptical eye and wondered why anyone would believe it. To be honest, at first I thought people must be either ignorant, or they didn't really believe it at all. I thought, come on, they really know deep down that there isn't a god. Funny, they thought the same thing about me, that deep down, I must really believe there is a god. Instead of butting heads over the idea, I figured that Christians who professed to really believe in God must really believe. And as you would expect, when I began to correspond with Christians, I found that most were not ignorant at all. Many very intelligent people believe in God and believe that Jesus rose from the dead. [*I make it sound like I was surprised. I don't think I was. I mean, most everyone I knew at the time was Christian, so I had to know that being a Christian didn't mean a person was stupid.*]

The next logical question was, why? Why would anyone believe that a god exists who created humanity especially for the purpose of worshiping and adoring him? Who would believe that this great, superior, supreme being would torture parts of his creation for not believing in him? What sort of creature would do something like that? To me, of course, only an egotistical monster would. To the fundamentalist Christian, God loves us! He loves me but he's going to send me to Hell.

Granted, not all Christians believe Hell is a place of torment and not all even believe that Hell exists. Most of the Christians I interact with, however, [*On the Internet, mind you. The Internet is its own crazy world, isn't it? And ten years ago even more so.*] do believe in Hell as a punishment for all manner of sins, not the least of which is nonbelief. They are quick to defend their all-loving god, however, when I protest such behavior on his part. "God isn't sending you to Hell, you're sending yourself there," I am told.

But God created Hell. Didn't God set up the garden, the temptation of the tree–didn't he let the serpent have a go at those newly created innocents Adam and Eve? Didn't God set up the whole scheme? The whole plan? Knowing full well what would happen? He's terribly irresponsible, incredibly stupid, or just plain mean.

Why do people believe that the stories in the Bible are at all factual? The most recent research exposes the Old Testament stories of the Hebrews as untrue. Archaeological evidence since the Seventies does not confirm the Bible in history, but shows instead that it is not reliable history at all. The Old Testament is nothing more than the exaggerated stories of a nomadic people in need of a great heritage–they simply created one. [*It should probably be pointed out here that proving a city existed, even one with the name given it in the Bible, isn't evidence of the truth of the Bible. I'm sure I go into that somewhere. So, that's not the archaeological evidence I'm talking about. I'm talking about evidence that there was no large population of Israelites in Egypt at the time, and no exodus. There is evidence that the Israelites didn't conquer Canaan. They were themselves originally Canaanites. These sorts of findings and more were documented in the book* The Bible Unearthed *by Finkelstein and Silberman.*]

You can find, with a study of the *Gilgamesh* epic and the *Egyptian Book of the Dead*, that the story of Genesis is borrowed heavily from Egyptian and Babylonian myth. The New Testament stories of Jesus are also born out of earlier and current mythical ideas. Jesus most likely was, as the evidence suggests, a Jewish version of the prevailing pagan gods. You can read the evidence of the similarities between the myths of Osiris-Dionysus, Bacchus, Adonis, and Jesus in many available books.

The well-read Biblical Christian will tell you, most likely, one of two things regarding the fact that earlier myths resemble theirs. Either the earlier myths arose out of man's yearning for God, a precursor of the True Word of God, or Satan planted all those earlier similar myths to confuse us. [*Admit it: that's just sad.*] Of course, there are Christians who will simply deny any correlation between other myths and Christianity. This is a difficult position to hold in light of the early Church fathers' defense against their critics who pointed out the similarities.

Joseph Wheless, in *Forgery in Christianity* (Kessinger), quotes Justin Martyr in his *Dialogue with Trypho* as saying:

> For when they tell that Bacchus, son of Jupiter, was begotten by [Jupiter's] intercourse with Semele, and that he was the discoverer of the vine; and when they relate, that being torn in pieces, and having died, he rose again, and ascended to Heaven; and when they introduce wine into his mysteries, do I not perceive that [the devil] has imitated the prophecy announced by the patriarch Jacob, and recorded by Moses? ...And when he [the devil] brings forward Aesculapius as the raiser of the dead and healer of all diseases, may I not say in this matter likewise he has imitated the prophecies about Christ?...And when I hear that Perseus was begotten of a virgin, I understand that the deceiving serpent counterfeited this also.

Wheless also quotes Tertullian, Bishop of Carthage (c.160-220 CE) who claimed: "You [Pagans] say we worship the sun; so do you."

[*Forgery in Christianity was a fabulous book. But, it's not really a good source to cite. It's old, for one thing. Really, really old. It's one of those books that you'd read and then need to verify what it says with some other source. So, I did.*

Despite the fact that Wheless ought not be considered a good source, the quotes listed above are verified.

Tertullian made his statement about sun worship in Ad nationes, *and Martyr's quote is from chapter sixty-nine of his Dialogue. Both are documented in the Catholic Encyclopedia, a copy of which you can find at New Advent online.]*

I don't accept the explanations that similarities between Christianity and paganism are due to Satan's handiwork or human yearning for God. Those sound very much like poor excuses made by people who simply choose to believe their own myths are true while others are false.

The Christian defense that there are no real similarities between their theology and pagan myths is based on the supposition that Christianity is unique. Yes, they say, you might find some vague similarities, but no other religions are exactly like Christianity. No other gods came to earth and died exactly in the way Jesus did or for the same reasons. This defense belies an ignorance of human cultural practices.

No one claims that Christianity was taken wholesale from another religious belief. No one claims that someone else's theology was adopted and simply renamed. That's not how cultural borrowing works. Humans adopt bits and pieces of other cultures, taking what they like and leaving what they don't. Then they add to it to make it uniquely theirs. All religions are unique.

The skeptic claim is that pagan gods incarnated, died, and were resurrected. The ideas were current–floating around, ready to be adopted and made into new religions. The gods most often cited as similar to Jesus are Osiris and Dionysus of Egypt and Greek theology. But some other gods incarnate worshiped at the time were Inanna, Tammuz, Zalmoxis, and Mithras. The following is a brief look at these pagan gods and their similarities to Jesus.

[I can't attest to the veracity of any of the following stories of these particular gods. No doubt some of it is true, some of it not quite true, and some of it could be false. I only know that these are things I learned during the time I was researching earlier religions and their relation to Christianity. Do I care that some of it might not be accurate? Not really. I'm not a historian and this is not a history book. This is a book about how I realized I was an atheist. And it doesn't change the conclusion that the Jesus story wasn't fully original.]

Osiris

The cult of Osiris was in existence from 3000 BCE. His annual passion play, commemorating the events of his life, death and resurrection, was celebrated until 400 CE. Osiris was an Egyptian god. When he was born to Rhea a voice was heard to proclaim that the lord of creation was born. Osiris established laws for Egypt then set out to civilize other lands. In his absence, Isis, his wife and sister, ruled Egypt. When Osiris returned to Egypt, the evil Set (or Typhon) tricked him into getting into a coffin. Set locked him in and tossed the coffin into the Nile.

Isis cut a lock of hair in grief over her husband's death and sought out his body. Once she found it, she sought out her son Horus. But Set found the coffin while Isis was away and cut Osiris' body into fourteen pieces, hiding them throughout the land. Isis found all the body parts, pieced them together and Osiris was resurrected and rose to reign eternally in Heaven.

So, Osiris was a god who at one time possessed human form to rule the earth. He was killed, resurrected and is now ruler of the dead in Heaven.

Dionysus

Dionysus was a Greek god born of a human mother. His Roman counterpart, Bacchus, was spoken of by Justin Martyr as quoted earlier. He actually had two lives, one divine and the other mortal; he was resurrected twice. First, Zeus (Jupiter in the Roman pantheon) came to Persephone, a goddess, disguised as a serpent and she bore Dionysus as Zagreus. Jealous Hera, Zeus' wife, provoked the Titans into killing Dionysus. They tore him into seven pieces, boiled and ate him. But his heart was rescued. Zeus used a potion made from Dionysus' heart to impregnate Semele, princess of Thebes. Hera, jealous again, tricked Semele into asking Zeus to reveal himself as a god, at which moment his divine fire incinerated Semele and she was cast to the underworld. Her fetus (Dionysus), who was said to have danced in his mother's womb, was taken out of her ashes by Zeus and sewn into his thigh until he could be born. So it was said he was twice born or born again.

The cult of Dionysus had spread to Italy by the third century BCE. It reached Rome in 496 BCE and became very popular there by the second century BCE. In the earliest festivals celebrating the life of Dionysus, believers tore apart a live animal and drank its blood, believing they were partaking of the god's body and blood–sharing in the essence of the god. By the mid third century his followers called him the Redeemer; he was the god of wine. He was said to have risen from the dead each year to rule the winter months and was celebrated as rising in March and dying in December.

So, Dionysus was a god popular in Rome, born of a goddess, killed and resurrected via birth of a mortal mother, born twice, the Redeemer, celebrated in the eating of his body and drinking of his blood, and in his death in December and his rebirth or resurrection in March.

Inanna

Inanna was a Babylonian goddess worshiped long before Ishtar (Babylonian), Tammuz (son lover of Ishtar) or Dionysus. Inanna was the Queen of Heaven and Earth who entered the underworld upon hearing the cries of her sister Ereshkigal. Before entering the first gate, she told her servant Ninshubur to wait three days and three nights for her; if Inanna failed to return, Ninshubur was to seek help. At each of the seven gates to the underworld, Inanna was forced to part with one of her signs of dominion and power until she was naked before her sister. The judges of the underworld ruled against her and she was killed by being hung from a hook on the wall. Ninshubur contacted the God of Wisdom, who created two beings from the dirt under his fingernails; the beings descended into the underworld, healed Ereshkigal of her pain, and as a prize, asked for the body of Inanna. Inanna was resurrected and returned to Heaven. The Semitic goddess, Ishtar, replaced Inanna during the decline of the Sumerian kingdom. Ishtar is considered to be an incarnation of Inanna.

So, Inanna was a god who descended twice, first from Heaven to Earth, then to the underworld; she was judged, crucified, and resurrected.

Tammuz

Tammuz was worshiped by the Phoenicians, Hebrews, Canaanites, Babylonians and Assyrians by his title, Adonai, meaning Lord. Sumerians worshiped him as Dumuzi, the vegetation god and husband of Inanna, who showed the people how to approach the gods.

Tammuz died young in the winter and descended into Hell or the underworld. Through his death and rebirth, the fields and flocks were recovered. Women were required to weep and mourn for his return to ensure the rebirth of the earth. The prophet Ezekial, chapter eight verse fourteen, expresses his frustration with the continued practice in the Old Testament.The cult of Tammuz spread to Phrygia and Greece where he was worshiped as Attis and Adonis.

So, Tammuz was Lord, died young in winter, was mourned by women, descended to Hell and was resurrected in spring.

Zalmoxis

We have very little information on the worship of Zalmoxis. Herodotus wrote of him in his *Histories* of 440 BCE. He said that the Thracians worshiped Zalmoxis and believed that when they

179

died, they went to live eternally with him. The Greeks claimed, according to Herodotus, that Zalmoxis was a man, a former slave of Pythagoras who was freed and after amassing wealth returned to his own country to school his people in the arts of civilization. Zalmoxis, they said, built a huge hall in which he feasted with the elite of his countrymen all the while building an underground chamber. He taught his doctrine of eternal life and then disappeared, descending into his chamber. For three years his people mourned him as dead. In the fourth year, he rose out of his chamber and the people then believed his doctrine.

So, in Zalmoxis we have a story of a god/man who descended into a tomb of sorts and then arose out of it, and preached a doctrine of eternal life.

Mithras

The Roman cult of Mithras was very secret. What we know about it today comes from outsiders such as early Church Fathers writing about it in order to attack it, philosophers appealing to its doctrines, and artifacts from the thousands of underground temples dedicated to the god.

Roman Mithraism arose at about the same time Christianity did causing Christians to claim that we can't be sure whether Christianity is copied from Mithraism or vice versa. But the earliest record we have of the pagan cult is 67 BCE when Plutarch wrote about a band of pirates in Cilica practicing the secret rites of Mithras. Thus, Mithraism in Rome predates Christianity, unless the Christians would like to change their time line. The earliest physical evidence dates to the first century CE and Mithraism was at its height in popularity in the third century. It was eventually eclipsed by Christianity and exterminated in the purge of all religious practices deemed heretical.

Roman Mithraism, however, is related to, and has its roots in, the Persian god Mithra, at first a minor deity, but later a full-fledged god worshiped very much like Jesus. The similarities between Mithra and Jesus are numerous and amazing. Both were born of a virgin mother on December 25, performed miracles, and were known as the "light of the world." They were both considered saviors of mankind, were both killed and resurrected. Mithraism and Christianity are both based on the dual nature of good and evil, and incorporate baptism, a sacred banquet, and resurrection.

[*None of the above matters. That's right. I said it doesn't matter. If no god in history was anything remotely like the Christian gods Yahweh, Jehovah, or Jesus it wouldn't matter. If there were never any other gods that people believed in and worshiped throughout all of history, it wouldn't make the Bible or its gods any more true. Originality in storytelling doesn't equal truth. If the stories in the Bible were unique, they'd still be fantasy. Why? Because snakes don't talk, humanity didn't start with two people, there wasn't a worldwide flood, there was no exodus, and people don't rise from the dead; there isn't a god anywhere around telling us what to do, how to worship, or how to live. There is no evidence that any gods exist.*]

These aren't the only gods similar to Jesus, but the point isn't to try to figure out which gave rise to the Christian god–they all lent ideas to the surrounding cultures. The point, which is so obvious and yet so quickly dismissed by Christians, is that at the time Christianity had its beginnings, people readily accepted gods incarnating as human men, suffering, dying for our salvation, and resurrecting. None were exactly like Jesus–all of them were unique. But Jesus was nothing new–the ideas surrounding him were not original.

People at the time were very superstitious. They believed that men could be gods. Even the Bible shows us in Acts, chapter fourteen, that the people of Lystra believed Paul and Barnabas to be Zeus and Hermes incarnated. Gods becoming men was not an original idea. People also prayed to statues, believing they would be healed by them; miracle workers abounded; people followed every new Messiah, sometimes to their deaths. To characterize the people of that time as rational, sensible people who were convinced despite themselves of the (capital T) Truth by the miraculous life, death, and resurrection of Jesus is simply inappropriate, if not disingenuous.

To claim that Christianity is unique is not saying much. There were other gods before Jesus who did miraculous things. Why should we believe the stories of the others were false and Christianity's is true? Because it is the only story that is still believed by large numbers of people today? The number of people who believe something or how long the idea survives has no bearing on its validity. The fact that the main ideas of Christianity were accepted by pagans in various forms before the story of Jesus erupted is proof that Christianity is not special and evidence that it is not any more valid than its older, pagan versions.

Ancient people all over the world worshiped the Sun. They watched its rising and setting location travel from north to south throughout the year and experienced the changes its path produced on Earth. The winter solstice is that time when, because of the tilt of the Earth, your hemisphere is leaning farthest from the Sun so that daylight time is very short and the Sun's path is at the lowest arc of its travels. Solstice means "sun-standing-still." The Earth seems on the brink of death; the Sun seems to be slowly disappearing–the warming, life-giving light may die out altogether. Without the intervention of man–his supplications and ceremonial offerings–the Sun may not turn again, retrace its path, and renew the Earth. The winter solstice has been celebrated as the annual birth of various Sun gods for thousands of years.

The Sun begins its northward path again at the solstice in late December (winter solstice in the Northern Hemisphere; summer solstice in the Southern) and finally, the daylight and nighttime hours become equal–the Sun is midway through its path to the north–at the spring or vernal equinox, when Earth is thrust into rebirth–it rises again from the dearth of winter.

This is the origin of Christianity–of all religion. [*All religion? I don't think I'd go that far.*] Christians aren't worshiping the son of God; they are worshiping the Sun god who is born in December and resurrects the Earth in spring. Jesus isn't coming back some time in the future; he returns every year. It was only the determination of a small sect of early followers of the Christ cult to claim their Sun god was actually the promised Messiah that confused the issue and led to the belief that Jesus was a historical figure. And because he failed to do what the Messiah was supposed to do, his death and resurrection were reinterpreted to point to a future, physical return. Because of that, Christians no longer worship Jesus as the original pagan, Jewish, Sun god–they now worship a supposedly real man/god who will return, not at each winter solstice, but in the future. They worship a vengeful god created by an oppressed Jewish population. They have, in essence, destroyed the beauty of the religion.

Chapter Nine

Morality

If the Bible and my brain are both the work of the same Infinite God, whose fault is it that the book and my brain do not agree?
                                              –Robert G. Ingersoll

Where do you get your morals?"
That's the question I get most often, as if morals are bought and sold at a shop somewhere and being an atheist is like being an anti-shopper so how can I have any morals? My answer to the question has never been accepted by any theist. It is this: same place you do. I get my morals from my family, community, society, and culture. They are taught to me from birth. I learned some better and more quickly than others. I didn't learn some until later in life. Some of us never learn all of them. Some of us learn about morality but something is wrong with our wiring

and we don't feel the guilt and shame or, more important, empathy necessary to keep us abiding by the moral laws of our society.

Theists are repelled at the thought that we get our morals from our culture. That would mean that morality is (gasp!) subjective and situational. They say "situational ethics" as if it's a disgusting concept and not what's been going on for millennia. And worse, they confuse situational and subjective ethics with individual ethics. They make statements like, if there is no absolute morality, we can all just do whatever we want. Christians who say things like that belie their ignorance of society and culture, not to mention ethics and morality. [*Belie...is that the proper word? I'm going to say...no. Why don't I just say that people who say things like that don't get how societies and cultures work?*]

People are inculcated [*Inculcated? Holy crap. Where did I get these words. Did I really talk like that back then? I mean, no, of course I didn't talk like that. I've always talked like someone with squirrels in her brain. But I did have a tendency to write rather high-browly (I've just made up that word—high-browly. It means in a high-browed manner. Ooops. I've made up another word. Damn it, you know what I mean), especially when I got into defense mode. I mean, preciseness is very important to me and let's face it, some words just fit better than others. But inculcated? I don't want people to have to stop reading and look up words—although, if it's the ebook version, I have to admit I love the Kindle function where I can instantly see a definition. I mostly use it to get an aha! when I see an author misuse a word.*]

Only kidding! Seriously. Joking. Anyway, better word: instilled. People are instilled] with the morality of their cultures and communities. Yes, they make individual decisions; that's why people still steal and cheat. But the more unfavorably certain actions are looked upon by the greater society in which a person lives, the harder it is for him to commit those acts. That's why you have fewer people murdering than you have lying. Committing acts deemed atrocious by society requires a lack of the fundamental emotions necessary to moral behavior, such as empathy and shame, often producing a psychological rift between the individual and society—in other words, a psychosis. [*By god, I'm smart.*]

Christians can rail against the morality of their society all they want but until they realize that the majority view is what creates the moral climate, they will only cause friction and discord. While morality is related to law, all the variations of personal moral values can't be legislated. Morality isn't something that can be forced on others; rather, we epitomize and exemplify our personal standard for others to judge. Discussion and persuasion, not attack and denigration, are the proper means to moral unity and understanding. [*Moral unity. Not philosophical conformity. In other words: exemplify morality; mock religion.*]

Christians try to force a morality onto society that doesn't fit because they claim we do not get our morals from our culture. So, I ask them, "Where do you get *your* morals?" They tell me we all get morals in two ways: God lays his moral law on our hearts and he outlined it in the Bible. I am also told God's moral law is absolute—uncon-

187

ditional and not limited by restrictions or exceptions. What are these absolute morals that God has outlined for humanity? There are none, if the truth be told. God's moral law is subjective and situational. [*The moral law of the god of the Bible is subjective and situational. God's moral law is subjective and situational. (I just wanted to say it again. Just in case you didn't take it in the way I'd hoped.) I can do that because I'm the author.*]

Is the moral law a separate and distinct set of laws, existing somewhere apart from God? Is it a set of laws that even God must obey? Is morality separate from God? If the moral law is separate from him, God is subject to it himself and must uphold it; but God fails to do so.

If murder is wrong, then he is guilty by his acts in the Old Testament. "I, on my part, am about to bring the flood waters on the earth, to destroy everywhere all creatures in which there is the breath of life; everything on earth shall perish." (Gen 6:17) "At midnight the Lord slew every first-born in the land of Egypt..." (Exod 12:29)

If lying is wrong, God is guilty of breaking the moral law. "So now, the Lord has put a lying spirit in the mouths of all these prophets of yours..." (1Kings 22:23) "And if the prophet be deceived and speak a word, I, the Lord, have deceived that prophet..." (Ezek 14:9)

Maybe that's what happened with Isaiah and his false prophecy of Damascus? Or maybe the Bible is just stories that someone made up and God is not guilty of lying and murder at all. If so, how do you know what is true about God and what isn't? If these things are true of God, it means that he can break the moral law while holding us accountable to it—and we have no recourse in the matter. He's more powerful than we are and apparently 'might makes right.'

However, I am told that God and moral law are one and the same—the moral code isn't above God because nothing is above God—he is supreme. God created the moral law or the law is part of his nature. That means that morality is subjective—it is subject to the will or nature of God.

If God says murder is good, murder is good because God is the author of morality. If God says infants being dashed to pieces (Isaiah 13:16) or bashing babies against rocks (Psalm 137:9) is good, then it is good because God says so. If God says that raping the virgins of your slaughtered enemy (Num 31:18) is good, then it is good. If God says that sending she-bears to maul young boys for teasing a bald priest (2Kings 2:24) is good, then it is good because God authored it. Whatever God calls good and moral, is, by definition, good and moral. What you or I may think of it is of no consequence. That's subjective morality—it emanates from the subjective mind of God.

I'm also told that God has written his law on my heart. [*I keep wanting to snark this heart business, but I'm forcing myself to let it go.*] God has instilled me with the knowledge of right and wrong—sort of like getting my morals as hand-me-downs instead of having to buy new. That is how I know that murder is wrong, even if God doesn't get the chance to tell me. That is why I am held responsible for my sin, even if I didn't know about it, because God wrote the law on my heart. [*There it is again. There's a lot of talk about our hearts in Christianity. I know what they mean, but it still bugs me.*]

When I feel that slaughtering an entire enemy village–young boys, babies, the elderly, every living thing–except the virgin girls, is horrible, I think it's horrible because God has instilled me with a sense of right and wrong. Yet, what *I* find horrible is an act sanctioned, even commanded, by God in the Bible. Something God ordered, I find repugnant. How can this be?

Do you find any of the following morally wrong or bad in any way?

- a worldwide flood that kills babies, animals, everything (Gen 6, 7)
- human sacrifice (Lev 27: 28,29; Judges 11: 34, 39)
- a man offering his virgin daughters to a mob [*for some sex until you die action*] (Gen 19:8)
- the murder of the first born sons of an entire country (Exod 8)
- slavery (Exod 21: 2, 4-6, 20,21; Lev 25: 44-46;)
- using women [*sexually, of course*] and casting them aside (Deut 21: 10-11, 13-14)
- taking captive virgins for your [*sexual*] pleasure (Num 31)
- death penalty for idolatry and heresy (Exod 22:20)
- killing your family members for practicing another religion (Deut 13:6, 8-10)
- death penalty for menial labor on the Sabbath (Num 15: 32, 35-36)
- death penalty for all manner of silly things (OT laws)

- massacre of an entire people, capturing their virgins as [*sexual*] booty, slaughter of helpless women and children (Num 31)
- massacring an entire people for something their ancestors did (1Sam 15:1-3,8)

All of these atrocities and more are sanctioned or commanded by the god of the Bible, the supposed author of my moral values. Here's the crux of the problem. By my moral standards, the Christian god is a mass murderer, a cruel tyrant, a torturer of frail and imperfect beings. Before I read the Bible, I had been told that God was love itself, that God loved me, that God so loved the world he gave his only son to die for my sins. But when I read the Bible, I didn't find that to be true. I found God to be disgusting.

If a person claims that any of those things I listed above are good for any reason whatsoever, they are immoral by the standards of Western society. I have heard people try to explain in what manner it was good for God to command those horrible deeds, good for all of us, good for God's people, even good for the victims. It's a disgusting display of the destructive power of belief.

I've been told that I do not, cannot, have God's perspective but if I did, I would see that all God's actions are good and that once we are in God's presence we may be able to understand them. God had adequate reason to act the way he did and the outcome will be best for all. This sounds very much like 'the ends justify the means,' a concept I've heard degraded by Christians as immoral. I don't care what good may come of the murder of children—it is wrong under all circumstances. The ends cannot justify the means, by my moral standard. I find it incredible that an omnipotent god could use no better means to reach his goal.

I've been told that my problem isn't with God; it's with Satan. Satan is causing me to misunderstand God, to see God's actions as evil. If I were a Christian and filled with the holy spirit, I'd see that God is good and all the bad things he did in the Old Testament were really good things.

I do not want to be filled with a spirit that would make me see horrible things as good. I don't think this holy spirit is a good spirit. How can it be right to see murdering young children (Num 31:17) as a good thing? I have to wonder who is really blind to the truth here. [*I have to wonder? I don't need to wonder—it's pretty obvious.*]

I have been told that as the creator of humans, God has the right to do with us as he pleases, including ordering, committing, approving of, or not interfering with murder. This is blatant 'might makes right' thinking and I disagree. Humans are sentient beings. We reason, we feel joy and suffer pain. Once a deity creates sentient beings, his rights over them are severely limited.

How dare I judge God by my human morality? I dare because I do have moral standards and obviously mine are higher than the Bible god's. My standard of what is good and fair, loving and kind, forgiving and merciful is higher than that of the Christian god. If, as Christians claim, my morals came from God, something is amiss. [*Amiss. Cute word. I daresay something is amiss.*] If he gave me my moral standards, he is either above them and I am supposed to turn a blind eye to his violation of his own laws, or the god in the Bible isn't the god who created me and gave me my morals.

If God is indeed above the law, free to murder and torture humans, my moral standard tells me I must turn against him. Might does not make right. Murdering and torturing beings that are weaker than you are is not moral. I cannot, will not, worship an immoral god.

Also, I must judge God—we all must judge God. According to Christian theology, God wants me to come to him of my own free will to worship, love, and serve him. I can't choose God without first making a judgment about him. When Christians choose God and Jesus they make a judgment—they judge them worthy. I do not. Of course, I also don't believe that the god of the Bible exists, and it's a good thing he doesn't, the way I see it.

Morality and the Bible

[Slavery] was established by decree of Almighty God...it is sanctioned in the Bible, in both Testaments, from Genesis to Revelation...it has existed in all ages, has been found among the people of the highest civilization, and in nations of the highest proficiency in the arts.

—Jefferson Davis, President
Confederate States of America

I've heard several Christians attempt to apologize for Jesus' lack of outrage against slavery by claiming that the institution didn't mean the same thing back then as it does today. By my moral standards, the indenture of one human being by another is bad; it is never good. Looking at the scriptures regarding slavery, detailing the punishments for beating or killing a slave or servant, it is apparent that slavery in ancient times was not much different from slavery throughout history. The attempts to tone it down, to make it seem that in Biblical times it was an honorable or caring situation is a blatant and immoral attempt to rationalize one's belief.

Others have told me that Jesus didn't speak out against slavery because the people of ancient times weren't capable of accepting such a dictum. That, to me, is ridiculous. Jesus told us to "be perfect, just as your Heavenly Father is perfect." (Matt 5:48) That is impossible to live by and yet, he told us to do it. Of course he would have told us to stop owning slaves if he thought we should.

Jesus was supposedly the son of God, the greatest prophet ever to walk the earth and I am asked to believe he didn't bother to leave us with important rules. In actuality, he didn't need to. God left the explicit, exhausting rules for living in the Old Testament. Christians don't want to live by those laws so they imagine that Jesus somehow nullified them by "fulfilling the law." Yet, Jesus said he hadn't come to change the law one jot or tittle; "until Heaven and earth pass away, not the smallest letter or the smallest part of a letter will pass from the law." (Matt 5: 17-18)

Why don't Christians live by most of the Old Testament laws? I can think of three reasons: there is a passage somewhere in the Bible in which someone contradicts Jesus; the laws in the Old Testament are too tedious to follow; or, by today's standards many of those laws are immoral.

When I ask about the laws of God in the Bible, I'm generally offered the Ten Commandments but those traditional ten aren't the right ones. The traditional Ten Commandments are taken from Exodus, Chapter 20, though they aren't labeled as such in the text itself. The story goes like this: Moses led the people out of Egypt to Sinai and there went up the mountain to have a few words with Yahweh. Yahweh told Moses to remind the people how great a god he was, evidenced by his nastiness in dealing with the Egyptians, and to find out if they wanted to be his chosen people; the people agreed. Then Yahweh told Moses to tell the people not to touch the mountain when he was on it (or they'd get stoned to death or shot with an arrow), not to sanctify themselves, and above all not to have intercourse with any women! [*Because sex is really dirty. It's a wonder the followers of the Abrahamic religions manage to reproduce at all.*] After doing so, Moses went up the mountain again to get the commandments of God.

The traditional ten are laid out in Exodus Chapter 20, verses 2-17; but God didn't stop there. He continued in verses 22 through 25 and then Chapters 21, 22, and 23 with more laws–laws regarding slaves, personal injury, loans, social intercourse, and religious practices. There aren't ten commandments; there are dozens.

The people down at the base of the mountain weren't behaving themselves [*probably due to sexual frustration*] and when Moses came down with his laws (for I suspect he wrote them himself and made the rule about not coming up the mountain while God was on it just to keep the riffraff from finding out the man behind the curtain was himself [*Right. Like the dude actually existed and did all that stuff.*] he smashed them to the ground in anger. No matter, "The Lord said to

Moses, 'Cut two stone tablets like the former that I may write on them the commandments which were on the former tablets that you broke.'" (Exodus 34: 1)

The problem is that the second set Yahweh gave Moses was not the same as the originals. God said: "But you, on your part, must keep the commandments I am giving you today." (Exodus 34: 11): And the real Ten Commandments are [*Drumroll, please.*]:

- Don't worship other gods or make covenants with people you defeat in war
- Don't make molten gods
- Keep the Feast of Unleavened Bread
- The first-born of your livestock and sons is to be given to God
- Work six days and rest on the seventh
- Keep the Feast of Weeks
- Don't sacrifice animals at the same time you sacrifice with leavened bread
- Don't keep the sacrifice of the Passover feast for the next day
- The first fruits of the soil must be given to God
- Don't boil a kid in its mother's milk

I am at a loss as to why Christians don't claim these as the Ten Commandments. Either they don't actually read their Bible, or they just don't find these ten appealing. More importantly, if we follow any of the commandments issued by God in the Old Testament, why don't we follow all of them? I am told it is because Jesus fulfilled the law so it's no longer necessary. If that is true, why do we still revere the traditional Ten Commandments? [*It's a twisty, crazy, mixed up religion.*]

Why are we allowed to eat rare meat (Leviticus 19:26), live after committing adultery (Leviticus 20:10) [*Granted, in some places in the Middle East you aren't...if you're a woman, anyway.*], and work on the Sabbath? Why do Christians pick and choose which laws of the Old Testament are still binding and which are not? Could it be because some laws of the Old Testament still appeal to them and others do not? Could it be that Christians, just like the rest of society, adopt moral laws using their own, their families', and their culture's guidance instead of a supposedly absolute morality imposed upon them by a deity? [*Uh, yeah.*]

If Jesus fulfilled the law and made the Old Testament commandments unnecessary, then the traditional Ten Commandments are outdated. Jesus, in Matthew chapter 19, verses 18 and 19 said the commandments to follow are:

- Do not kill
- Do not commit adultery
- Do not steal
- Do not lie
- Honor your father and mother
- Love your neighbor as yourself

There aren't ten of them and he left out one of the greatest. Jesus said the greatest commandments were to love God with all your heart and your neighbor as yourself. The first could be considered a rendition of the commandment to have no other gods before Yahweh. The second is a rule of social behavior found in Leviticus 19:18, in which we are also told not to take revenge or hold a grudge against fellow countrymen. Jesus says these two are the greatest commandments–that "the whole law and the prophets depend on" them. (Matt 22:36-40) If we put them all together, we have only seven commandments according to Jesus.

Jesus didn't say to ignore any of God's other commandments. In fact, he said quite the opposite: "Do not think that I have come to abolish the law or the prophets. I have come not to abolish but to fulfill. Amen, I say to you, until Heaven and earth pass away, not the smallest letter or the smallest part of a letter will pass from the law, until all things have taken place." (Matt 5:17-18) If fulfill means to end, then Jesus contradicts himself. [*Egad!*] Heaven and earth haven't passed away as far as I can tell, so all things haven't yet come to pass...so why are Christians daily ignoring the law of Yahweh? Because morals change; *there is no absolute morality.*

Do not kill. If that is one of God's absolutes, why do so many conservative Christians support the death penalty? If "do not kill" really means do not murder, it's not absolute after all. Murder is a relative term. When is killing murder? When is it an act of war? When is it justifiable? "Do not kill" either means no killing of any kind under any circumstance, or it is a situational, subjective commandment.

There is no absolute morality handed to us by a god. Our morals have developed and changed throughout the evolution of our species. I get my morals the same way Christians do. The big difference is that somewhere along the way, they were told that it is immoral to not believe in and worship their god. In that respect, no matter how good and moral a person I am, I will always be

198

immoral in the eyes of many Christians.

I've been told that atheists and practitioners of other religions borrow moral codes from Christianity. Christianity, they say, brought morality to the world and we benefit from it while reviling it. We are unappreciative sycophants flailing against the very philosophy that supports us. This is untrue [*to say the least*].

Christianity is not the originator of morality. Law is a reflection of each culture's morality. The codification of laws originated within the moral systems of human groups. The earliest known codification of laws was done by the King of Ur about 2100 BCE. Hammurabi codified a comprehensive set of laws during his reign in Babylon from 1795 to 1750 BCE. But even before laws were organized and written down, societies lived by their own moral codes. All cultures survive by adhering to codes of conduct. To claim that Christianity was, or even that the Hebrews were, the first to bring about a moral code for humanity is ludicrous and shows a terrible lack of historical understanding. Mankind created systems of morality and conduct on its own, long before the Hebrews adopted the warrior god Yahweh and long before pagan Jews created their own risen savior.

[*But of course the Christians will just say that God's moral law originated with mankind, not Moses and the Ten Commandments. That guy just wrote the laws down. The reason humans had moral laws in societies before that was because God gave us the moral law. You know, that old laying on our hearts stuff. All those earlier laws are just humans feeling the God in them. Or*

199

Satan. Either way, my argument doesn't cut it.]

Chapter Ten

What's My Problem?

In some awful, strange, paradoxical way, atheists tend to take religion more seriously than the practitioners.

—Sir Jonathon Miller,
British physician and theater director

Many Christians with whom I've spoken are genuinely concerned about my atheism. They seem to feel that if I only understood God, the Bible, and Christianity the proper way, I'd come to believe in those things. At least one has offered to study the gospels with me, to answer my objections, and explain to me where my misunderstanding occurred. I appreciate their feelings [*No I don't. I think they're creepy.*] and their kindness [*Even creepier. Most of the time they were the types who'd call me 'friend' in their initial correspondence. "Hello, friend. Can I call* you friend?" *Cringing*.] and I understand their strong faith in what they believe. [*Eh, not really. I get it intellectually. As in, this is why humans believe weird shit. But when I read about some of the stuff people believe and the crazy stuff they do, I really don't get it. I think there is something seriously wrong with the species.*] I've studied Christianity from an objective viewpoint and learned from Christians themselves enough to know that the explanations meant to convert me fall far short. [*That was obvious, wasn't it?*]

The quick answer to why I don't believe what they believe is because I'm a rationalist. The long answer is that, aside from simply not believing in gods, I find the Christian faith to be false and immoral so that, even were I to be a supernaturalist, I would not be Christian.

Rationalism

I am not a scholar or a philosopher–I'm an average person [*Well. I don't know. Oh, okay. I'm average.*] with an interest in the differences between believers and nonbelievers. I don't pretend that we will come to any agreement; I certainly don't expect others to accept my reasoning against their beliefs. [*Comes from all that butting my head against the brick wall that is 'belief.'*] I only want it understood and accepted that I, and most other atheists, have not dismissed Christianity without thorough consideration.

Rationalists claim reason–not subjective experience, authority, or spiritual revelation–is the primary basis of knowledge. That is why I don't believe what others believe–I am unwilling to allow someone else to tell me what is true, to assume gods when the evidence doesn't support their existence, and to accept an answer because I feel I must have an answer when there isn't one to be had.

Science

I accept the scientific process as the best method we have for determining the nature of our reality. I understand that many people, not just Christians, are wary of science because it doesn't agree with their ideas regarding supernaturalism and the spiritual realm. [*It was really tough for me to like System of a Down's "Science," but somehow I managed to even sing along. Ugh. Stupid song.*] Science doesn't delve into that realm because there is nothing there to be objectively studied. The evidence suggests it doesn't exist.

There is no conspiracy in the scientific community against the supernatural as Christians, astrologists, and chakra practitioners are wont to claim. [*Are chakras even still a thing? Don't answer that. I don't want to know.*] There is simply nothing there for science to deal with. If it can't be tested, measured, or authenticated–if its effects can't be reproduced–we can't know anything about it and it is, therefore, equal to nonexistent. I understand that many won't agree with that because they have accepted the existence of a supernatural realm that can only be verified through subjective experience and spiritual or authoritative revelation. As a rationalist, I do not accept those as evidence. [*Because they aren't evidence.*] They are, as far as I can discern, products of the human psychology–they are in your mind only. If they can't be objectively researched, we can never be sure of them and certainly can't claim any knowledge of them.

The scientific method is a valuable tool. It has brought us from the Dark Ages through the Enlightenment to this great age. [*Not to imply that the scientific method popped into existence shortly before the Dark Ages.*] I trust the scientific method; it has enabled us to objectively and rationally study our reality. Too few people know what the scientific method is. In the scientific community, claims are based on evidence; theories are tested and peer-reviewed. People suspicious of the scientific method often point to arguments and disagreements among scientists as evidence that scientific claims, such as evolution, aren't valid. "Scientists can't even agree on it," they say, "so how are we supposed to believe it's true?"

If we look closely at the scientific community, however, what we find is a system of checks and balances that allows us to evaluate theories and findings and reasonably accept conclusions. Scientists disagree; that's the beauty of the search for reality. There is no science dogma to which scientists must adhere. New findings are subject to peer review and unbiased testing. [*Not that every claim actually gets retested, unfortunately.*] Scientists do disagree on some aspects of evolutionary theories, such as how it occurred, but the vast majority of scientists agree that evolution explains our human origins.

Christians also claim that scientists are biased against the supernatural and God and try very hard to ignore any evidence that might lead to anything but a naturalistic conclusion. Just imagine if a scientist could come up with objective evidence for the supernatural. If anyone could offer repeatable, testable evidence that proved ESP, chakras, angels, the effectiveness of prayer, or God, he'd be a celebrity. He wouldn't be ridiculed or banished from the scientific community if his theory had objective, testable evidence to back it up. But no such evidence exists.

Evolution

Creationists make it sound as though a 'theory' is something you dreamt up after being drunk all night.

–Isaac Asimov

I accept the facts that show us our evolutionary heritage. The subject of evolution is a big one with Christians. Many accept the facts and simply attach evolution to their god's plan but there are still those, the loudest it seems, who deny the facts, claim evolution is "just a theory," a lie, and that creation as told by the Bible is the truth. I will not discuss the various evolutionary theories here– hundreds of books are available to anyone who wants to learn about them. [*Even evolution books for dummies and idiots.*] I wanted to include evolution here for a particular reason.

I don't *believe in* evolution. I am not an *evolutionist*. Phrasing it that way is a blatant attempt on the part of many Christians to make acceptance of the facts of evolution into a faith so that they can claim it is no different than what they do when they choose Christianity. That is a lie and a rationalization made for the express purpose of avoiding the fact that they have no evidence to support their view that a god created the world and humans, as described in the Bible—there is no evidence for Creationism. Creationism, therefore, is something that necessitates a belief. You must *believe in* Creationism because it is not based on facts.

I don't *believe in* evolution—I don't have to; I simply accept the facts that I have seen and read about. The difference between a rationalist and a Creationist is evident in this debate. The Creationist already knows what is true for him—an authority has given him his truth in the Bible. [*Because people around him, most likely his parents, told him he's a Christian and that book has all the answers.*] All the facts [*he encounters*] must support that truth. No facts that dispute it will be accepted; worse, facts can be created, made up, or *fabricated* as long as they support his truth.

The rationalist, on the other hand, is free to accept facts as they are. He creates a theory based on those facts. A scientific theory doesn't mean a guess, an assumption, or a made-up story. A scientific theory is an explanation based on supporting facts. The great thing about science is that theories change. When new facts are discovered that contradict long-held theories, they aren't ignored, they aren't banned, they aren't called heresy or changed to fit the theory—they *change the theory*. [*Well, eventually. After the scientists get over their human knee-jerk reaction to being shown they're wrong.*] Rationalists are free to accept new ideas—we have no authority that tells us what is true. Creationists find facts to fit their truth. Rationalists discover the truth that fits the facts. One position is noble, the other is not. One is honest, the other is not. One is truth, the other, a lie. [*Take that, liars!*]

Truth

There aren't any versions of the truth.
–Dr. Ian Malcolm
Jurassic Park II: The Lost World
(Universal, 1997)

What is truth? Some people talk about Truth, with a capital T, as if it is an ultimate idea that transcends all life and reality. When I say truth, I'm talking about plain, simple, factual truth. Not a truth for me, different from your truth—and not an ultimate, great truth. I'm talking about *the* truth; the only one.

I've heard it said that one person's truth is another's lie. This is not the kind of truth I'm looking for. Let's say that Person A believes the moon is made of green cheese. Person B believes the moon is made of ham. If every person holds his own truth, then both of these persons are correct. But neither is correct—the truth is that the moon is a rock. That truth will never change and it doesn't matter what people believe about the moon or how many people believe it; there is a truth with regard to it that can be discovered.

I want the truth. I don't want to believe in something. If there isn't an answer to a question, like, how did life on earth arise, then I will have to wait until there is or die without it because I would rather be without an answer than believe in something that may not be the truth.

In the final chapter of *Does God Exist?* (Prometheus, 1993), a debate between J.P. Moreland and Kai Nelson, Peter Kreeft discusses "The Choice of a

Lifetime," how to decide what position you will take after reading the debate and discussions pertaining to it. He starts out fine in highlighting the advice that we should be honest with ourselves and we must look at all evidence on both sides. But from there he digresses into a disgusting display of emotionalism and the threat of Pascal's Wager. We should look at lives, he says, to determine the truth–and people's lives have been changed for the better with Christianity. We should try living our lives as if we were Christians and then as if we were nonbelievers and see which one is more satisfying–as if this will lead us to the truth. Finally, he speaks of the possibilities: either God exists or he doesn't and we either believe in him or we don't–and only the one combination of those choices (he exists and we believe) will earn us "the infinite prize of eternal life. Faith," he says, "is a 'no-lose' bet and atheism is a 'no-win' bet."

This is how we should determine truth? We imagine a frightful scenario of eternal torture versus a paradise and then see what feels good or hedge our bets? This is why Christianity is akin to snake oil to me, and its apologists fearmongers. I don't determine what is true by how I feel–I want the facts.

Why I am not a Christian

Certainly my rationalist view affects the manner in which I interpret and understand theism. It is because I am a rationalist that I am atheist. But what is it that makes me think I would not be Christian even were I to accept a supernatural realm? There are many tenets of the Christian faith that, when viewed objectively, show it to be false and immoral. Much of Christianity only makes sense when viewed historically as layer upon layer of apologetics were created to explain discrepancies and contradictions.

The omni god and free will

Epicurus said,

Either God wants to abolish evil, and cannot; or he can, but does not want to...If he wants to, but cannot, he is impotent. If he can, but does not want to, he is wicked... If, as they say, God can abolish evil, and God really wants to do it, why is there evil in the world?

When you discuss the Christian god with Christians, you begin to get a picture of it and its attributes. God is omnipotent, omnipresent, omniscient, and omnibenevolent. In other words, he is all powerful, everywhere, all knowing, and all good. God gave us something called free will. Free will is supposed to explain why the world is in the state it is while there is an omni God at the helm. Free will is the excuse Christians invented for God's ineptness and inattention. [*Snap!*]

The Christian god cannot possibly exist. Christians have unwittingly defined their god into non-existence–he has disappeared in a puff of illogic. No entity can have all the omni attributes and offer free will at the same time.

God can't be all powerful; he can't do absolutely anything; he is limited. Christians say, for instance, that he can't do something that is logically impossible, such as create a rock so big he can't lift it himself, or create a square circle. Christians get exasperated when atheists and skeptics play logic games like that with them. They think we're being facetious, but we're just pointing out that no entity can be all powerful. There is no conceivable way for God to be omnipotent. He is limited by logic, and any limit imposed on him makes him less than all powerful. [*I'm pretty sure at least one Christian told me that God can, in fact, create a rock so heavy he couldn't lift it and still be able to lift it. Naturally he can make a square circle after that. Logic is just different with God.*]

God is supposed to be all good and can't do anything that is not good. Therefore, he is again limited. I've been told that God can't kill himself or cease to exist. There are plenty of things that God can't do. [*He can't have sex because there's only one of him and he can't masturbate because that's just wrong; it'd grow hair on his knuckles and he can't have that.*] In the Bible, God is certainly not described as omnipotent. He couldn't help Judah defeat a certain population because they had iron chariots (Judges 1:19). That's silly, of course, to think that a god could be bested by iron chariots–but it's in the Bible. [*Don't look there; look at the leaves!*]

Jesus is God, I'm told, and yet, in his home town, he couldn't work any miracles because the people there didn't believe in him (Matt 13:57-58). That always made me wonder...he wasn't powerful enough to overcome disbelief. Only people who already believed in him would believe in him. [*Right. It's just like psychics. You believe they have some psychic ability so you buy into what they're telling you. You aren't skeptical.*]

Christians sometimes explain God's power problem by redefining the word "all" to mean "all within his capability." Using that definition, I too am all powerful because I can do everything within my capability. [*I am the all-powerful Dianna! Powers subject to wily Christians' definition of 'all.'*] God can't do anything he wants to do. He is bound by the rules of logic (and steel) and by his own good nature. Therefore, he is not all powerful. He is more powerful than man, I'll give you that. He's just not omnipotent. [*Meh. I don't care much for the first part of this argument against omnipotence. We get what they mean, right? Being logically inconsistent—the rock argument—is just obtuse. I should have just stuck with the steel chariots argument and said, "Look. You take all the Bible or none of it. Why on earth would you follow a book that clearly shows your god to be incapable of melting the crap out of some steel chariots? What kind of god is that? Your whole religion is based on silly stories.*]

God is not omniscient. The Bible is clear on that point. In Genesis, God didn't know where Adam was or that he'd eaten from the forbidden fruit (Gen 3:9-11). He didn't know why Eve ate the fruit and offered it to Adam (Gen 3: 13). And he didn't know what happened to Abel (Gen 4:9). [*Christian apologist: God was just being polite in not appearing to assume things that he obviously already knew, especially with Eve. You know how women get.*]

God can't be omniscient if mankind has free will. If we truly have choices to make, God can't know what we will choose before we choose it. If God knows what we will do, our future is already told. His prior knowledge eliminates our freedom of choice, making it an illusion. [*It's fun to watch apologists leap through their apology hoops trying to make us able to change our minds with God still knowing our choices in advance. You should watch it sometime, if it won't make you feel too dirty.*]

Christians tell me that God knows everything there is to know as it happens; this wouldn't include the future. But then, they also tell me that God knew that man would rebel and he would have to send himself down as Jesus to die on the cross for our salvation—he knew all that from the beginning of time. Others tell me that we have complete free will, but God just knows the choices we will make ahead of time. I'm confused. Does God know everything, including the future? Or does God only know the past and present? It's really very simple, I don't know why Christian doctrine is always making things difficult: either we truly have free will and God is not omniscient, or God is omniscient and the future is already set— we can't do anything to change it.

God is not omnibenevolent. He punishes people—an all-good being wouldn't be able to punish anyone. [*A being that is all good, that is love incarnate, wouldn't even know how to hit someone, hurt someone, make someone sad, much less kill him.*] He commands people to murder others in the Bible (Num 31) and is vengeful (Deut 32:35). God allows evil in the world. He doesn't stop the murderer or rapist from their designs against innocent humans. [*He wouldn't even be able to create a being who could do those things.*] Christians say that is because he gave us free will.

That's fine. But it shows that God can't be all good. He could be good–just not all good. No omni-benevolent creature could allow evil to flourish when he is powerful enough to stop it. [*That's the truth of it, right there.*]

If God is omnipotent and has the desire for all mankind to be saved, all mankind would be saved. Anything an all-powerful God wants, he gets–because he's all powerful. I'm told that this doesn't happen, that all men aren't saved because there is something else that God wants. He wants us to have free will. I don't think it says that anywhere in the Bible. It says, "All things are possible for God," (Mark 10:27) and that God is "not wishing that any should perish but that all should come to repentance." (2Peter 3:9) Nowhere does it say, "...but more than this, God wants you to have the free will to turn away from him and not be saved." It's just not there. Free will is something that Christians made up to explain inconsistencies in their religion.

There are some Christians who don't believe in free will. They find plenty of support for their position in the Bible: "The Lord brings to naught the plans of nations; he foils the designs of peoples. But the plan of the Lord stands forever; the design of his heart, through all generations." (Psalm 33:9-11) "Our God is in Heaven; whatever he wills, he does." (Psalm 15:3) "In the beginning I foretell the outcome; in advance, things not yet done. I say that my plan shall stand, I accomplish my every purpose." (Isaiah 46:10)

It is very clear by those verses that God has a plan and nothing we do can change it. Whatever God wills is done. That means that God wills some people to be Christian just as he has willed that I should be atheist. He wills that some will be homosexual and some heterosexual. He wills that some should be slaughtered in war, maimed, raped, or tortured and he wills that others should die peacefully. God is in control, not us. Nothing has gone wrong with this world that God has not willed. The fall of man, sin, evil, Satan, murder–it's all God's will. [*If atheists aren't allowed to make judgments about their god,*] Christians have no right to judge what God has willed.

As Epicurus noted, if God is in charge, there is no free will. If God is all good, there can be no evil. If God wanted to stop evil and had the power to do so, he would. He's either powerless to act, making him useless, or he's vile and mean. Or, maybe, he's just fiction. [*Snap again!*]

The Trinity

The Trinity is a very strange concept but it had to be invented. Some early Christians believed that Jesus was God. In order for the tribulation on the cross to make sense, he had to be a man, too, because gods can't suffer and die. The only answer was that Jesus was God and man–fully God and fully man *at the same time.* That is, of course, impossible and illogical but it must be believed if Christianity is to make any sense at all.

Strangely enough in the Old Testament it is written that, "God is not man that he should speak falsely, nor human, that he should change his mind." (Num 23:19) Nonetheless, early Christians, for whatever reason, ignored the scripture and determined that God was, indeed, man–at least for a little while. Obviously man has a problem with

214

telling the truth. As Paul said, "...every human being is a liar..." (Rom 3: 10) Why we are expected to believe anything Paul said after that is one of my big questions. How are we are supposed to believe Jesus' words as well, considering that he was fully man? Knowing God's penchant for sending lying spirits to the mouths of prophets (1Kings 22:23), it is well within reason to distrust the entire story.

The Trinity divides God into three parts: the Father, the Son, and the Holy Spirit. They are three separate entities but they are each God at the same time. They are one and three and impossible to believe. If God can be three and one, I fail to see the problem with his creating a rock so big he can't lift it. If he must stay within the realm of logic, what is he doing mixed up with the Trinity?

God sent himself down to become a man. [*No, no. God had sex...wait. The Holy Spirit had sex...* Somebody *had sex with Mary to impregnate her with himself. Or was it himselves?*] He was still himself but he called himself Jesus and walked the earth–while he was still in Heaven and called himself the Father. He had himself tortured and killed (though he couldn't die because he was God) and buried. He rose again, though he was already alive. He ascended into Heaven where he had been the whole time.

Remember that nonsense poem we [*really old people*] recited in school?

One fine day in the middle of the night
Two dead men got up to fight
Back to back they faced each other
Drew their swords and shot each other

That's the Trinity for you. It makes no sense.

[*Now, wait a minute. Not only was God also man when he was Jesus, we are supposed to believe that the Trinity has always existed. Jesus is eternal, too. So that means...Jesus had sex with his mom! Cue: Ray Stevens, "I'm my own grand-pa."*]

The family thing

One of my biggest questions regarding Jesus involves his miraculous birth. While it is extremely difficult to believe the mythical element of virgin conception–of the Holy Spirit, being God [*Uh, and Jesus too*], actually impregnating a woman–that's not the problem. [*Not that it isn't a problem.*] My confusion arose when I read about Jesus as a grown man and his parents' and the townspeople's reactions to him.

In the beginning, Mary was approached by an angel who told her she would conceive a child by a holy spirit (meaning God, the Father, and the son Jesus, too...Jesus is his own father!). [*Duh! And boinked his own mother. I can't stress this e-nough.*] This angel said to Mary of Jesus, "He will be great and will be called Son of the Most High, and the Lord God will give him the throne of David his father..." (Luke 1:32) An angel visited Joseph, Mary's fiancé, too because he was thinking of breaking the engagement. The angel told him that Jesus would "...save his people from their sins." (Matt. 1: 21)

Jesus was born in a manger and three wise men from the East headed over to pay him homage–his birth was apparently a glorious and renowned thing. But...for some reason it was all forgotten. The people in the town of Nazareth didn't think Jesus was anything special. I suppose I can buy the theory that Mary and Joseph didn't tell anyone about the relationship between their son and God (that he was Jesus' real father) and that Jesus was the promised Messiah. You'd think after all the fuss with Herod killing baby boys, people would have been on the lookout for a Messiah of about the right age who could have escaped the massacre. When Jesus showed up, they didn't find him special; no one seemed to remember his family's secret flight out of the country during Herod's slaughter. I can accept the theory that they didn't recognize him because God had a plan; God blinded them to the truth. [*Such a drama queen.*] But what I can't believe is that Jesus' own mother and brothers didn't know who he was.

Jesus' brothers, according to John, didn't believe in him. (John 7:5) How could that be? How could they have been raised with the son of God/God himself and not known it? Why would Jesus' relatives claim he was insane? (Mark 3: 21)

Worse is the behavior of his mother and father. They accidentally left him behind in Jerusalem [*Sure it was an accident. I bet they were trying to unload the arrogant little cuss and when people asked where he was they were all like, "Oh, right, Jesus, I guess we'd better go find him...the little shi–ah, shhweetheart."*] and went back to find him in the temple teaching. "When his parents saw him they were astonished." (Luke 2: 48) Why? Didn't they remember he was the son of God/God? Jesus explained to them that it was natural for them to find him in his father's house, but "they did not understand what he said to them." (Luke 2:50) How can that be? How can two people experience a miracle in their lives, take an adventurous sojourn into Egypt to rescue the savior of mankind from Herod (Matt 2:13-14) and forget all about it? It isn't possible. If God blinded Jesus' parents to the truth, why did he bother sending the messenger angels? Why didn't he just wait until Mary was married to have sex with her–then no one would have suspected anything for him to have to cover up. It just doesn't make sense.

The problem was evidently caused by a later insertion of a virgin birth story and a parallel to Moses' escape from Pharaoh into the narrative. That's what happens when you create and expand myths; they become convoluted and nonsensical.

The problem at home

When Jesus went home to Nazareth he couldn't work miracles there because the people didn't believe in him. According to Matthew, "Jesus said to them, 'A prophet is not without honor except in his native place and in his own house.' And he did not work many mighty deeds there because of their lack of faith." (Matt 13: 57-58) Why do you suppose people in a person's home town don't believe he is anything special? Could it be because they know him? Maybe they knew he wasn't who he claimed to be. Why would their lack of belief have anything to do with Jesus' ability to perform miracles? If you had to believe Jesus could do miracles before he could do them, how do we know the stories of the miracles aren't just due to imagination and the desire to believe? Wouldn't Jesus have wanted to perform miracles for people who didn't believe in him so they could be saved? [*Don't be silly. Obviously God wants some people to go to Hell. What's the point of having one if you can't send people there?*] Being that he was God, he should have been able to make anything he wanted to happen easily come about.

Some Christians have told me that it is precisely this sort of problem in the gospels that can be used as evidence of their validity. Because the gospels do not always show Jesus in a good light and perfect, they must have been written by people trying hard to be objective. If everything was perfect about Jesus, about the Bible—if the gospel narratives had no contradictions—that would cause them to suspect something was amiss. As they are, they show the work of honest men. [*Right. It's the all-perfect word of God when they want to hit the gays over the head with it, but it's an honest, fallible telling when they can't explain why it's so fucked up.*]

That is one way to look at it, I suppose, but there is another explanation. If you accept that the stories of Jesus' life began orally and weren't written down at the same time, you can see the building of the myth come to life before your eyes. Mark is acknowledged to have been written first in about 70 CE with the rest through about 110 CE when John was composed. If you line them up in that order—Mark, Matthew, Luke, and John—you can watch the building of the cult of Jesus from basic information on his teachings to full-fledged miraculous conception and godhood. When people retell and rewrite stories for their own audiences, elements are added and changed causing conflicts and errors in the manuscripts. That is why the gospel stories are contradictory and grow more and more mythical with the years. [*That's just too logical; believers don't accept logic on principle.*]

As to the character of Jesus, we may never know in what manner the authors of the original stories meant their works to be interpreted. If we consider, however, that early followers of the cult may not have accepted Jesus as a historical figure, but as symbolic, or even as a mere man, the fact that he wasn't presented as a perfect god makes sense.

The truth about the parables

Timothy said that God, our savior, "wills everyone to be saved and come to knowledge of the truth." (1Tim 2:4) Did Jesus/God want people to be saved? The disciples asked Jesus why he taught in parables and he said, "...so that they may look and see but not perceive, and hear and listen but not understand, in order that they may not be converted and be forgiven." (Mark 4: 12) God contradicts himself. He does and he doesn't want everyone to be saved.

According to the Bible, many people didn't believe Jesus' teachings so Isaiah's prophecy could come true: "He blinded their eyes and hardened their heart [*sic*], so that they might not see with their eyes and understand with their heart [*sic*] and be converted and I would heal them." (John 12:40) So I have to wonder which is correct. Does God want everyone saved or not? If he wants everyone saved, why would he blind eyes and harden hearts to prevent it? [*He's just diabolical; it's one of his cutest attributes.*]

These are just some of the questions and issues I have about the story of Jesus and Christianity. I am sure apologists have answers to all of my problems; they can smooth away any contradictions and make sense of atrocities. I have little doubt I've heard the excuses before. None of them are convincing to me. I think perhaps we should just agree to disagree. [*And avoid each other—I'm not too keen on hanging out with people who don't have a problem with insanity.*]

Chapter Eleven

But, What Do I Really Think?

With or without religion, good people can behave well and bad people can do evil; but for good people to do evil—that takes religion.

—Steven Weinberg
(as quoted on the Internet)

[*Clearly I had no real source at the time. The quote is from an article titled, "A Designer Universe?," derived from a speech Weinberg had given at the Conference on Cosmic Design put on by the American Association for the Advancement of Science, in Washington, D.C. April 1999. The quote at the conference was somewhat different: "Religion is an insult to human dignity. With or without it you would have good people doing good things and evil people doing evil things. But for good people to do evil things, that takes religion."*]

Literalist Christianity is an immoral lie. [*Wow. I really handed it the world there didn't I? But why only "literalist" Christianity? It's all a lie.*] I realize that may be shocking to most people. [*It shocked me.*] The majority of the world has been deceived into believing they are educated about Christianity, its precepts, its moral goodness, its historical base, and its history. Most Christians have never read the Bible. [*Remember, it's not important how many people read it, just how many buy it and keep it on the bestseller list. It's all about the validation.*] Most Christians have never studied history as told by the opposition or by true historians. [*Right. Real historians with PhDs, not agendas. Not David Barton. He may be a student of history, but the only things he is an expert at are rewriting it and distorting it.*] Most Christians don't even go to church. Those who do simply accept what their pastor tells them and what they read in books written for the express purpose of defending the Christian lie. Most Christians will continue to be deceived because instead of truth, they want comfort. The comfortable path is generally the path you're already on. Change isn't something humans enjoy. Most of us will only accept it when it is forced on us.

Searching for truth is an active pursuit but it isn't an easy one. It takes diligence and discipline. It takes a commitment to put aside one's longings and emotions for objectivity. It takes an understanding of what bias is, how it invades our thinking and how to purge ourselves of it. To add to that, the truth about our reality isn't an easy one and humans aren't very big on difficulty. We generally take the rutted path–or remain on the road we find ourselves walking along.

I started my educational journey through the precepts and history of Christianity with a reading of the Bible. It was after this reading that I came to the firm conclusion that Christianity was immoral and even if it were true, I would not be able to worship its god.

The Bible

Evidence against the validity of the Bible abounds. One of the most fervent [*Fervent. Fervently. I must have had a little obsession going on with this word.*] claims of Christianity is that the Bible is historically accurate. I used to counter this claim with the obvious conclusion that just because the Bible is historically accurate in some spots doesn't make its mythical claims any less fallacious [*Fallacious!*]–and that was true. However, with more investigation I have found that modern archeological evidence destroys the historicity of the Bible. The Bible is far from historically accurate. It is, after all, the exaggerated claims of a backward and oppressed people.

Hell and a loving god

The concept of Hell is immoral. Many Christians have managed to distance themselves from the idea because they agree that eternal punishment is not in line with a loving and just god. Modern, mainstream Christianity seems to be of the opinion that God equals goodness and love. This all sounds acceptable and is probably what keeps mainstream Christianity alive.

Fundamentalist, conservative Christianity may continue its claim that God is love, but it doesn't hide its acceptance of God as vengeful and cruel in its perceptions of the Rapture, when the blood of the wicked will fill the streets, and Hell, where the screams of tortured souls will be pleasure to the ears of the saved. Normal, well-balanced, loving people don't accept those ideas as well they should not—they are immoral.

Looking at Hell from the literalist perspective we see an entity creating an imperfect being and then punishing it for its failings. At worst, the punishment is an eternal torture and at best, simply the absence of the presence of God. Mainstream Christianity has struggled with this problem of Hell. How does Love create a place of torment and punish people eternally for crimes committed in this very short lifetime? While we can give some credence to the idea of punishing extremely bad behavior for some length of time, the condemnation of nonbelief and mistaken belief seems unnecessarily cruel. [*Seems?*] How is it the fault of the Muslim for believing Islam when he was raised to believe it? How can a just god punish him for it? How can a just and loving god punish an agnostic for honestly claiming that he feels he can't know whether or not a god exists? [*Really. Punish him for being an arrogant sonofabitch instead.*]

One answer I have received from Christians is not helpful [*Only the one?*]: God doesn't send us to Hell, they say, we send ourselves there by denying God. But the Christian god is said to have created Hell; and he created humans with an imperfect nature—if we were created perfect, there would have been no fall, no matter how much temptation God placed in the garden. Perfect creatures don't

226

make imperfect choices. How can sin be the fault of the imperfect creation? God creates sinful beings and then punishes them for the way he created them.

It is God who must be imperfect, for a perfect god could only create perfect creatures. A perfectly loving god could only love those creatures. God must be imperfect (not hard to believe after a good reading of the Bible) and he punishes mankind for his own sin. [*Not that I think imperfection is a sin, or even a flaw.*]

Some Christians believe that their god creates some humans knowing they will end up in Hell; I've heard that some humans are created for the express purpose of going to Hell. Proverbs 16:4 says, "The Lord has made everything for his own ends, even the wicked for the evil day." This doesn't sound like the Christian concept of a loving god to me at all. [*It's sick is what it is.*]

One Christian told me that all people, even Muslims in the Middle East, know that Jesus is our savior and the only reason they don't consciously seek this truth is their own sinful natures. So, a Muslim born into and raised in Islam is inherently at fault for not accepting the truth he knows, that Jesus is the savior, and shunning Islam. Talk about elitism!

Another answer is that no one knows who will be in Hell and who will not. Some Christians say that they have no doubt there will be atheists in Heaven. Some believe that Hell may be only temporary. I appreciate that these people are honest about their aversion to the concept of eternal torment for humans but I don't think their ideas are Biblical. Jesus very clearly said that all those who don't believe in him were condemned and that Hell is an eternal punishment. (Matt. 25:46; Mark 16:16; John 3:18)

Many people claim that Hell is not Biblical at all. They say that Hell is a modern concept added to the Church in later days. The condemnation of Jesus, then, must mean something else. And what of Revelation and its bizarre story of a vengeful god destroying the wicked in a second coming? Either believe the entire Bible, or don't believe any of it. Why pick and choose? By what criteria do you believe some of it true and the rest false? If it isn't all true, is it the word of a god? And if not, why believe any of it? [*I think it's the silky smooth, thin pages and the funky language. And some people think the less sense something makes, the more important it must be. It's like those really stupid people who think they understand quantum physics. They watched that movie* What the Bleep Do We Know!? *and go around saying, "I'm really into quantum physics." They don't know what the hell they're talking about.*]

I've heard others say that Hell isn't permanent; that the punishment will fit the crime and some even believe that eventually every human soul will be in Heaven. I, personally, think they're making all of that up to make an immoral deity into something palatable to modern theism. [*Because that's exactly what they're doing.*]

Heaven

What will Heaven be like? Will everyone be good in Heaven? Some Christians have told me that living in Heaven, in the presence of God who is pure love and goodness, humans will no longer sin. But Adam and Eve lived in God's presence and they still sinned. Some say that in Heaven, we'll have free will just as we do now. People who do bad things will be cast out of Heaven immediately. If humans can be good all the time in Heaven, or bad people will be cast out, why didn't God create us in Heaven to begin with—why the passion play? [*Because he's a drama queen, that's why.*]

The purpose of the Earth creation, some have said, is a test. Our loyalty is being tested, our faith and belief, our obedience. Why? Why can't we know now that God exists; why can't we live in his presence and have a chance to know him and love him? Why do we have to just believe that he exists because other people tell us he does? Why would an all-knowing deity need a test? [*I told you; he's a freakin' drama queen. He's up there (up?) right now wringing his (probably very hairy) hands together with glee watching us try to figure this bloated, convoluted, ridiculous religion mess out. He's a creep. It's a good thing he's fictional.*]

Such a test, in the opinion of many, is unfair but I am told that God, as usual, has his reasons and I am always assured that his reasons are good ones. Because he is God and god is defined as good, anything he decides is good—whether I think so or not. [*Stupid me, getting my moral judgment from God and then using it to say he's not moral.*]

Heaven just doesn't make sense. If we get tested and only the good people get to go to Heaven, why didn't God just create only those good people? If only the people who believe in God by faith without evidence get in, why didn't he just create people like that in the first place? [*Too easy.*]

Others have told me that Earth is like a training ground. An oak begins as an acorn, they say. This life isn't a test, it's our infancy and here we must learn to trust in God. Right...those of us who fail to learn get tossed into the flaming abyss. It always boils down to Heaven as a reward, a prize to be won, not by using our brains, but by turning away from everything our reason tells us is true and instead believing in something nonsensical and contradictory. I can handle that. I can see that brownie points could be awarded to people who use faith. But that doesn't make the situation moral.

[*That scenario would mean, basically, that God wants stupid people in Heaven with him. So, eons ago...um, er...4,000 years ago, God created human beings and they were stupid. He waited and waited and let them get smarter until a whole heck of a lot of them realized he's a douchebag, or not even there. Soon he'll take all the stupid ones (the stupidest apparently being Christians and probably only those who reject reason and logic the most) and cast everyone else into a lovely little Hell where he and the stupidest humans ever made can glorify in our screams of torment. What a great plan! Only a really wonderful god would come up with that sort of plan. I'm starting to like him.*]

The fall of man

The fall of man, as described in the Bible, makes no sense. It goes pretty much like this: God creates Adam and Eve and they are perfect (or simply good, depending on the apologist). God sets them in a garden where he also plants two trees,

230

the tree of knowledge of good and evil and the tree of life. God only mentions the first tree to A&E and tells them not to eat any of its fruit—if they do, they'll die. Along comes a serpent, wily and cunning. Who let him into the garden? Where did God disappear to? The serpent tempts Eve. Eve, we must remember, is innocent; she hasn't eaten from the tree of knowledge of good and evil yet, so she obviously doesn't have any knowledge about them. Eve is perfect and living in the presence of the divine and holy god but, for some odd reason she is tempted by the serpent. The serpent claims that God is a liar; he says, "No, God knows well that the moment you eat of it your eyes will be opened and you will be like gods who know what is good and what is bad." (Gen 3:5) So, she eats the fruit and gives some to Adam. [*And all hell breaks loose. But don't blame God!*]

The problems with this story are enough to cause a person some pause. [*Ya think?*] Why did God allow his creatures to be tempted in such a manner? Why did he put the tree in the garden at all? Many Christians tell me that it was all part of the plan—that God knew what would happen—but, that is despicable. To create beings that you know will disobey you if you plant the right temptations in their home and then to punish them and all their progeny for it is not the behavior of a just and loving father.

Even worse, the serpent told the truth! Adam and Eve did not die when they ate the fruit as God said they would. Many Christians have tried to claim that God didn't mean they were going to die right then, he meant that they were immortal until they ate the fruit and then God cast them out and let them succumb to physical death later. This is not possible, however, if you believe the Bible. The scripture clearly shows that after A&E ate the fruit of the first tree, God was quick to hustle them out of the garden "lest they should eat of the tree of life and live forever." (Gen 3:22) Adam and Eve were not immortal to begin with. God said they'd die the day they ate the fruit. God lied. The serpent told the truth.

I suppose it is possible, as I've been told by one Christian, that God was letting A&E eat from the tree of life to get their daily dose of immortality and only stopped them from doing so after they figured out good and evil. We can't have immortal beings knowing good and evil—like gods. Unfortunately, the Bible doesn't say anything like that.

Why did God lie? If he wanted a fallen, sinful man, why didn't he just make him that way? Why, instead, go to all the trouble to make mankind's sinful nature look like man's fault? Something is very fishy there. [*Duh. We can't tell people we speak for God, and to stop masturbating and enjoying sex, and to stop having affairs and lying—we can't force them to live by the morals we think are best by threatening them with the wrath of God if we don't make it look like they're the problem. God can never be the problem!*]

To fix the lie problem some Christians tell me that God didn't mean "die physically," but that Adam and Eve would "die spiritually." The Bible doesn't say that. It says nothing about the spirit or spiritual death—it says Adam will die. In trying to argue for a spiritual death, Christians are adding their own words and ideas to God's in order to force some sense out of the story. That is a sin according to Revelation, which says,

> I warn everyone who hears the prophetic words in this book: If anyone adds to them, God will add to him the plagues described in this book, and if anyone takes away from the words in this prophetic book, God will take away his share in the tree of life and in the holy city described in this book. (Rev. 22:18)

I think the author is only referring to his particular book, Revelation, which is, in my opinion, the ravings of a lunatic but some Christians tell me the warning refers to the entire Bible. If that is true, how can they claim that the word "spiritually" should be added to Genesis 2:17 and 3:3? Why does it never occur to these Christians that maybe it's just an imperfect story written by humans thousands of years ago?

Christians also claim that with the fall, mankind invited sin into the world. Paul says in Romans 5:12, "Therefore, just as through one person sin entered the world, and through sin, death, and thus death came to all, inasmuch as all sinned..." However, God doesn't say anything about that in Genesis. According to the Bible, the curse of the fall had nothing to do with mankind suddenly having a sinful nature.

Here is the punishment mankind received for the original disobedience: Women get intensified pangs of childbearing and an urge for their husbands [*Oh, my! That's just awful!*] and men will be our masters. [*Like that's going to work.*] And men

233

get cursed ground; they'll have to work hard to get food from it. [*Poor darlings.*]

That's it. That's the sum total of the curse on Adam and Eve, nothing about mankind now being filled with sin. Strangely enough, God had already put Adam in the garden in the first place to "cultivate and care for it." (Gen 2:15) I guess the ground in Eden was easier to work than the cursed ground outside it after the eviction. The way I see it, early Christians added the concept of sin to the Genesis story and in truth, the curse wasn't much of one.

All through the Bible God sets people up only to punish them, tortures and murders humans unnecessarily (assuming you haven't bought into the it's-man's-own-fault-he's-wicked excuse the god of the Bible would have you believe), and wreaks havoc wherever he can. And yet, we are supposed to believe God equals love and justice. Something just isn't right with this story.

The ultimate blood sacrifice

In the Old Testament, Yahweh was pleased with the smell of burning animal flesh (Gen. 8:21; Exod. 29:18, 25, 41; Lev. 1:13, 17; Num. 15:7, etc.). I have been told that later in time a sacrifice was again necessary for the sins of mankind. No ordinary sacrifice would do this time. This time, it would be one final, huge sacrifice: God would send himself down to earth as his own son/self [*by boinking his own mother*] and offer himself up as a savior. [*People actually believe this stuff?*] This last sacrifice was supposed to be the greatest and most meaningful of all but, it doesn't make any sense.

Why does the Christian god punish innocent people for others' crimes, as he did with Adam's progeny (Rom. 5:12) and King David's son (2Sam 12:14), and forgive others' crimes by punishing an innocent man/god, Jesus? Where is the justice in this system? How could we have possibly come up with the fairness of our justice system if we were instilled with Yahweh's manner of justice? It is an abhorrent and irreconcilably unfair system. Under any normal circumstances a Christian would agree but, because this is his god we're talking about, he defends it as somehow meaningful, good, and just. Until Christians can explain to me how it is meaningful, good, and just that an innocent person must pay for someone else's sins, we will have to be at odds. [*Have to be at odds? God, I talked funny back then.**]

Another problem with Jesus' sacrifice is that there doesn't seem to be one. What exactly was the great sacrifice? Jesus spent a few hours on a cross and died—but he is God! After he died, he got to live again and, better yet, go back to Heaven. What was so great about the short time on the cross?

I've been told that the sacrifice was in his taking all of our sins onto himself. But, again, he is supposed to be God. I don't see how an omnipresent and omnipotent god could have a problem with taking on all of humanity's sins, considering he's everywhere already and all-powerful, and considering it was his decision to inflict the sin in the first place. "It's because God is pure goodness," one Christian told me. "It is excruciatingly painful for him to abide sin, much less possess it himself." If this is true, how is it that God murdered the first-born of Egypt or the poor guy who steadied

235

the "ark of the covenant" to keep it from falling (2Sam 6:6-7)? How is it that a purely good being engages in such cruelty, especially if it is painful to him? "Because he loves us," is the answer. It sounds like grasping at excuses to defend the indefensible to me.

My position with regard to Christianity is a harsh one. I believe it is a lie and an immoral one at that; but I know that Christians are not immoral people, in general. As with people of any other religion or philosophy, there are good and bad. One of the biggest problems I have with Christianity is that it can so easily be used for bad people to justify their hatred, intolerance, and vile acts against others. [*Same with Islam. Holy moley.*]

When we look at the history of Christianity, we imagine Christians must be ashamed but, for some reason, they aren't. The Inquisition, the Crusades, the witch trials and burnings, the support of slavery in the southern United States—all are explained away as the acts of people who were not true Christians. But the hateful people who carried out these horrors were good Christians who believed they were following the word of God—the Bible—and they were. For every evil act and bigoted attitude expressed by man, a supporting scripture can be found.

How do Christians respond to that? "Don't blame God," they say. "It's not the fault of God's word, but of fallible mankind." I don't buy it. God himself (or a wise prophet) [*Or just some guy writing fanfic.*] once said:

By their fruits you will know them. Do people pick grapes from thornbushes, or figs from thistles? Just so, every good tree bears good fruit, and a rotten tree bears bad fruit. A good tree cannot bear bad fruit, nor can a rotten tree bear good fruit. (Matt 7:16-18)

If the Bible were truly the word of an all-loving supreme being there would be nothing in it that could remotely be misconstrued and used for evil purposes. No omnipotent deity could create such a horrible, misunderstood book without meaning to. Either the Christian god is as evil as his book, or he didn't inspire the book, or...he doesn't exist at all.

[*And, oh my god, no. Just because I said the word 'god' doesn't mean I believe he exists. Just because I handle money with 'In God We Trust' on it doesn't mean I secretly believe in God, or that I'm a hypocrite about separation of church and state. Does it even have to be said that god is a figure of speech? We say it in exclamation all the time and it doesn't mean we're really talking about a particular god.]

Chapter Twelve

The Voice of the Collective

I don't think of Christianity as a cult. [*Sometimes I do. Like when Christians are babbling and handling snakes and falling on the floor in seizures. Sometimes it looks like a cult.*] Cult is a funny term, after all; it has many definitions and its usage may be determined by the user's feelings more than any truth in his claim. Originally cult meant, basically, religion–there was no negative connotation. Today, the most negative view of cults is of small radical groups of people "brainwashed" into following a charismatic leader, often into some type of violence. Brainwashed is another funny term–it really just means heavily indoctrinated under significant pressure to conform.

But the word cult can just mean any group of people following a charismatic leader. Its members are indoctrinated into the beliefs of the group and those beliefs are interpreted and taught either by an individual leader, a group of leaders, an organization of leadership, or a combination of all three.

In the opinion of some Christian groups, a cult is a breakaway sect of Christianity that doesn't follow the mainstream. Their definition of a cult cracks me up. A cult, they say, is a group of people who claim to be Christian–but they embrace a doctrine (taught by an individual, group, or organization) that denies one or more of the core doctrines of Christianity as taught by the Bible. It just seems to me that you could label Christianity as coming out of Judaism and denying one or more of the core doctrines of Judaism. Then you could describe Protestantism as a cult originating out of Catholicism and from there every new sect of Christianity could be said to be a cult. It's as if what they are saying, without hearing themselves, is that any group newer than their group is a cult. [*Yes. That's exactly what they're saying.*]

The major sects that Christians seem to point their fingers at and label as cults are the Jehovah's Witnesses and Mormons. These two groups claim to be Christian while denying core doctrines such as the Trinity or the deity of Jesus–and of course, they each claim to be the One True Faith. "Cult!" cries the Biblical Christian who actually has the correct doctrine and belongs to the real One True Faith.

Christianity as a whole isn't necessarily a cult–it's too divided and broad. But each sect, each denomination, each home church is its own little cult appendage, a new branch that will one day be able to point the finger at the newbies and cry, "Cult!"

Christianity could be said to be a cult because it has many of the traits we associate with cults.

What makes a cult? In general, a cult is considered to be a group of people devoted to a charismatic leader. Cults employ manipulation to persuade and control members. Some of the forms of manipulation are: isolation from friends and family; pressure to conform to the group doctrine; information censorship and management; suspension of individuality and critical thinking; and promotion of dependence on the group. Cult groups might also physically debilitate people using drugs, fasting, marathon praying, etc. to enhance the potency of their other methods in controlling members.

Cults, like any other group type, range from the extreme, like the Christian doomsday cult of Jim Jones, to the moderate sects of mainstream religions. People don't generally call Christianity a cult simply because it has become widespread, accepted, and it's not considered dangerous.

Still, Christianity is much like a cult. It is based on the charismatic leadership of Jesus as interpreted by the charismatic leaders of the individual churches. Christianity calls people to be reborn into new beings and to surround themselves with other Christians; new Christians, especially, are often told to be wary of non-Christians who might lead them away from their tenuous, newfound faith. There is much pressure from other Christians to conform to the standard doctrinal interpretations of the sect. Information is often withheld regarding responsibilities and practices until a new Christian is further indoctrinated into the faith. Afterward, reliance on scripture, as interpreted by the sect, is paramount and all other data is considered "worldly" and of Satan. While even the most evangelical adherents will deny it, critical thinking and individuality are to be set aside–total reliance on the doctrine of the sect and an ethereal holy spirit is promoted and expected.

[*It's true. A lot of Christians, if not most of them, will tell you that theirs is a rational belief system that encourages questioning and doubt. But as soon as they start in on the virgin birth and world-wide flood and their rejection of evolution, they're setting aside their critical thinking skills–if they ever had any.*]

Christianity appears very much like a mild, culturally acceptable cult. But because of the negative connotations of the term, a better description might be a Collective. [*Oh, yeah, right. That's better. That'll go over just fine. Why didn't I just call it a cult? No, no, I get it. Collective is better because Christianity is like the umbrella cult under which a bunch of other cults practice their own brand. Never mind.*] The Collective of Christianity is broad and varied. There are many pockets containing different sorts of people. It is difficult to talk about the Collective as a whole and yet all its members share in it. Those on the outer rim of the Collective don't bear as many of the Collective markings as those toward the inner circle. In the inner circle are the evangelicals and Biblical literalists. As you travel outward, adherents become more and more liberal, accepting less and less of a literalist interpretation of the Bible.

It appears that the inner Collective of Christianity has a code language–Christianspeak. [*I totally made that word up.*] Listening to one Biblical literalist is just like listening to all of them.

They have a standard set of zingers that they hear and repeat–they acquire learned responses to certain accusations or questions. Sometimes the code is merely a terse slogan, such as "God is good" or "Jesus saves." Other times phrases are strung together, creating the semblance of a language that can go on for paragraph after paragraph. For example: "All humans are unregenerate in the Spirit and hate the thought of putting their hearts under the Will of the All-Loving God; only through His grace is the Truth made known to us, allowing our sinful natures to be cleansed in the Redeeming Blood of Our Lord Jesus Christ."

What you have, in actuality, is a language built around an idea without substance. God is invisible and unknowable and yet he is assigned attributes– attributes that are in reality meaningless: omnipotence, omnipresence, omnibenevolence, trinitarian. In order to make these attributes meaningful, they are themselves imbued with more nonsensical ideas: almighty, supreme, First Cause, love itself, Father, Son, Holy Spirit. From there, more vague words and ideas are added until Christians are speaking without actually saying anything. [*Oh, snap! Talking heads.*] Their language is spattered with words and phrases like: glorification, justified, regeneration, righteousness, salvation, sanctification, tribulation, gifts of the spirit, let Jesus into your heart, be filled with the holy spirit, sins of the flesh, cleansed by the redemptive blood of Christ, etc.

Biblical Christians absorb this code language in church and from books and pass it on, sometimes adding their own slant or embellishment. If an outsider stops them and starts asking what exactly they mean by the things they say, they sometimes get thrown off...but only for a moment or two. Just like the Grinch inching his way out of a tough spot in the chimney, they maneuver around difficulties with more Christianspeak. [*Snork. The Grinch in the chimney!*]

How Christians approach atheism

Over the years I've heard (and read) plenty of questions and comments from Christians. I understand that it's difficult to relate to atheism when you are well entrenched in god-belief; it's difficult for theists to be in my shoes. One of the problems I have seen with Christianity is that its adherents accept certain ideas about atheism proffered by the Collective that make them comfortable.

The following are the most frequent questions and comments I hear from Christians. Any atheist approached with these comments is likely to have heard them dozens of times already, and couched in very little variety of Christianspeak.

"How can you be an atheist?"

I really enjoy this one because it expresses their bewildered shock at the sheer audacity of atheism. "How can you possibly not believe what I believe?" I was never indoctrinated into theism or supernaturalism. (Neither was I indoctrinated into atheism.) Once evidence of gods and a supernatural realm were presented to me, I found the propositions to be without merit. I don't see the outrageousness in that position.

**"How did the universe get here?
How did the Earth get here?
How did we get here?"**

What do these questions have to do with
believing in gods? I don't understand why answers
are so urgently required. Life is a mystery–and
there are scary things happening around us. I
suppose it's comforting to believe you are protected and will live forever...but, what these
questions imply is that if we don't have the answers, there must be a god. I don't see the connection.

**"If there is no god,
what is man's purpose?"**

I personally don't believe that mankind has a
purpose. [*Ugh. Did I really write that? Was my
book hacked?* Mankind has no purpose. *There.
That's the way I should have answered that
question.*] But if he does, I don't know what it is
and, frankly, no one else does, either. Why can't
man have a purpose if there isn't a god? Isn't there
any possible chance that aliens from another
galaxy spawned life on earth as a science exper-
iment? [*Jeez. I suppose. If we're going to get all
weird and 'out there' about it.*] That hypothesis
seems just as likely to me as the idea of a god who
created humans for the purpose of worshiping
him. [*Right. So we're back to the beginning. Mankind has no purpose. That doesn't mean you can't
have one. Maybe your purpose could be to raise
your children or teach kids or drive a race car or
all three. Go for it.*]

"You are denying god."

I am of the opinion that the verb 'deny' is an active word. I can't deny something that isn't there and I have no god-concept—to me, god isn't there. I can't deny something I don't believe exists. I don't accept the existence of gods because I haven't seen any evidence that they do exist; but I don't deny any existing gods. All they need do is present themselves to me and I'll willingly accept that they exist. After that, we can deal with their demands.

"You just don't want to live with the consequences of obeying God."

This is usually said with a flair for self-righteousness and it is a flagrant insult. [*Mercy me, I've been insulted! Flagrantly! Say that word ten times fast.*] I live a moral life on a par with the Christians I know. The only meaningful difference is that I don't worship a god. If that's the worst crime I ever commit, I at least commit it for good reason—I can't worship something that I don't believe is there. To pretend to worship when I don't believe would be dishonest. [*And creepy.*]

"Pray to God for a sign."

I have been told to get into a dark closet and pray to God fervently [*There's that word again.*] and he will show himself to me. Not necessarily there in the closet and not as a physical presence, but I will receive some sign. What is to be taken as a sign from God? If I should feel a twinge, is that a sign? If I get a letter with money included a few days after my closet time, is that a sign? If I *almost* get in a car accident a week later, is that the sign? What of all the other times these things happened without the closet beseeching of the god? How do I tell the difference between coincidence and a sign? How can such mundane occurrences be signs of the existence of the almighty god of the universe?

[*One day fairly recently I went to the Publix (the best grocery store in the southeast) and as I was leaving, I met a guy out front with a dog. He asked if I could spare some money, so I gave him some and told him to take care of his dog. He probably said bless you, to which I responded, no thanks, I'm an atheist. ('No thanks, I'm an atheist' is a running joke in our house because before this, I gave some college kids some gas money at the gas station and the one who took it said, "Bless you," and I said, in a bit of a snotty voice I guess, "No thanks, I'm an atheist," and drove off before he could respond. My kids teased me about it the entire way home. It just pops out of my mouth! What am I supposed to do?) Anyway, so this guy with the dog was all like, no way, an atheist? And he told me that he was going to pray for me and just wait and see, I'd have a revelation, a come to Jesus moment and I wouldn't be an atheist anymore. I said, sure, sure. And he said, really just wait and see! So, uh: hello guy at the Publix with the dog. It doesn't work like that, dude. Just because I'm a girl doesn't mean I'm not too rational for your hocus pocus.*]

I read an article in the newspaper recently about a woman who lost her trailer in a tornado. She prayed to God to save her roof. He saved the roof, but nothing else...except her life. She claimed that God answered her prayer. Fine–I just don't see it. I read in a *Dear Abby* column recently too, about some women who found a few pennies on the ground outside a car dealership and took it as a sign that their dear departed wanted them to buy a car at that place. It was really just a sign that someone dropped some pennies and didn't pick them up.

[*Recently some woman saw the face of Jesus in a moth and said it was a sign. People see him in cut trees, waffles, and French toast. These are the stupidest, weakest signs imaginable. What's wrong with God? Is he trapped in another dimension and trying desperately to get a message through?*]

I won't give supernatural meaning to normal occurrences without good reason to do so. God is just too subtle for me; he's going to have to hit me hard over the head. [*My cousin once said that a feeling I got of love for just everybody—you know how that happens sometimes? You feel so good and happy and you just love everybody?—that was God trying to get through to me, laying himself on my heart, apparently. Way too subtle. I think I was just really happy.*] I've heard he's not willing to do that, which only leads to my belief that I am closer to right on this one: there isn't a god there. People have been taught he's there, they are comfortable with the idea of him being there, they believe he's there; but that's not enough for me. [*It shouldn't be enough for anyone.*]

"You are atheist just because you choose to be."

I can't believe that anyone just wakes up one morning and decides to be an atheist. I think that Christians believe this because to them, atheism is a belief system and a belief system is something you adopt–they *became* Christians actively by saying a prayer and dedicating their lives to Jesus. [*Whatever the hell that even means.*] People tend to project their own views onto others and that is why Christians so often think that atheists choose to be nonbelievers; but it's not true. Atheism isn't something I decided to believe; it's the label I felt best described my lack of belief. Atheism isn't a club you join; it's just a word that describes nonbelief in deity.

I've read posts by believers doubting their faith on The Secular Web message boards. They say, "I'm thinking of becoming an atheist." You don't decide to *become* an atheist. You think about what you believe and if you decide you no longer believe it, maybe the atheist label describes your newfound position.

I don't choose to be atheist. It is just something that I am.

"Atheists say there is no god but to know that, you would have to know everything and you don't.
So really, you're an agnostic."

[*We've been over this before, haven't we?*] If it makes Christians more comfortable to use agnostic instead of atheist, they can do so, but they would be wrong. If truth and honesty and correctness mean anything to them, perhaps they might rethink the whole thing. [*I guess we have our answer. Oh, snap!*]

Agnosticism is related to atheism. Atheism means without theism–without belief in deity. Agnostics believe that we can't know the truth of the proposition regarding the existence of deity; they usually have no belief in deity as well. Anyone who has no belief in deity is an atheist. [*Whether you like it or not, bub.*]

I am sure there are many atheists who say, "Gods do not exist." That is a plausible assertion considering the lack of evidence of gods in our world. I realize that to Christians there is ample evidence but to the skeptic it's all subjective emotionalism and hearsay. That's not evidence to a rationalist. [*It's not evidence at all! Did I have no spine ten years ago?*]

As to the idea that we need to know everything to know whether or not gods exist, that may be true but then we have to know everything to know whether or not gnomes, fairies, invisible pink unicorns, and gabblecronks exist. Are Christians agnostic with regard to those entities? Or are they willing to say that they don't exist?

"Jesus was either Lord, liar, or lunatic. He wasn't a liar or a lunatic so he must have been God."

This is a beautiful example of the Collective and Christianspeak–they heard one guy say it (C.S. Lewis) and now they repeat it again and again as if it makes sense. They call it the "Trilemma," but it's really a false dilemma. The choices offered are all meant to lead to the preferred conclusion of Jesus as Lord. Lewis offers only three choices as if they are the only options available to us: He was a perfect god, a pathological liar, or a crazy person.

Christians are unable or unwilling to think outside the box, outside the Collective-approved quips. If they could, they'd see other possibilities:

maybe Jesus was just a man with some good ideas, elevated to godhood by zealots; maybe he really believed what he was saying but was just mistaken; maybe he was talking about a different god; maybe the people who quoted him got it wrong; maybe he didn't exist and people made the stories up; maybe the theology is patterned after a pagan god. There are other options.

"If you believe in God and you turn out to be right, you haven't lost anything, but you've gained eternal life.
If you don't believe and you are wrong, you've lost everything and will suffer an eternal torment."

The funny thing about Pascal's Wager is that whenever someone says it to me, they presume that I've never heard it before when I've heard it dozens of times, and they act as if it is a profound argument when it's anything but. [*Do you suppose there are Christians out there still doing it? Still trying to convince atheists with it and not realizing it's so stale?*] Pascal's Wager can be approached several ways.

People don't choose to believe or disbelieve a proposition. I can't just start believing that gods and a supernatural realm exist. Try to make yourself believe something that you don't. Believe that the moon is made of green cheese. Believe that an Invisible Pink Unicorn is in your closet. You can't do it. You'll know that you are lying to yourself. I can't believe something that I don't, no matter how much evil Christians threaten me with.

Pretending that I believe in something that I don't, in my opinion, would be dishonest and therefore, I would lose a great deal—my self-respect. I can't imagine anyone else would respect me if they knew I was pretending. Deeper than merely pretending, however, is the issue of believing in something because you've been taught to, told to, or because it's habit. I think that sort of belief is also dishonest—but I agree it is not a purposeful deceit...we can't help being human. Believing in something when there is no evidence of its validity is wrong, in my opinion. People who do so haven't thought much about what they believe; they aren't living consciously.

Another problem is the idea that a god would accept my belief and admiration simply out of respect for the odds or fear of punishment. Is that love? Is that a relationship? Is that justice? Is that what your God wants from me?

Pascal's Wager can be used against Christians too. While some may agree that Allah is the same god as theirs, they don't believe the Koran is the word of their god, and yet, it is claimed that Muhammad is the latest prophet of the God of Abraham. If they don't believe in Muhammad they've rejected Allah and they have lost everything. There could exist some other god than the Christian god—we don't know because we don't know everything. [*Snap!*] How can they know if they're worshiping the correct god in the proper way? Be careful, you may have chosen the wrong god to worship and for that you may pay the ultimate penalty.

And finally, let's suppose that the god Pascal's Wager is designed to support does indeed exist. This god will make nonbelievers suffer simply because they could not believe. In my opinion, that is immoral. No one should be punished for what he believes or doesn't, and certainly not forever. I will not follow an immoral leader and I would not worship an immoral deity. Belief in the torture of your enemies is a slippery slope (no matter how much you may claim to "pain" for them and their fate) that can lead to immorality. [*What? I'm not sure what "belief in the torture of your enemies" is, but considering torture of your enemies a good thing, or even acceptable, is immoral. Worshiping a god who tortures people is immoral. Period.*]

"God loves you, whether you love him or not; he wants you to know him."

[*Cue: The Partridge Family, "I Think I Love You."*] All God has to do is show himself to me. Convincing me of his existence isn't forcing me to love and worship him. I can still reject him–no free will problem there. But, let's face it; if someone I've never met wants a relationship with me, I'm going to have a problem if he never bothers to introduce himself. Christians say, "But he is trying to reach you through his word (the Bible) and through other Christians witnessing to you." Sorry, doesn't work. If someone wants a relationship with me and just sends me his autobiography and his friend to tell me about him, it's not going to do it for me, especially when his autobiography is filled with immorality, con-tradiction, and error...although, he could still exist, he'd just not be as great as I was told he was.

The only answer I seem to get is that I have to really want him to come into my heart (like heart worms?) before he will. How can I want a deity that I don't believe exists to do something? I have

253

to believe in him before he'll lead me to believe in him. [*That's pretty much how it has to work.*] However, if Christianity is true, it is the Christian god himself who decides whether or not I will believe. "So it depends not on a person's will or exertion, but upon God, who shows mercy...he has mercy upon whom he wills and he hardens whom he wills." (Romans 9:16-18) It has nothing to do with me, or Satan, or anything other than the will of God. If this god has willed that I should not believe, why do Christians find it necessary to vilify me? Aren't they, by doing so, saying that God's will is evil?

God is just too subtle for me...either that or he doesn't want me to believe in him...or he just doesn't exist and people are making it all up because they really want there to be more to life than...this.

"There are no atheists in foxholes."

That's not true, of course–I've communicated with atheists who did go to war and fought and watched others die. There have been plenty of atheists in foxholes. [*There's a whole organization devoted to them now: Military Association of Atheists and Freethinkers.*] What this statement means to say broadly is that, when the chips are down, so to speak, when atheists are faced with death or harm or even a tough exam, they pray to a god. This is infuriatingly elitist and untrue. [*Aw, did the mean Christians make me mad?*] Atheists go through their lives just fine without having to appeal to a deity. Christians like to say things like that to make them feel sure of their beliefs. What it does, however, is evidence how insecure they actually are. [*Maybe. But certainly it's all about their idea that atheists really do, deep down inside, know there's a god. We just don't want to admit it. They just can't stand the fact that some people don't believe what they believe. And when you believe something really silly, it's important to vilify anyone who doesn't—otherwise you end up looking, well, silly.*]

"Darwin and Madalyn Murray O'Hair now know that God exists."

This is another phrase that helps Christians feel secure. They have the truth and everyone will find out after they die that Christians were right all along. The way I see it, if you have to think things like this to make yourself secure in your beliefs, you ought to take a good hard look at yourself and see if there is anything there that needs to be right more than needs the truth because you can't determine truth if your ego is in the way. [*Look at me, lecturing the Christians on being honest with themselves.*]

I heard the Christian groans in my head after that statement. They've told me I am the one with the ego problem. [*Well, it did sound pretty arrogant.*] I reject God because of my egotistical view that I am in control of my own life. The difference is that I am first looking around me at the evidence of reality. Truth isn't about what I feel, want, think, or imagine; it's about what is factual. [*Let's clear this up. I'm arrogant and egotistical. But that doesn't have anything to do with being an atheist. I don't reject God because of it. If I were a Christian, I'd be one of those arrogant elitist ones. Ooh, I'd have such a time*] *looking down my nose at other Christians, and Muslims, and agnostics—well, no change there. I'm telling you, I'm just egotistical. That's all there is to it.]*

The Darwin fish being eaten by the Truth fish

Have you seen it? What this bumper sticker means is that an ethereal, elusive, ultimate Truth based on subjective experience and revelation from a transcendent entity and interpreted by your local preacher trumps physical evidence. What Christians are saying to the world when they put this sticker on their cars is, "Don't confuse us with the facts."

[I have one of those with the Darwin fish humping the Jesus fish.]

"Why do you pick on Christianity?"

[Why not?]

Christianity is the religion of my culture. It's all around me; it's on every street—it talks to me in the pithy sayings on church signs, some of which are quite rude. Most everyone I know believes in gods and demons, a man being crucified as a blood sacrifice (like that's a wonderful thing) then rising from the dead, and that one day the streets will run red with the blood of the wicked.

Because Christianity is the prevalent religion in my society, it is the religion I studied. I found that Christianity isn't what most Christians think it is, at least it's not what they keep telling me it is. I found it to be immoral, and speaking out against immorality can't be bad. I found it to be a lie, and striving for truth is a good thing. *[I'm so very noble.*]

"Don't you like anything about Christianity?"

Yes, I do! [*Wait. What? I do?*] I love the architecture of many churches, especially the older ones. [*That's true.*] I enjoy the music, especially at the winter solstice. [*For pete's sake, just say Christmas. Cue: Tim Minchin, "White Wine in the Sun"*] Some beautiful works of art were inspired of religious passion. I appreciate that it was Christianity that brought Santa Claus and reindeer into my life (though I can't give it credit for the Easter bunny and egg hunts; the pagans have my gratitude for that). If belief in Christianity has turned some rotten people into good people who wouldn't otherwise have conformed, I'm glad. [*I just hope they never read this book.*]

I appreciate that Christianity evolves. While there will always be those who need to maintain a dogmatic Biblical belief, Christianity also appeals to loving and tolerant people who can glean from it a positive and accepting religion.

Chapter Thirteen

How to Approach an Atheist

Christian (initiating the conversation): How did you become an atheist? Were there certain events in your life that propelled you in that direction? Or is it something you just woke up believing one morning?

Atheist: I'm not sure, but maybe you meant to ask why I'm an atheist, instead of how I became one. "How" implies I had a choice.

Christian: Ahh. You don't think you had a choice in the matter?

Atheist: No, I don't. I did figuratively "wake up" over a period of days; but not to "believing" something...atheism is a lack of belief.

Christian: I'm curious to know why you say that atheism is not a belief.

Atheist: A—without; theism—belief in deity. I am without belief in deity. Atheism is not a belief.

Christian: Certainly it is! Certainly, it is your faith. True?

Atheist: Why did you even ask? I said it wasn't a belief. You seem to be calling me a liar.

Christian: You seem to have a disdain for Christians. True?

It was all downhill from there. Though the conversation above is a very abbreviated and paraphrased form of one I actually had, it is typical of my conversations with theists.

It's important for atheists and Christians to communicate, to share our feelings and thoughts. There is no reason why we can't accept each other and treat each other with respect. [*Right. Because I'm so respectful of them.*] We can honor people without having to laud their beliefs—we only have to acknowledge that we don't agree. [*I suppose that much is true. I can probably look past the fact that someone believes the Earth is only 4,000 years old and Eve was made from a rib and...no, no I can't. I can respect some kinds of Christians, I suppose. Universalists, for instance. But those conservative Christians who really do think Adam and Eve were the first humans? Nope. Not interested in honoring them.*] But all too often, the conversation ends without any real communication having taken place. Naturally, from my perspective, the problem is on the side of the theists who don't seem willing to hear what the atheist is saying. Perhaps I am wrong [*I doubt it.*]; nonetheless, I offer some tips to Christians in the hopes of bettering our chances of real communication. No matter the intention, to debate or to befriend, I hope that this information will offer Christians an insight into the difficulties they may face in such an endeavor.

Accept the atheist's definition of himself

This is very important. Think about what you call yourself. The term Christian doesn't mean the same thing for everyone. There are Christians who don't accept other professed Christians as such. Just as an atheist must learn what a Christian means by his label, the Christian should take the time to learn what the atheist means. The biggest problem I have encountered with Christians is their insistence that they know *what* I believe and the reasons I don't believe in their god. I am always told that I don't believe because the thought of a god is abhorrent to me or I don't want to subject myself to a higher authority.

If you want to engage an atheist, first discover what he means by the label. You must be willing to accept his definition of atheism and his reasons for labeling himself so. If he says he doesn't believe because he sees no evidence for gods, you must take him at his word. Admittedly, this causes problems for the Christian who would like to convert such an atheist but you can attempt to outline what you consider evidence for God and hope for some agreement from the atheist. [*Why? And wouldn't it be a good idea to ask if the atheist in question is even interested? Because in all likelihood, she's not. Why don't you just leave the atheist alone? I suppose if he's your son...by all means, tread carefully and listen to him. But otherwise, why bother with conversation on the topic at all? Do you get extra brownie points with God for converting an atheist?*]

Understand atheism

Accept that atheism is not a religion–it has no

dogma. There are no principles of atheism. Atheism is nothing more than lack of belief in deity. If you want to know what a particular atheist holds to be true, you have to ask him. You'll get into trouble if you assume you know what a person thinks, feels, and believes just because he calls himself atheist. In order to have an honest, friendly, open discussion with another human being, you have to be able to accept him as he is, not as you have prejudged him or expect him to be. [*This goes for atheists talking to other atheists too.*]

Atheists are normal everyday people, just like Christians. Some of us are rude and obnoxious. [*Raises hand.*] Some of us are quiet and sweet. [*Raises hand. Hey, "I am large, I contain multitudes." —Walt Whitman*] Some are well-read and intellectual. [*Ooh, ooh, raises hand!*] Some are couch potatoes. We are regular people. If you meet an offensive atheist, don't judge all atheists by him. How do you like it when non-Christians judge all Christians by Jerry Falwell or Jim Bakker? [*Wow. Those guys are dead, aren't they? Let's update that to Ken Ham (Shudder. Dude, put a mustache with that beard.) and Dinesh D'Souza.*] All atheists don't think like Madalyn Murray O'Hair. [*Am I old or something? Old references.*] Atheists are very different from each other—the only thing we are sure to have in common is lack of belief in deity. [*Apparently Jim Bakker is still alive. And, okay, I am also something of a couch potato.*]

Forget Pascal's Wager
The first time I heard Pascal's Wager was from

my teacher in a low-level logic class in college. [*Hard to believe. I still shake my head when I think about it...and the fact that I didn't say anything. Sometimes I wonder if he was challenging us to challenge him. But nobody did.*] I remember thinking, "Hmmm, was that logical?" Atheists don't believe that gods exist—we believe they are fiction. Threatening us with God's wrath is meaningless to us—and not a little humorous. It's difficult to take someone seriously when they repeat Pascal's Wager, no matter how cleverly they think they've disguised it. It shows an acute lack of understanding of atheism and the wager itself. [*It shows us that you're stupid. There, I said it.*]

Never tell the atheist he is going to Hell

Atheists know that according to Christian theology we are destined for eternal torment but we don't believe that Hell exists. Threatening us with the prospect is meaningless; it doesn't scare us any more than the boogeyman does.

On the other hand, if you don't believe in the traditional concept of Hell, don't offer this idea to the atheist as if you are assuring him that, despite his atheism, God still loves him. Doing so is rather self-righteous. Your best bet is to stick with discussions of what Hell may or may not be. Any attempts on your part to declare a truth without any evidence will be seen as dishonest. [*Well, then, they're screwed. Like I said, why bother? Just leave atheists alone.*]

Don't try to prove the Bible is true by quoting it as your source

Atheists don't believe that gods exist; therefore

we don't believe that any gods have revealed themselves, certainly not in a book written by men. Quoting from the Bible to show the atheist that there is indeed a god and Jesus was his son will get you nowhere fast. Quoting the Bible to try to prove your moral stance is superior because it is derived from the highest authority in the universe will get you into trouble too, especially if you happen to have come across one of the many atheists intimately familiar with the book. You're likely to hear quoted scripture that reveals the ugliness and immorality of your god. [*Oh, I don't think they should worry about that. They can just use one of their handy apologetics deflectors. 'You're taking that out of context,' for example. Or, 'That's not the correct interpretation. To get it right, go to this other scripture here, and then this one way over here, and then this one back here. Put them all together and what it's saying is what I say it's saying, because I'm a Christian so I'm the one who knows. Not you. Satan's blinding you to this obvious truth.'*]

You can't prove the Bible is the word of a god by quoting the scripture in the Bible that says so. You can't use the book to prove the book is true. If you want to argue that the Bible is the word of a god, you'll have to find some outside evidence to support it. [*They'd have done that already if such evidence existed. Duh. What they actually do is just claim that history and archaeology have already proven that the Bible is true and therefore the word of God. All they have to do is say so and you're supposed to believe it.*]

If you are debating the historicity of Jesus, the Bible could be used as one source but you can't

264

expect the atheist to accept the Bible as anything more than fiction until it has been shown to be true. Suppose I tried to convince you that Scarlett O'Hara was a real person. I could quote parts of *Gone with the Wind* to try to prove it to you but that wouldn't be forceful would it? [*Face it, you'd think I was nuts.*] I would have to prove to you that *Gone with the Wind* was true; then you could accept it as evidence that Scarlett really lived.

[*I know I'm repeating myself but sometimes repetition is necessary if you want the information to get through certain thick skulls.*]

Accept the atheist's reasons for feeling what he feels

Our society vilifies certain segments and when that aspersion succeeds in damaging the emotional health of that segment, society lays the blame for it on the behavior of the group in question. A perfect example is homosexuality. A portion of our society despises homosexuality; they consider it immoral, vile, dirty, and ugly. They want no part of it themselves (at least not consciously or publicly) [*Snap!*] and don't want homosexuals to be open about their lifestyles. Homosexuality, they say, is a shameful behavior and should be wiped out; if they can't abolish it, they can at least force homosexuals to keep their affairs in the closet where they (the presumably good and moral people) won't have to see them. Then these people have the audacity to claim that most homosexuals are depressed and hostile and dare to say it is the result of being homosexual. [*Rotten people!*] I'd be rather depressed too, and not a little angry, if an outspoken portion of society considered me to be abnormal, unacceptable, even vile. [*Uh...but they do.*]

Not strangely enough, that is precisely what "good" Christian people do to atheists. [*Told you so.*] I am happy to say that a large portion of society has become more accepting of homosexuality and they now decry violence and bigotry against gays and lesbians. [*And what do you know?! Gay marriage bans are failing all over the place. It's wonderful, isn't it?*] As well, it is no longer considered honorable to be racist or misogynous. Unfortunately there is one prejudice that it is still quite acceptable to hold–that against atheists. It is still permissible to call your enemy an atheist, as if that is the worst thing a person could be. No one will contradict representatives or authorities who call atheism immoral and tell us all to leave the country if we don't like good 'ole God-fearing American values.

[*In April 2012, Rhode Island state representative Peter G. Palumbo referred to atheist student activist Jessica Ahlquist as "an evil little thing" on local radio. Did the country freak out? Hell no. Just the atheists. If you call buying up and wearing t-shirts with "evil little thing" printed on them freaking out.*]

Atheism is labeled as the destroyer of our national greatness, the aberration that pollutes our good country, communist, Satanic, etc. All the evils of the world can be put at atheism's door and no one will dispute it; no one will stand up for the rights of the atheist community except atheists themselves.

Atheists will deal with this societal ostracism in various ways. Many aren't bothered by it at all;

they have a community of friends, realize that their understanding of the world isn't widely held, but aren't bothered by what other people think and say about them. Still, most people want to be accepted and liked; it's a normal human desire. Feeling that you are different is difficult enough without knowing that what makes you different is considered evil and abhorrent to many others. [*I admit, despite having a website, having written this book (twice now), having sued my local school board over graduations in a church, I still don't tell many people I'm an atheist.*]

Some people never admit they are atheist; it's the last thing they would ever do. I don't blame them. I think it must be a sad way to have to live, never being fully honest with other people, maybe not even yourself, but being empathetic, I can understand it and I would not look down on the atheist who can't or won't admit it to others, even to himself. Some admit what they are and remain unhappy with the reaction they receive. When you encounter an atheist who seems angry, try to feel what it must be like to be in a small and denigrated minority. [*There are too many Christians who just can't do this. That's why they argue against the separation of religion from government. They lack empathy. We should be afraid of them, if you ask me.*] It's a natural human reaction to be angry at one's situation when so many people hate you for it and make no qualms about expressing that hatred—when so many people tell lies about what you are and who you are and everybody else accepts those lies as if they are true. It's not an easy situation in which to be.

When an atheist expresses anger or sadness,

even depression, you mustn't assume that it is atheism that causes those feelings. [*You mustn't? Is mustn't even still a word?*] It may be the reaction of the Christian community the atheist lives in that causes those feelings. [*You mean the United States of Christianity?*] If people were more accepting, tolerant, and loving of people who are different from them, the different people could be happier. Of course, that's never going to happen because when you have a dogma that must, without question, be believed, you have to vilify and demonize anyone who refuses to accept it. But because mainstream Christianity demonizes atheism doesn't mean individual Christians must go along with it.

If Christians want to approach atheists in hopes of learning more about them, friendship, or trying to convert them, they should understand the situation atheists are in. Too often the atheist is told his anger arises from his denial of God, from his anger at God, or from his unwillingness to submit to God. Christians won't score any points with that attitude. [*This is the stupidest section of this book, isn't it? Christians who actively engage in debates and confrontations with atheists don't give a shit about any of this. Atheists don't either, if you ask me.*]

On the other hand, many theists are surprised to find that the happy well-adjusted family down the street, the mom active in the PTO, or the homeschooling family next door is atheist. [*They're surprised all right. Then you get the "I'll pray for you" crap.*] That's not the atheism they are presented with in church and in books written by Christian apologists. Unfortunately, people

268

you'd least expect can turn out to be atheists–
that's a result of the prejudice of Christian society.
More and more atheists and non-Christians need
to speak out in this country if we hope to be
accepted. [*Nope. I say we skip right on past
acceptance from conservative fundamentalist
Christians and just keep going with the margin-
alization of faith and bigotry. It's happening.
They know it's happening. And there's nothing
they can do about it. We don't need their acceptance.*]

Be willing to take as much as you give

One of the biggest problems I've encountered
and witnessed in the atheist/Christian dialogue is
the Christian unwillingness to be wrong. I know
that Christians believe they are correct; of course
they do; people don't believe things that they know
are wrong. And yet, the Christian expects the
atheist to admit a possibility that he is wrong.
Christian/atheist discussions are usually one-
sided. The Christian takes the position of teacher
and expects the atheist to be his student. The
Christian tells the atheist what he must do to find
God, but is unwilling to take the opposite course
and apply it to himself. As well, the Christian often
insists that the atheist concede that gods are
possible but is rarely willing to agree that the
absence of gods is also possible.

A Christian might tell an atheist he must pray
to God for him to reveal himself. In order to do
this, however, the atheist must first admit that a
god possibly exists to which to pray. Then he must
be fervent [*Jesus, did I love that word or what?*]
in his desire for this god to reveal his presence.

269

The atheist must take a humble attitude of supplication before the greatness of this god, and beg him to reveal himself, to manifest his spirit in the heart of the atheist. I have heard atheists accept this challenge, but logically, they want the Christian to take a part in it as well. If the god in question does not reveal himself, the atheist might propose, is the Christian willing to admit that it doesn't exist? No, the Christian says, because he claims for himself the correct position and will not admit that he could be wrong. Why should the atheist accept all the necessary criteria for the test and the consequences of the result while the Christian accepts nothing when the test fails?

If I ask a Christian to do the closet praying routine for Isis or Osiris, Odin or Shiva, he thinks my request is ludicrous. Why? Because the Christian does not accept that he could be wrong. It is the atheist who must accept fallibility and when the test doesn't work, the atheist is blamed. He didn't pray hard enough; he didn't really believe it could work; he wasn't earnest. Never is the possibility that the god in question simply doesn't exist considered.

A Christian might also tell an atheist to live for a specific period of time as if he believed in God; pray to him, seek his guidance and wisdom, read and study the scripture for a period of, say, three months. The Christian assures the atheist that, if he truly lives this way, immerses himself in the idea of Christianity, he will experience the presence of God and will feel the great joy and love of being Christian–he will come to know and believe in God. But the Christian is never willing to apply the test to himself. He is not willing to live as if he doesn't believe for three months to experience that his life would be no different, or maybe better as a nonbeliever. Neither is he willing to accept that he is wrong if the atheist does as he is asked but returns to atheism at the end of the specified time.

[*Some Christians may have done this test. But the problem is that you can't just stop believing something that you believe. So even if a Christian attempts to live as if he didn't believe, he still does. Same for an atheist who goes to church and studies and hangs out with Christians. It's really just an exercise. You might learn something, but I can't imagine it having any effect on your beliefs or lack of them.*]

These are unfair tests. They assume their conclusion—that the atheist is the one who is wrong and simply needs to perform a certain way, think or feel a certain way, and he will see the rightness of the Christian position. The existence of God is debatable; he either does or does not exist. That all people don't agree that a god exists, and that this God hides and must be sought out is evidence that he isn't real. It has certainly not yet been shown that he is. The Christian must be just as willing to accept he is wrong as the atheist.

Determine what proper evidence is

Christians might, early in the dialogue, determine what the atheist would accept as valid evidence for God or Jesus. They will find that most atheists don't accept the evidence that they have as evidence at all. [*Because it's not.*] If they did, they'd be Christians. They mustn't [*I said mustn't again. Lordy.*] assume, then, that the atheist is only atheist because he hasn't seen the evidence.

271

Try to imagine being an atheist in this Christian-dominated country. It is highly unlikely that a person who knows he's an atheist and is willing to be labeled as such has no knowledge of Christianity and the evidence claimed in favor of it.

Rationalists require that deity be researched in an objective manner. The fact that we can't answer a particular question is no reason to insert god as the answer. Miracles must be beyond mere stories and legends; they must be verifiable. Considering the power and superiority of the god in question, the things that pass as miracles today are nondescript. Is that the best a god can do? [*Apparently. There are no real miracles. Miracles don't happen.*] Prophecy must be accurate beyond the odds and must be specific, not vague and so symbolic as to be interpreted in many different ways. [*There is no such thing as prophecy. No. Such. Thing. Why am I talking as if there is and Christian apologists need to make sure they use only the accurate prophecies in debates? I bought a bunch of books on Biblical prophecy a long time ago thinking I'd write a book just on that but I got bored.*]

Christians should be warned, however, that a request to know what it would take to convince an atheist that God exists or that Jesus was his son might produce an odd response from an atheist friend. [*I can not believe I wrote 'atheist friend.' I mean, come on. If they're friends, they're probably not acting like this—debating Christianity. This is aimed at Christians trying to argue with atheists. It's the Christians who come at you with 'friend.' It's weird. It's as if they have classes on converting people and one of the lessons is on how*] to get a nonbeliever to trust you. "You've got to be her friend, make her feel like you care about her." It's creepy when they call you friend in the very first email they send you. They also often come at you right off the bat talking about how depressed and hopeless they felt before they found Jesus. It's like they think atheists are depressed and hopeless (which, of course, they do) and they think if they start out saying "I was there, I know how you feel," and then call us friend, we'll be primed for their Jesus cure. It's sad. That's what it is. Sad and creepy.]

Too often, atheists are approached with just such a question and when they give their answer, are attacked for it. The atheist is told that he is making demands on God for a sign, which is an affront to God. The atheist is told that he is presumptuous to claim God owes him any evidence at all. I have also heard atheists called to account for not humbling themselves before God, for daring to even ask that God make himself known to them, a lowly, wretched human! So you see, often the question of what evidence I might accept for God and Jesus is really just an excuse to berate me. If I don't seem happy to answer the question, that would be why.

[So, what would convince me? It's hard to say for sure. I think that if the face of a god appeared in the sky and talked to us, and everybody saw it, not just me and a few other people (because then I hope I would wonder if I wasn't just crazy) I would wonder if it was a god. But I wouldn't accept it right away, because there could be some cool new technology I don't know about that could put a hologram in the sky and make it look like it *was a god. So I'd need more than that. If people prayed over the sick and dying and the sick and dying were healed right away, that would add evidence to the god in the sky theory. If people prayed to have this god regrow lost limbs and it worked, and these stories were verifiable, for all of us to witness, I'd start believing. I might still have a bit of skepticism in me. I'd be wondering if this wasn't some weird elaborate hoax. But if it kept on long enough, if the god hung around and maybe drew really bad people, like people who molest and murder little children, up into the sky and made those people disappear in a puff of smoke—I'd be all in. Yeah, I think that would do it. I'd believe that there was at least one god and he was up there somewhere in the sky somehow. That would be freaky, wouldn't it? Everything we know to be true would be wiped out. But it wouldn't matter. Who needs science when your god is right there to explain things for you?*

It's funny when you think about it. If there was a god, he or she could totally do that. And why not? Why is this god who supposedly loves us, and wants us to know her, nowhere to be seen? That very point right there should be enough for people to realize there just isn't one. But that would mean certain things that Christians don't like. In fact, if you take it further and admit that there is not only no god, but no afterlife, no reincarnation, no supernatural at all, it means things that all religious and superstitious people looking for something comforting to believe in don't like.

It means that we die—this is it, this life is all there is and there's nothing more. It means that bad people who are not punished in this life get

274

away with the bad things they did. No purpose; no justice. What could it be about the human psyche that makes accepting these two things so difficult? So difficult that people invest themselves so deeply into believing they aren't true. They must build a belief system that enables them to turn away from that stark reality.

I get the death part. Sentience sucks, doesn't it? But the justice...Christians are big on justice. Must just be one of those human things, which would explain why people go to see public executions. Humans are so creepy.]

Avoid pat stories

There have been many stories spread around the Internet that some Christians offer as evidence for God. What they show, in actuality, is the gullibility of the believer who passes them on.

In one story, an elementary school class is being lectured by a teacher who points out that you can see the trees and the birds but you can't see God so he obviously doesn't exist. Then a little girl pipes up and claims that the teacher must not have a brain because no one can see it. What a laugh we all have at the atheist teacher's expense...being bested by a child. Unfortunately, none of the children suggest they cut the teacher's head open; then they would all be able to see her brain. Or, perhaps a CAT scan would serve. You see, we *can* see the teacher's brain. We have seen human brains, so we know they exist. [*Duh. Seriously, this is the level of thinking those people engage in.*]

We can't see the wind but we know it exists because we can witness and measure its effects in the world. We can't see air but we can analyze its molecular structure and its effects on the animal and plant life forms that use it. We can measure gravitational pull. We experience the emotion of love. All these things we cannot see can be experienced, studied, and discussed objectively. God is invisible and is not experienced objectively.

Another fable we get is the story of the logic professor in which he argues with a Christian student and gets flustered because the Christian student maintains his position. The professor holds up his piece of chalk and declares that if there is a god let him stop the chalk from falling to the ground–then he drops it. The chalk, instead of falling to the floor, lands in the cuff of the professor's pants. [*I lost a quarter once at school and my friends and I searched for it for the longest time. I found it in the cuff of my corduroys (yes, I'm that old). My friends accused me of having faked the whole thing. So you see, Christians think things landing in cuffs is so unlikely it's either faked or supernatural.*] Or the professor proclaims that if there is a god, he will stop the chalk from breaking when it hits the ground and the chalk drops, bounces off something, and hits the floor without breaking. Then all the students follow the Christian out into the hallway where he witnesses to them while the professor is humiliated. [*That was a great story, wasn't it?*]

What exactly is this story supposed to show us beyond the credulity of college students? We are supposed to believe that it was a god who caused the chalk to fall into the cuff instead onto the floor? We are supposed to believe it was a god that caused the chalk to bounce off something and land softly so it wouldn't break? Is that the best a god can do? Couldn't a god have suspended the chalk in midair, levitated it to the chalk board, and wrote with it, "I exist?" And the horrible characterization of the college professor belies a prejudice against the intellectual community that I find disheartening. [*Stupid people don't like smart people.*]

Christians should avoid stories such as these when dealing with their atheist friends. If they serve you and your Christian friends, keep them between yourselves. [*It's really no business of mine what you share with your friends. I'm just trying to say that you'll get nowhere with a rationalist with stories like that.*]

Don't belittle education

Rationalists at least (I can't speak for all atheists), hold education in high esteem. "Intellectual" is not a dirty word. Why is it iniquitous for so many believers? [*Iniquitous? Did I write this book with a thesaurus open on the desk? It's not even the right word. Contemptuous would make more sense.*] From this side it looks like Christians don't like it because in order to educate yourself you may have to give up some, if not most, of your beliefs. [*Oh, I don't know. I think I've seen enough to realize that people can learn quite a lot, have a number of degrees, a great vocabulary (and never use the wrong word like yours truly), do all the maths, and still believe in the stupidest things.*] The hierarchies in control of the Christian churches are well aware that the more educated a person is, the less likely he is to believe in a literal

Christianity. The natural answer is to demonize intellectualism. [*I don't think you need religion for that–just widespread ignorance.*] If a Christian wants to open a dialogue with an atheist, the last thing he should do is claim that revelation, interpreted from a very old book or by his local preacher, is more accurate than scientific research in explaining our natural world. If a person can't respect science and learning, he may not want to approach an atheist at all. [*Exactly. Just don't.*]

Don't attack subjects you don't know much about

If Christians want to attack evolution they'd better learn as much about it as they can. [*But they think they've learned everything they need to know from the Christian books they've read.*] If they want to attack an atheist's logic or morality or philosophy, they'd better do their research. True, they're likely to come across some atheists who can't offer good responses to their attacks. The best they'll get in response is a quizzical look–the atheist is thinking that what he's hearing doesn't sound quite right, but he's not sure why. If the Christian keeps at it, the atheist is likely to go to the computer or library and start learning about the subject.

From experience, I know that most Creationists know very little about evolution. They've taken all their information from the Creationist propaganda machine [*Ooh, the sinister propaganda machine!*] which is a poor choice if you want to engage a rationalist on the subject. [*It doesn't stop them from doing it.*] Don't get your information from the pulpit or a book or website built on the foundation of refuting the subject. Go to the books and sites that deal with the science or philosophy behind the subject as told by those who adhere to it. [*Yeah, right. Like they're really going to do that.*]

When I wanted to learn about Christianity, did I read about it at an atheist site? In a book by an atheist? No. To learn about Christianity you have to read Christian books and talk to Christians. I understand that many Christians will claim that I have misrepresented their theology here; but what I have learned about Christianity has come directly from Christians–from their books, their websites, personal conversations, and emails. I recognize that they are all very different; atheists are all very different also.

On the other hand, when I wanted to learn about the history of Christianity did I read Christian books? No. I read books by historians. When I wanted to learn about evolution, I read science books. To learn what Creationists believe I looked at Creationist books and websites. Don't let the opposition tell you the facts about a subject. Go to the best educated people in that subject for your information. [*I'm pretty sure I just went over how these kinds of Christians don't think educated people know what they're talking about.*] You don't have to believe what they say, but you'll at least be getting closer to the facts and less propaganda. Then go to the opposition for a response and see how they fare.

The problem with people who have a dogma to which they adhere is that they tend to look at others in the same light. If they have a truth that must be defended, they assume that people who study and talk about evolution must also have a truth to stand by. Dogmatic people are suspicious of science. That is a real problem and I don't know how to help with it except to say that you needn't [*Needn't. Mustn't. These are such snotty words, aren't they?*] accept everything the opposition says as truth, but if you want to discuss the matter intelligently with its proponents, you must at least be versed in the subject from their viewpoint. [*Yes, but it's pretty clear they don't care about discussing stuff intelligently. Why did I write all of this? Seriously. Look below there where I'm going to talk about evolving from monkeys. Yes, people actually said that to me. People have said all this stuff and not just one people, lots of people. (Yes, I said people and I'm sticking to it.) Why on earth would I think that any of what I'm saying here could possibly make a difference to someone who would say, "If we evolved from monkeys why are there still monkeys?" There is no hope for those people.*]

To put it bluntly, if you try to offer Creationist rhetoric to an intelligent atheist, he may laugh at you. [*Maybe not to your face. And after a while it just gets sad and we can't even smile about it.*] I have yet to see anything offered by a Creationist that wasn't pure baloney. [*Finally I tell it like it is!*] There are intelligent skeptics of evolutionary theories [*Where?*]; but they are hardly Creationists.

Never say we evolved from monkeys

The first time I heard a Christian deride the theory of evolution by saying he "didn't come from no monkey" I thought it was a fluke. What's one person with a misunderstanding of speciation, after all? We can't all be scientists. But again and again I hear the same refrain from theists: evolution means we evolved from apes or monkeys. Worse, I get the question, "If we evolved from apes, why are there still apes? Why don't we see the apes changing into humans?" I have, more than once, stood at my door teaching a basic lesson on the origin of the human species to Jehovah's Witnesses and I'm not exactly a scientist. How is it that a non-scientist can understand these theories better than many Christians? Dogma–I don't have one. [*Sure, sure, it's just the dogma. Really, there's also that little thing called intelligence. We don't all have the same amount of it and that's just the way it is.*]

Let me explain briefly here that humans did not evolve from monkeys or apes. [*I still can't believe this has to be explained.*] Monkeys, apes, and humans are all primates–we share a common ape-like ancestor. Monkeys evolved into monkeys. Apes evolved into apes. And humans evolved into humans. I can't believe the standards of science education in this country are so poor that I should have to explain that. [*Well, you know how it is. If you teach children they "came from apes" they'll act like apes. Have you ever seen someone walking down the street and just–bam!–saw evolution? Just suddenly saw it–we're really just tall goofy hairless apes. Happens to me a lot, actually.*]

Mind your Truth

"You can't understand the Bible until you are filled with the holy spirit."

"You don't understand the Truth because you are blinded by Satan."

"Worldly knowledge is foolishness to true Christians."

These things might be true, if what Christians believe is true. What they appear to be, however, is excuses–reasons Christians, as they have done from the inception of the religion, offer to explain why others question their beliefs. If the sciences seem to refute Biblical teaching, it's because science is "of the world" or scientists are blinded and biased. Only spiritual truth is real truth, all else is meaningless. The reason everyone is not Christian is because Satan blinds men to the truth or because they are willful and disobedient. These are handy justifications to keep Christians from looking objectively at their beliefs. All you have to do is believe that you have the truth, the one and only truth, and the reason other people don't accept it has nothing to do with your beliefs–the problem is not your dogma, it's the nonbelievers themselves. That is a very convenient excuse to carry around. If someone is going to approach an atheist with these ideas in mind, I have to wonder why they would bother.

[*A business downtown once put this on their sign: "The truth is more important than the facts. –Frank Lloyd Wright." I took a picture of it and the owners of the business happened to be out front pulling weeds. They asked me if I liked it and I said, not really. I didn't explain it to them. The problem is that there is no truth without facts, so if either was more important than the other, it would be the facts. There isn't any big truth to be worked out. There are only things we know and things we don't. You don't have any truth without facts. And Christianity has no facts. Figure it out from there.*]

Chapter Fourteen

The Way I See It

What is tolerance?–it is the consequence of humanity. We are all formed of frailty and error; let us pardon reciprocally each other's folly–that is the first law of nature.

–Voltaire

All religion, every bit of it, is had through hearsay. Everyone is talking about the god who is there, but where? No one knows what it is, where it is, how it is, or why it is but they talk about it just the same, as if they know. No one ever experiences god personally. [*Christians will say this isn't true but it is. The easiest way we can know this is that people from all the religions claim to experience their gods personally. There are either lots of different gods or what people are experiencing is not supernatural at all. The most likely explanation is that humans interpret heightened emotions and physical sensations as god.*] We listen to other people talk about it and read books. Other people tell us what to believe; they interpret our subjective feelings as "god," but we can never know for sure because god is hidden.

Nonbelievers are expected to accept hearsay as valid evidence for god. That is how god wants us to know about him, we're told. He won't come directly to us—he sends his believers as mouthpieces and his holy book as instructions. When we question believers, we realize that they know nothing beyond what they've been told by someone else or read in a book written by men. Occasionally someone comes on the scene saying something new—even traditional Christians admit those people are making it all up. Jim Jones wasn't a Christian, they say. Neither was David Koresh. They were false prophets. Listen to us, they say, we are the true prophets. Shadow play, hearsay, illusion, hope, self-righteousness, and power—that is religion.

I don't believe that there was a conspiracy to take a Jewish carpenter and turn him into a god for the purpose of blinding the masses to gain power and wealth. I don't believe anyone purposefully deceived anyone else in the conception of the theology. I believe people were misguided by a misunderstanding of mythology and some cunning, unscrupulous people took advantage of the situation. It's not Christianity's fault; it was a natural mistake and a product of our culture that we would rally around a figure of salvation such as the Christ/Messiah. That's where we were in our history and clearly, many are not ready to move beyond it as yet.

I think Christianity is a lie because I don't

believe that Jesus ever existed. I believe he was a mythical product of pagan Judaism, a pagan god, linked to the would-be historical figure of the Messiah. It is understandable that some thought he was a real man but, to me, it's a lie. [*It's a lie to me? I was really bending over backward to make this all out as just my opinion. Didn't want to step on any toes, I guess. Here, let me stomp on some. There is absolutely no evidence to show that Jesus ever existed. None. Nada. Zip. Therefore, it's reasonable to claim he did not.*] All that is needed for me to change my mind is evidence to the contrary.

Another reason I can't accept Christianity as truth is because I don't believe that humanity is a vessel of sin that must be redeemed to be in the presence of a god. If a creator god exists, if we are God's children, we can't be so disgusting to him that we require a savior. What sort of perfect, loving entity creates loathsome beings?

I think of Christianity as the epitome of the parent/child relationship–an extension of it in adulthood–an escalation of it into something sacred and holy. The parent/child relationship at its best exemplifies unconditional love and acceptance. I would never punish my child for being human and certainly not forever. "But you are not God," is the response I've heard. To which I reply, that's correct–God would be unfathomably more accepting and loving than I, as a human mother, could be. How could I, as the created, be more beneficent toward my child than the omni-benevolent creator himself? If we allow our god to be anything less than we are, we debase the concept so that it becomes the ultimate expression, not of the greatest, but of the vilest of man—we make it ugly.

[*A Christian mother once tried to explain the goodness of Hell to me. She said it was like tough love. She'd apparently had to use some with one of her kids—had to put him out of the house. It's the same with God, she said. What she did for her son was best for him. And God sending people to Hell is just like that. Except that she wouldn't put her son out of the house for merely a lack of belief, would she? And if he reformed, she'd take him back, wouldn't she? She wouldn't force him out of her life forever. "But I'm not God," she said.*]

Christianity gives people what they need. I can understand the anxiety that scientific advances bring to our society. The more we progress technologically, the more fearful we become; the more we learn about the vastness of the universe, the smaller and more insignificant we feel and the more we begin to think that everything we do is for naught. [*Do people still say 'naught?' Other than poets, I mean.*] Salvation religions play on that fear. They say, "Yes, you are an insignificant worthless creature...but you belong to a powerful father/god," thereby offering you hope that you have meaning and purpose, that you are significant, that your life will not end.

I can understand all of that. Part of me thinks it is all right to let people indulge their yearning—don't take away their solace; they need it. Another part of me thinks that a lie, no matter how comforting, can only be harmful in the long run. I do believe that the lie of salvation religions has been very harmful to our world.

Christians often point out to me the good that

Christianity has brought about. They are either not well versed in history or choose not to consider the horrors that Christianity and other salvation religions have caused. Think how much more good might have come if we'd learned earlier that this life is the only life there is and that there is no other world, no Heaven. Long ago we may have stopped warring; we may have started helping our planet instead of abusing it; we may have actually seen the true worth in our fellow humans and learned what love really is.

[*We might not have burned people to death or hanged them because we were stupid enough to think they were witches. Maybe some of us wouldn't still be stoning women to death for having sex outside marriage, or whipping them for being raped. Maybe we wouldn't have tortured people for apostasy or fed people to lions. Sure, I suppose we'd still have fought over land and power, but I bet we'd be better off without the idea that we had a god and he needed us to punish people for disobeying the laws we think he made.*

Whenever atheists talk about the horrors that people have committed in the name of religion, Christians point to communist and other godless regimes and claim that atheists have killed more people for atheism than Christians ever did for God. What they fail to understand, because they just don't want to, is that those regimes didn't murder for their god or their religion, they did it for power and control. And that's what religion is, really. Power and control. So sure, humans would probably be just as vile without religion, but they would have to work a lot harder to justify it and they probably wouldn't be quite so gleeful about it. And anyway, "You guys murder people, too" is hardly saying much for your religion.]

We can never do those things on a global scale until we stop looking to the hereafter for consolation and into the ancient past for values.

I don't like Christianity for several reasons. As good as the religion is for good people, it is even better for bad people. People use Christianity to promote hate and intolerance—they use the Bible to support their efforts to treat others despicably. Christians tell me this isn't the fault of their religion; it is the fault of sinful mankind. I don't see it that way. I think of god, if it exists, as a great and wonderful force. Christians tell me God is all-loving and this all-loving, omnipotent being gave us his word. How could the word of such a remarkable being have anything bad in it at all? How could it possibly be misused if it was all good?

The supposed word of God, the Bible, is not all good. It is filled with acts of murder, torture, rape, incest, deceit, hatred, war, vengeance, and lust. [*I forgot misogyny. Not that I want to engage the feminists or anything, but it's in there.*] It is not the book of a loving deity; it's the book of tribal men. If a god existed that loved us and wanted us to live with him in a paradise, he would produce, even through inept men because he's so powerful, a book that was clear and unambiguously good. It would have nothing in it that could be misconstrued. That's why I will never believe that the Bible is the work of a god. My idea of god is different from most Christians'. My idea of god doesn't reflect man's idea of himself, it *transcends* it.

Some people have been shocked to hear me claim their religion is immoral. Others simply disagree–they have a different idea of morality than I do. What is immoral about Christianity? The biggest immorality is Hell. There is, by my moral standard, no justification for eternal punishment. Christians have wrestled with the concept of Hell for centuries and they've altered their interpretation to suit the changing morals of our society.

While some Christians continue to maintain that Hell is a tortuous and eternal punishment for sinners of all kinds, others have made different claims. Hell, some say, may not be eternal; the punishment will fit the sin or crime–but that is not a Biblical perspective. Many people are uncomfortable with the Biblical view; they take from it pictures of Christ and God that are palatable to them and claim that the parts they don't agree with or find discomforting are symbolic or tribal history, not the message of God.

Christianity is inexorably [*I like that word: inexorable.*] linked to the Bible. If you're not going to take the whole thing, why take only parts you like? If you've decided that Hell is anything other than eternal torment (Matt.25:46), you've re-created Christianity to suit your sensibilities. If you can do that, how is it that you can claim that any part of the Bible is the true word of your god? As long as Christianity is part of the Bible, it will be immoral. Maybe one day, a thousand or so years from now, there will be a new Christianity, totally separate from the tribal war god, Yahweh. That will just be more evidence that man makes reli-gion, not gods.

Christianity furthers elitism and intolerance. Many conservative Christians try their best to adhere to the entire Bible and that, while noble, is what will forever leave them with an immoral social outlook. The Bible offers ample justification for intolerance and hatred of other religions, other sects of Christianity, nonbelievers, homosexuals, and women. As long as the Bible is looked on as the word of their god, Christians will have to defend iniquity and injustice.

Luckily, most Christians don't read and study the Bible as if it were the absolute, pure, inerrant word of their god. They read it as an ancient history with many (questionable) morality tales and lessons. Anything that they don't agree with or find immoral, they simply dismiss. Christianity is, in fact, evolving and changing. [*We can only hope it continues to change for the better, toward more progressive ideas, and doesn't go backward into the Dark Ages like Islam is doing in parts of the Middle East.*]

Christians are no more immoral than anyone else. [*Maybe.*] There are moral, upstanding Christians, just as there are moral upstanding Jews, Muslims, pagans, Wiccans, and atheists. The problem with Christianity is that immoral people can use its holy book for their own pernicious means.

Immoral Christians aren't immoral only because they worship the god of the Bible. They mold him to fit their moral views. They easily interpret his wishes, using the scripture that fits, to align with what they believe to be true. Corrupt Christians claim that they are perfectly just in their misanthropic behavior [*Misanthropic? Really? This should just be 'immoral behavior.'*] because it is God-ordained. But is it possible for a good, moral person to become immoral by adhering to a literal interpretation of the Bible? I believe so. [*That's a big fat yes.*]

It begins with Hell and elitism. The normally good person accepts that some people are less deserving of Heaven than they themselves. Worse, people who merely don't believe the way they do are deserving of eternal torture by the god they call loving. These good people begin to equate love with torture, with Hell, with evil. They allow themselves to become bigoted against certain others in society. They don't call themselves bigots (what bigot does?)—they call themselves the righteous, the good. What does that do to a person's idea of morality? Punishment is love; torture is justice; bigotry is goodness. It's a short, slippery slope from that point to hatred and intolerance of all but those they agree with in every aspect of life.

Many Christians openly oppose tolerance. Tolerance to them means acceptance of sin and evil. But tolerance is appreciating our differences, allowing that we are not the only standard bearers, and realizing that we cannot make all the rules for all the people. Tolerant people understand that no human has the only truth about deity. No one knows for sure if there is one. Those who believe that the Bible is the word of the one and only god only *believe* it. They don't *know* it to be true because there is no god here and now substantiating their claim. They must *believe* it because there is no evidence to support their position. Someone else could be right. The Muslims could be right. The Hindus, the pagans, the atheists could be right. Theists can't know for sure.

Intolerance is adamantly proclaiming that your way is the right way and everyone else is wrong—your interpretation of the word of your god in your holy book is the only right way. That's intolerance, elitism, and bigotry. It's very unattractive and seamy but there will always be a segment of society that requires the feeling not only of being right, but of being one of a select few who are. It's an immoral view, an immoral attitude, and an immoral way to live. I want no part of it.

Since realizing I was atheist, I have faced many theists, most Christian, who have mislabeled me, misunderstood me, and despised me. It seems from this side that Christians can't stand to look at the possibility that they are mistaken and they have to make atheists into something we are not to make themselves feel more secure. They hate us for pointing out to them—by our mere existence—that they could be wrong.

I am often reminded of the story of the *Emperor's New Clothes* by Hans Christian Anderson. If you recall, the emperor commissioned two scoundrels to make him a set of new clothes from the finest fabric in the world—invisible to ignorant and stupid people. When the emperor found he couldn't see the cloth, he knew he had to keep his ignorance secret. He then paraded his new outfit in front of the populace, confident that only stupid people would think he was naked. All the people admired his clothes so no one would think they were dumb. But a small boy, as children are often more honest and forthright, stood in front of the throng and declared, "The emperor is naked!" The boy was scolded; but gradually everyone began to agree that the emperor was, indeed, naked. The emperor, too embarrassed to admit the truth (that he'd been had), continued on his merry, naked way.

Atheists are like the honest boy who didn't understand why everyone was claiming clothes when no clothes could be seen. The adults didn't appreciate his honesty because it forced them to question their willingness to believe. Atheists don't want to pretend we see things that aren't there just to keep believers from feeling threatened.

I can't help that I don't believe what Christians believe; I can't help that I've come to think of their religion as a lie. I think they are wrong, just as they think I am. They believe their position is correct as strongly as I believe mine is. [*At least I have evidence on my side.*] Our only options are hatred and intolerance or love and acceptance. [*Or polite distance.*]

I don't think Christians are stupid, as I have been accused by some. I think they are credulous–willing to believe more easily than I am. I am more skeptical. I don't know why; I just am. That doesn't mean there is something wrong with me or that I am bad–it doesn't mean that I am better than believers, or that they are superior to me. We're just different. We should, both sides, be able to accept that simple fact: we are different. [*I may not be better as a person, but a strong desire for facts and truth and scientific inquiry is better than belief–better for individuals and better for society as a whole.*]

I imagine that many people will claim I have misrepresented Christians and maligned Christianity–I've pointed to a small subset of Christians, they may say, and attacked their brand of the theology, instead of seeing Christianity as it really is–liberal, loving, and tolerant. I hope that is true. I hope there is a huge majority of Christianity that doesn't adhere to the doctrines of Hell and Biblical literalism. If they are out there–where are they?

According to recent statistics, there are some thirty million Americans who do not subscribe to any religious identification–where are they? Hidden? They are quiet, independently living their lives without stirring up trouble, marching on Washington, or typing out scathing replies to others on the editorial pages. [*Editorial pages don't exist much anymore, do they? Now it's the comments sections at click-bait 'news' sites.*] I feel it's time they stood up and were counted–it's time to let the world know we are here in all our varieties, under all our labels (or without label), and we won't allow a theocracy in this country.

Perhaps the same independence and complacency infects the majority of liberal Christians who I am told are "out there," because the Christianity I am confronted with regularly, via the bookshelf, television, and Internet is evangelical, radical, and pro-theocracy. [*This is still true.*] If liberal Christianity is the norm, it needs to stand up and denounce the aggressive "religious right" that would lead this country away from its base of freedom for all people.

This is the way I see the religious: the principles they accept of their theology reflect their true personalities. Intolerant elitists become hateful extremists, taking all the worst parts from an ancient book to further their selfish aims. Kind, loving moderates take from the religion of their culture gentle, peaceful teachings, and practice acceptance.

Which sort of believer are you?

[See? The original book still had some merit. It just needed a shot of snark here and there. I hope it wasn't too offensive for you. You know, despite what you might think, I was raised like everyone else and taught that it's best to be nice to people, to not offend them on purpose. It's not nice to mock people's beliefs, sure. And while I find some satisfaction in it, I don't really like to hurt people's feelings or anger them. It's just that...

Keeping quiet about things is always good for people in power, for majorities who see nothing wrong with forcing their rules on minorities. A lot of the reason they see nothing wrong with what they're doing is living in the majority bubble, their viewpoints constantly being reinforced by those around them. Politely and sweetly telling these people that they aren't being nice and that what they're doing is wrong and what they believe is wrong won't get you anywhere but shouted down.

And why be so rude as to try to tell them that what they believe is wrong? Because what they believe—in this case, the entire Christian cultural phenomenon—is the basis for their oppression of others.

Pleasant doesn't get us anywhere. At some point we've got to get in their faces. We've got to shout, we've got to mock, we've got to call a bigot a bigot. It's necessary. And I make no apologies for it. Okay, so I made a few. I'm a little wishy washy about all of this meme busting. I suppose that makes me human.]

Chapter Fifteen

The Honesty of Atheism

The following essay was originally published in Russ Kick's anthology Everything You Know About God is Wrong *(The Disinformation Company Ltd., 2007). In it, I argue that atheism is actually the only honest position a person can take with regard to religion. That's right: it's the* only honest *position. If you ask me, "The Honesty of Atheism" makes the entire case for nonbelief. When I read it, I have no desire to snark it, so I'm leaving it alone. You may find parts of it a tad redundant. Think of this chapter as a precise and powerful summation of what you've just read. But don't skip it! No, no. Don't do that.*

Some time ago, after American Atheists president Ellen Johnson made an appearance on a national news program, an acquaintance of mine opened conversation saying, "I saw your leader on television last night." I was duly confused. Her statement was not much different from telling a Catholic the same thing after seeing Pat Robertson on television. The difference being that few, if any, atheists look to any particular person or organization as representative of their "beliefs."

But, then, atheists aren't so very different from any other group of people. While I've heard, and made, attempts to label us as fiercely independent, in reality we're pretty much like everybody else. As in the religious community, there are atheists who congregate with the like-minded and those who don't feel the need. Like the religious with their labels, atheists disagree on exactly what atheism is and who is and isn't an atheist. One thing that sets atheists apart, I suppose, is that, while the religious may claim other people of their faith are not truly a part of the flock, it is often atheists themselves who claim not to be atheists. I've yet to hear a Christian say he isn't one—in fact, they all seem to be clamoring for defining rights to the word. On the other hand, many atheists run from their label as if it's diseased.

A lot of atheists just don't like the word. They use various other labels to get around it: Humanist, freethinker, agnostic, nonreligious, secularist, materialist, and rationalist, to name a few. When put on the spot during the early stages of my atheism, I once told a woman, "We're not church people," in a polite attempt to turn down an invitation. Sometimes polite is an excuse for gutless.

Often we use one of our other labels as a "polite" way of saying we're atheist. For some reason, using the word that best describes our position with regard to the existence of gods is considered "in your face." Rude. Some atheists use these other terms because they don't want to alarm the general public. While I can sympathize, it's clear that the general public wouldn't be so outraged by the word if we'd use it more freely. Unfortunately, many atheists will outright claim they are not atheists when you try to pin them down.

While it's frustrating to have atheism misunderstood and mischaracterized by the religious, to hear it maligned by fellow atheists is disheartening. Much of the trouble in which atheists find themselves can be laid at their own feet, it would seem. Too many insist that atheism requires an absolute certainty or belief that gods do not exist. They prefer the word agnostic, mistakenly thinking it describes a skeptic, a doubter, or a person who just doesn't know.

The reality is that atheism is the only intellectually honest position a person can take–it is the only logical stance.

What is atheism? And why is it so misunderstood?

Let's be honest, right up front. People in the United States, for the most part, don't like atheism. We could debate the various reasons why: it casts light on their own doubts; they believe it threatens the moral fabric of our nation; they think it's Satanic; whatever–they don't like it and people tend to revile and slander what they don't like. For many, atheism is a steadfast refusal to accept the reality of the Christian God's existence. And that is, apparently, unforgivable and worthy of contempt.

According to the 2004 American Mosaic Project, a survey of U.S. households conducted by the University of Minnesota Department of Sociology, atheists are this country's least trusted minority. Americans rank atheists far below Muslims, homosexuals, and recent immigrants when identifying those who share their vision for America and those they'd like their children to marry. [1] These results should not surprise atheists.

Atheism has a long history as the term used for anyone refusing to fall in line and worship whatever gods are in vogue at the time. The polytheists called monotheists atheists for not worshiping local gods; their behavior was considered, at best, rude. The Romans, for instance, called the Christians atheists. With the growth of monotheism, atheism and paganism were seen as one and the same and reviled as evil.

Historically, the word was not intended to describe a person who "believed in no gods." No, the word atheist was generally used to describe a person who "does not believe in" one or more particular gods. Atheists of today, by virtue of living in a world in which the vast majority of god characters are no longer proposed as real, don't believe in any gods. There are only a few left, after all, to not believe in.

In today's America, there is a line not to be crossed in religion. Believe what you will about God or gods and you will be, at the very least, tolerated; but abandon belief in deity altogether, and you've committed an unforgivable act of reason. You have dared to suggest that the natural world is all there is. This will not do.

The agnostics are better tolerated because they seem to be saying they aren't sure. It is preferred that you be certain there is a god. To be unsure is at least admitting you are open to the possibility; but to be certain there is no god is to be unreachable. Adamancy in belief is good; adamancy in unbelief is evil.

This is a strange hypocrisy of belief. With it, you can claim you have knowledge when you don't, and call it reality. But you can then say someone who lacks your belief is making a claim of knowledge, and call such certainty delusion.

One reason that atheism is so misunderstood by religionists is because it must be. They can't fight its logic and honesty when properly defined so they make it mean what they feel comfortable attacking. The meaning of atheism is confused by atheists as a result of living in a society in which the term has been so maligned.

All our troubles with the word boil down to the difference between belief and knowledge. Atheism is nothing more, nor less, than a lack of belief in deity. Theism is "belief in deity." Atheism is without that belief. Regardless of whatever else a person believes or doesn't, if he does not believe in gods, he is atheist.

An atheist could believe in astrology or alien abduction or elves. He wouldn't be a rationalist atheist, but he'd be atheist just the same. A person could admit he has no idea whether or not there is a god; but as long as he doesn't believe there is one, he's an atheist.

Atheism is not a religion. Atheists like to say, "If atheism is a religion, baldness is a hair color," or "If atheism is a religion, not collecting stamps is a hobby." This does not mean that atheists can't have religions; but their religions would be god-less–and they would be individual choices, not something all atheists share.

Some atheists distinguish between strong and weak atheism: strong atheists claim no gods exist, weak atheists just don't believe in any. There is no real difference between these types of people. Either way, neither believes in gods.

Some say that strong atheists "believe" there is no god. I would hope they mean to use the word "believe" as a synonym for "think," though it's not the same thing. To believe there is no god is just as delusional as believing there is one–when we properly define the word "believe." Note the subtle difference between believing there is no god, and not believing there is a god.

The strong atheist is not one who "believes" there is no god. Instead, unlike the believer, the strong atheist bases his claim on evidence. In that respect, the basic difference between the strong and weak atheist is the weak atheist's hesitation to either state the obvious, or examine it. That is where the honesty of atheism lies. There is no evidence for the existence of gods, and some good evidence that they do not exist. The honest position is to admit that. All atheism asks of a person is the honesty to admit that no one knows whether or not there is a god–no one–and from that, to refrain from the delusion of belief.

Many claim the position of not knowing is merely agnosticism–but they're wrong. Let's take a moment here to realize that people use labels the way they want to use them. The other reason atheism is so misunderstood is that language is a fluid thing. We are all the time hashing out just what it means to wear a certain label, and unfortunately that process results in the invention of more labels–a few interestingly perfect, others completely useless, and some creating more havoc in an already confusing topic.

Agnosticism, for instance, in the public mind is doubt, being on the fence, not sure if there is a god or not. In the true sense of the word, as Huxley coined it, agnosticism is a claim of lack of knowledge about the existence of gods. The Gnostics of history claimed direct knowledge of God; Huxley, believing atheists claimed knowledge that there was no god, decided to call himself agnostic: he claimed to have no knowledge of the existence of any god. [2]

But Huxley was an atheist, whether he understood the word or not, because he didn't believe there was a god. When he said that atheists and believers had "solved the problem of existence"– atheists claiming knowledge that God did not exist, theists that it did [3]–he was wrong.

It is only by demanding that atheism requires certainty, or knowledge, that gods do not exist, that a person would find need for a word that describes a lack of knowledge of gods' existence. At their origins, atheism admits a lack of belief, while agnosticism admits a lack of knowledge. We are all without knowledge of gods–the agnostics are just the ones who admit it.

Defining gnosticism as "declaring knowledge of the existence of god or gods," there are agnostic theists who admit they have no knowledge of God's existence, but still believe it exists. There are agnostic atheists who admit they have no such knowledge, and logically refrain from belief. Naturally there are gnostic theists who claim knowledge of God's existence and believe one exists. One would think there would be no gnostic atheists–those who claim they have knowledge of the existence of one or more gods, but refrain from belief in them–but no doubt, they're out there rationalizing their disconnect daily.

In a 2003 Harris Poll, four percent of those calling themselves atheist/agnostic claimed to be absolutely certain there is a god. [4] I have conversed with a few former "Christians in rebellion." They claimed they knew all along that God existed, but they were either angry with him or just didn't want to live by his rules and so refused to worship him. They called this "atheism," now that they were back in the flock. [This attitude would explain why so many claim atheists know God exists and are only angry at him or want to lead licentious lives, as people often project their own failings onto others.]

Whether or not that unexpected four percent in the Harris poll was due to rebellious believers, functionally neurotic atheists, people using a strange definition of agnosticism, or people accidentally giving the wrong answer, we'll never know.

Of the four choices in the gnostic/agnostic theist/atheist range, gnostic theism is the more perplexing proposition. Belief is an active acceptance of something without evidence, or despite it. If you have enough evidence for a position, you don't need belief. I don't have to believe that being hit by a car can kill you; I've got lots of evidence of that–enough to know it's true. I don't have to believe my spouse loves me–he shows me by his actions that he does. I don't need faith in the sun's shining to expect it to do so–it has done so every day of my life. I have confidence in these areas, not belief. Confidence in something is only warranted when there is evidence to support it. Evidence is based on observation and repeatability. Belief is faith–acceptance without evidence.

If the gnostic truly had the knowledge he claims to have, he could share it with others; it would be factual, testable, and reliable because *that's what knowledge is.* If he had the knowledge he claims, he would not need the belief. We don't believe knowledge–we know it. And we know it because it is repeatable and based on observable evidence. Yes, much knowledge is probabilistic. There is no absolute certainty in matters other than logic or definition, for example; there are degrees toward certainty. Knowledge is what you have when you come very close to certainty.

Unfortunately, believers have managed to equate knowledge and belief with impunity–their belief is considered knowledge. But let the atheist claim that gods do not exist due to lack of evidence, and he is pounced upon with demands for proof there is no god. "You can't know everything," they say; "But you must think you know everything to say there are no gods." This is twisted logic.

Often atheists do make the claim that there is no god. We base this position on observation and evidence. There is just as much evidence for fairies as there is for gods, and yet, we aren't expected to believe in fairies. No one tells us that we must open our hearts to the reality of fairies before we'll see that fairies are very real. And more importantly, we aren't expected to prove they don't exist if we say we don't believe in them.

We have no knowledge of fairies—no evidence of their existence. We have stories about fairies, but that's all. When you don't have knowledge about something, you either remain without an answer or position regarding it, or you just believe what you've been taught or told or dreamt up. Only when you have knowledge, can you honestly take a position or claim to have an answer.

That is why belief in gods is disingenuous, and atheism is honest. There is no evidence for the existence of gods, despite the claims of believers. To believe is to dissuade oneself from seeking the truth.

Belief in God has become so ingrained in our society that it is the accepted norm. Claimants are rarely asked to show any evidence for their belief, or to even describe what they mean when they use the word "god." But when forced to confront skeptics, theists are adamant that there is ample evidence that a god exists. And in their endeavor to elaborate, we come to realize that the word "evidence" can be just as maligned as "atheist."

The "evidence" given for the existence of gods in our culture comes from Christian apologists, but can easily be transferred to other religious notions of god:

- Everything has a cause, so there is a God, who doesn't have a cause
- Life exists, so God exists
- Miracles happen, so God made them happen
- The Bible is so fabulous God must have

written it

- Biblical prophecy can only be explained by the existence of God
- Answered prayer proves God exists
- Subjective Experience proves God exists
- The effects of belief prove the belief is true
- The spread of Christianity proves God is the one, true God, and Jesus was his son

These arguments are taken very seriously by very serious people. Volumes are written on them. Syllogisms are presented and debated. It's all good fun for some, but these arguments can be dismissed very easily. They all require a leap of faith from what is unknown to an answer that has no evidentiary support.

For example, if everything has a cause, God must have one also. If God doesn't have to have a cause, some things are obviously exempt. To say that only God is exempt is cheating. To say that only things that "begin" to exist have a cause and God never "began" is cheating. Saying everything has to have a cause proves nothing except that you are assuming what you think will further your argument. If it has been shown that the universe had a beginning, it tells us absolutely nothing about whether or not there is a god. In other words, even if everything did require a cause, we still wouldn't know what that cause is.

Michael Shermer, in his book *Why People Believe Weird Things: Pseudoscience, Superstition, and Other Confusions of Our Time* (WH Freeman, 1997), outlines twenty-five fallacies that lead to errors in thought and allow people to accept invalid ideas as truth. Among these fallacies are the belief that bold and forceful statements and the use of scientific language make a claim true; problems with placement of the burden of proof; reasoning after the fact; rationalization of failures; and an inability to distinguish truth from false analogies, coincidence, and appeals to ignorance.

Belief in the veracity of the aforementioned "evidence" for gods is nothing more than Shermer's fallacies at work. We have no evidence for the existence of gods. What people have is lack of knowledge, and lots of faith. People react credulously to their incredulousness–the unknown is a vacuum that for millions of people must be filled with something to banish the gnawing discomfort of not knowing.

Millions either refuse to accept the factual evidence of evolutionary theory, for example, or are unable to understand it. They can't imagine that life arose for no reason and without the guidance of some greater being–so they believe there was one. People have a lot of emotion invested in life and they can't conceive of it just ending. They can't tolerate the idea that this is all there is–so they believe there is more after death. There are so many questions people can't answer, so they believe the answers given them by their cultural religions. The universe is so big and weird. How did it get here, anyway, and why is anything here at all? We don't know; people can't stand not knowing, so they *believe*.

The difference between a believer and an atheist is that the believer will believe a story that helps him deal with his lack of knowledge. The atheist will admit he doesn't know. That's enough for the atheist. It's not enough for most people probably because they are taught from a very early age that believing is a good thing. Believing is fun; believing makes you feel safe and happy. But that doesn't mean that the various things people believe about life and the universe have any basis in fact; they don't. If they had strong basis in fact, no one would have to *believe in* them—we'd all be able to *know.*

It is somewhat understandable that atheism would be equated with a certainty that no gods exist. The atheist says "I see no evidence that a god exists, so it probably doesn't." The important difference between that stance, and one of belief or certainty, is that the atheist awaits facts before accepting the existence of gods, while the theist believes. The atheist is open to evidence; the theist has already decided the question.

Belief is delusion. Belief is based on your feelings and ignorance, not on any factual evidence. If you had factual evidence for what you believe, you would not have to believe it...you would *know* it—and we could all share in that knowledge; we would all come to the same conclusion, the same god, the same story.

We can see now, the error of the theist promoting his god:

> *Theist*: Believe in him.
>
> *Atheist*: He obviously doesn't exist.
>
> *Theist*: You atheists think you know everything.
>
> *Atheist*: I don't have to know everything to assume your god doesn't exist. All I have to do is listen to you tell me to believe in him. If I have to believe in him, it's glaringly apparent he does not exist.
>
> *Theist*: Stop bashing me for my faith!

Atheist: Yeah, yeah, whatever.

There is no evidence that a god exists. If there were, we would all know that a god exists. Sure, there would still be deniers, just like those who refuse to accept the evidence of evolutionary theories. And that's what many believers would like to make of atheists: deniers. The difference is that we have a great deal of evidence for evolution; it can be found in the museums of natural history, in magnificent and scholarly tomes and journals, and more importantly, in the fossil record. There is no such evidence offered for their belief, only assertions.

We must always remain open to new evidence that would enhance our knowledge. But until such evidence arrives, the intellectually honest position is to refrain from believing in propositions for which it is lacking. To lack belief in what you can't know is to embrace the reality that *can* be known— to revel in the vastness of the unknown, to wonder, to muse, to imagine...and then return to what we know, to live as best we can in the face of it.

But this is unacceptable for the believer, who insists we all share his delusion. If you refuse, he'll claim you have your own. You will occasionally run into the senseless individual who will, with a straight face, tell you that there is no difference between lacking a belief and having one. Do not talk to such people. They can see your lips move, but there's someone else in their heads doing your talking for you, so just forget it.

Atheists don't know that gods don't exist; we're just fairly certain of it based on a severe lack of evidence for them. Believers try hard to paint the atheist into a position of absolute certainty so they can better attack him. Believers figure that atheism is a belief just like theirs, only opposite. "After all," they claim, "everyone believes something." Delusion needs company to survive. In company, it can hide and spread in the shadows of ignorance. We must bring it out into the light.

There's a trigger, somewhere in the human brain, I'm sure, that people just miss. Their thinking dances around it, avoiding logic by every means possible. One day though, for some of us, something hits it. Someone says something like, "I don't know how we got here and neither do you" and the trigger fires and they suddenly, though too often only briefly, understand lack of knowledge, lack of certainty, lack of belief. They get that it's all just different stories: the Jewish story, the Christian story, the Muslim story, the Hindu story, the Wicca story; and they get that the atheist just doesn't believe the stories are true.

Unfortunately, it rarely sticks because if they're all just stories, then the atheist is right. If we don't really know, then the atheist is the only one looking at the situation honestly. If no one knows, belief is just delusion, a salve for the mind, a bedtime story to soothe us into sleep.

And if no one knows, maybe the material world really is all there is. Maybe we really do cease to exist when we take our final breaths. Fear creeps in and sets the blocks of belief back in their places and the dishonesty begins anew. We cannot honestly admit we don't know because we cannot accept that we are a part of this earth and we will die.

"What a sad state of affairs," the believers lament. Perhaps. But sad doesn't mean false any more than comforting means true.

And so, we come to the truth at hand. As there is no evidence for gods (admitted by the theists who tell us we must believe in it before it will seem real to us; and as having to believe in anything is verification that it has no evidence for it and is therefore delusional), the only intellectually honest position one can take is that of atheism.

I myself do not believe in belief.

Notes:

1. American Mosaic Project main page: http://www.soc.umn.edu/amp/

2. *Encyclopaedia of Religion and Ethics*, 1908; Edited by James Hastings. Pertinent quotes can be found at: http://www.infidels.org/library/modern/mathew/sn-huxley.html

3. *Ibid.*

4. The Harris Poll #59, October 15, 2003 can no longer be found.

Chapter Sixteen

Why I Quit Atheism

That's right; I quit. Sort of. I wrote this essay in July, 2013. You might be wondering why I issued the second edition of this book if I've quit atheism. You'll just have to read the last essay, also known as Chapter Seventeen, to find that out.

I quit atheism this past June.

It's funny how events and ideas converged over just about a week. I was attending the Florida Tech Creative Writing Institute, four days of lectures and workshops on writing; it ran from Thursday through Sunday. On Saturday evening, I'd ended a brief engagement in yet another trivial argument with an atheist on my atheist Facebook page* and decided I was going to give up atheism.

Yes, I said I was arguing with *an atheist*.

I planned to delete the Facebook page and scale the Atheist View website down to the bare bones until its paid time ran out and then take it down. This was all very drastic so I decided I ought to sleep on it. When Sunday morning arrived and I was getting ready to attend my final day of workshops at Florida Tech, I told my husband, "I'm thinking of giving up on this whole atheism thing." I told him I was tired of arguing with atheists.

His response was, "What about the Poultry apologies blog?" That's a blog** in which I took articles on the Internet with silly grammatical or writing errors and made fun of them. I didn't see the connection, but told him that, yes, I was thinking about giving that up, too. I was tired, I realized, of arguing with people, of being angry and frustrated all the time. He was not happy. Let me paraphrase: "If you're not arguing with the atheists and you're not pointing out everyone's grammatical and spelling mistakes...where will all of your aggression go? Toward me, that's where!"

I had to laugh. Because maybe he was right. But I was at a point in my life where I just wanted to enjoy. Enjoy the Internet, mostly. Enjoy the good things in life. Enjoy my day without having to focus on all things negative. I'd already started trimming down my Facebook "friends" list. Don't you think it's creepy that we're all "friends," when most of us really don't know the people we're connected with at all? I'm not sure which is creepier, Facebook and my "friends," or Twitter and my "followers." I confess I do like Scrazzle and my "minions." [*Is Scrazzle even a thing anymore?*] Anyway, you wouldn't believe (well, maybe you would) what people post to their walls. And for years I was looking at it and starting my day off with it–essentially, I was getting pissed off every morning.

When I joined Facebook, I started "friending" atheists. It was as if all the atheists in the world were trying to connect and I was part of it. But after a while I stopped actively seeking out connections and just let them come to me. My wall was too crowded and I wasn't all that happy with what I was seeing. And then, about a year ago, I started to whittle away at the list.

People who posted pictures of suffering animals had to go. "But, wait," they would cry when I clued them in on my plans, "We're just trying to make you aware of the awful things going on." And I said, "You think I don't already know? And you think I need a picture on my wall of a dead and bloated dog tied to a tree during breakfast? Post a link instead. Be thoughtful of what you're showing people." But they didn't care. So, I "unfriended" them. I "unfriended" anyone who posted pictures of dead and suffering people, too. And children! How they loved to "make me aware" by posting pictures of dead or dying children. Maybe something is wrong with me, but when I see things like that, I cry. And I don't want to cry when I'm sitting at my computer trying to enjoy the Internet.

Anyone who posted pictures of nearly naked women in sexually suggestive poses–always an abundance of those. "Unfriended." And anyone who posted too many pictures of himself or herself, especially nearly naked in sexually suggestive positions. One guy posted a picture of himself masturbating. I had to suppose he didn't have his mother on his friends list. All gone.

Once I'd finally cleaned up my wall of the lovers of torture and sexual exhibitionism, most of whom were atheists, I was satisfied. Until June. When I decided to quit.

Sunday morning, after I told my husband my plans, I checked my email before going off to Florida Tech and coincidentally enough, there was a message from the leader of an atheist group near me wondering if I wanted to speak at one of their meetings. I was surprised. "I can't do that!" I said to myself. "I've just quit!" But, I decided I would do it anyway. I was still an atheist, after all, and maybe I could talk about how I'd just quit atheism.

This person, however, suggested that I talk about something else: "The Honesty of Atheism." He said that my article was still relevant. "Okay," I told him. "I'll take a look at it and see what I can come up with." After reading it, I was reminded of one of the lectures I'd sat in on at the Creative Writing Institute on Laura Riding Jackson.

Jackson was a poet and an intellectual. Born in New York, she lived in Europe for about fourteen years and after marrying Schuyler Jackson, moved to Wabasso, Florida, of all places. She and her husband lived in a Cracker Style house with no electricity, but she claimed to be happy. I can't imagine it. The man who spoke to us was with the Laura Riding Jackson Foundation, an organization formed to preserve her home after her death. He read some of her poetry. It was poetry all right– but I liked it.

But then he told us that Jackson and her husband set out to rewrite the dictionary. [The result was *Rational Meaning: A New Foundation for the Definition of Words and Supplementary*

Essays] Jackson didn't believe in synonyms. She believed that each word had a distinct and precise definition. I was instantly a fan. And I was reminded of it, when I reread "The Honesty of Atheism" because, at heart, it's about words and what they mean and how they ought to be used. And it was then, there in June, that I knew I was going to give up on atheism.

My history with atheism began in my thirties. I've never been a social person. As a youngster I was socially inept. Unpracticed. And too particular. The biggest problem facing me at adolescence was that I'd never found a voice. Growing up in my family, I learned that expressing my opinions or extremes of emotion was bad. Such things were too often met with derision, criticism, or even punishment. As a young teen, I learned not to have an opinion of my own. I believed whatever you believed. If you believed that abortion was wrong, so did I. And when I talked to someone who believed abortion was a right, I agreed.

I had very few friends and looking back now, I can understand why. I was what they called "two-faced." But I wasn't that way because I was a naturally backstabbing bitch. I was that way because I hated confrontation and was terrified of being wrong. So, if you hated Julie, so did I. But of course, I liked Julie and so couldn't be cruel to her (not that I was never cruel, because if the girls I was with at the time wanted to be cruel, I was cruel) so when with her, I hated the people who hated her.

Once I realized atheism, I started to find my voice. There I was, finally, with an opinion! And it was an opinion I could stand behind. Trust me, I'd thought about it. *A lot.* I'd even read the Bible (that pretty much cinched it). Atheism was logical. It made sense. It was honest. And so, I started to learn my own opinions on everything else, as well. I was growing a backbone. It was very painful.

At some point, I had this epiphany (if you can call it an epiphany when it's completely wrong). I thought that my social isolation, my lack of friends, must be because I'm an atheist. I'm not weird; I'm just trying to socialize with the wrong sorts of people. Once I find the atheists, I'll be just fine! I'll be like other people. I didn't for a second think there were any atheists living near me, or that there were more than, say, fifty, in the country. So, there wouldn't be parties. But there would be friends!

I believed that atheists, by definition, would be committed to reason, to truth and honesty, and to individual freedom.

My first foray into finding other atheists was in the AOL forums–this was back when AOL was the thing. While there, trying to learn and socialize, Christians would dart in and scream at us about how immoral we were and how happy they were going to be watching us writhing in pain in Hell for all eternity. Over time, I learned to give just as good as I got and began engaging in email lists, mostly designed for debating Christianity. But I became acquainted with other atheists that way, too.

After a while, however, I got tired of arguing the same things over and over again with new Christians–or the same ones who just couldn't accept logic and reason. So, I backed off a bit. I created a website, Atheist View, and then wrote my book. The book was cathartic—like a life dissertation. Here it is. This is what I think. Don't ask me any more stupid questions. And I got to the point where religion no longer bothered me. When Christians attempted to tell me how wrong I was about their beliefs, I either responded with sarcastic humor or ignored them. (I'm a big fan of sarcastic humor.) My time and energy was wasted there. And I no longer enjoyed the debate—probably because it was fruitless. It had become boring.

I sought more real association with atheists even though I didn't think there were any around. I created an email list; I think it was called Atheists of Brevard, and was surprised to see the list grow into the hundreds. At some point, my brother and I attended an atheism convention in Tampa, probably Atheist Alliance International, and there was a table set up there with information on starting up a local atheist group. I told my brother, "That's what I'm going to do." So, I founded Space Coast Freethought Association. We thrived for a while, with a newsletter, meetings, and a website. The group still thrives, I suppose, as a Meetup.

Our first meeting was in a local park and only my brother and I showed up. But the next month, a few more people were there. And the next month, more. Right away, we got crazy people. The first was a man who wanted us all to go to his house for our meetings, and for dinner. He told us that what he did was to go around to all the restaurants at night and get their leftover food, the stuff they were going to put into the dumpster. And he fed people with it. He claimed that the mayor had even been over to his house for dinner!

Every meeting it was, "Let's start meeting at my house." Nearly every day an email would show up on our list in all caps, "WHEN ARE WE GOING TO START MEETING AT MY HOUSE. I HAVE FOOD FROM LUCKY DUCKS." (Okay, so I had to recreate that from memory and it might not be completely accurate.)

I finally grew a pair and told him, "We are not meeting at your house." Luckily, I had a good excuse. We needed a neutral place where people would feel comfortable showing up and could easily escape when they decided they wanted to. That was the main thing I looked for when attending a meeting with people I didn't know, anyway.

So, we started meeting regularly in the local library. Where more crazy people turned up. There was the perpetual victim. Before she found us, everything bad that happened to her was because she was a woman. After she found us, it was because she was an atheist. I can tell you neither of those were the reason for most of her troubles. Then there was the Aussie who insisted that voting in our country ought to be mandatory—by law. That's right. If you don't vote, you risk going to jail.

There were the people you thought were wonderful and sweet—but they couldn't function logically. Like the sweet old man who believed that passages in the Bible told of aliens visiting earth. There was no other explanation! No one at that time could have described such a machine! Therefore: aliens. And then there were the people you respected, the ones you thought were intelligent, until they started appeals to authority and *ad hominem* attacks.

The email list was much worse than the meetings. We engaged in a lot of arguments. It was a wonderful learning experience, at least. I learned to argue out and parse my thoughts and opinions. But some others didn't seem to be able to examine their own arguments during the engagements. There were people who would change their stance on an issue mid-argument. If you quoted them verbatim, it didn't matter. They'd see it, and then claim it wasn't they who were changing stance, but you. There were people who would make bold statements of fact and refuse to support them with sources. And there were people who stomped their feet and called me names. I was always willing to label ideas and opinions, as opposed to people. I once called one man's opinion about some issue "fascist." He threw a tantrum, called me a diva, and stalked off.

There were liberals, conservatives, Objectivists, socialists, fascists, and more. All trying to convince me they were smarter than I was. And, well, I wasn't buying it. And sure, you can say that maybe I was the stupid one, the unreasonable one–those people certainly would say so. But I had some backup. I had some study and research and discussion with others to boost my confidence. I was never, ever the type of person to be confident in myself. I was always quick to be the one who admitted she was wrong. But I was finding that, more and more, that wasn't the case a lot of the time. And I was no longer willing to claim fault, where I was sure the fault wasn't with me.

I lost a lot of respect for a lot of people on that list. And no doubt, a lot of people lost respect for me—if they had it to begin with. But I learned something very important: Atheists can, and do, believe in a lot of weird things. Atheists are not immune to being unreasonable. But some things, you have to learn over and over again.

So I quit the group. I took to my website and blog. I started a Facebook page just for atheism. And through it all, I realized another very important thing: I don't like atheists any more than anyone else in the world. Just because someone is an atheist does not mean he is committed to reason. And I have a serious issue with that.

I like reason. I consider myself a rationalist—a person committed to accepting only observable, testable, repeatable evidence in determining what can be known to be true. Am I perfectly reasonable all the time? Of course not, don't be silly. But I strive for it. And I recognize stupidity when I see it. Unfortunately, I tended to not just let it pass. I'd learned to shrug off the religious who tried to argue with me, because I knew they would not, could not, be reasonable. I still hadn't learned the same about atheists.

Hence, finding myself once more in an argument with an atheist on Facebook in June. The Pope said something ridiculous like, wasting food is equal to stealing from the poor. I posted the link to the article in which he was quoted and said that it was stupid. I said, "Please. Every smart kid in America knew his mom was full of shit when she told him he had to clean his plate because there were starving kids in China." An atheist challenged me. He said, "Are you suggesting we do not have a culture of waste and it is a bad thing?"

Right then, I should have realized this person

was not reasonable. Nothing in my statement hinted at either of those things. I was talking about wasting food not equaling stealing. But, though I had learned my lesson over and over and over again and had backed off from trying to reason with atheists, once again, I had to learn. I replied, "I'm saying that me buying too much roast beef doesn't make me a thief."

It was as simple as that for me. You see, the word "stealing" means something. But he replied, "I think culture of waste says it pretty clearly. I find it hard to imagine any thinking person reading this piece and only finding fault with it."

So I handed him his ass. "Ah, well," I said. "Then there you have it. I'm clearly not a thinking person. Thanks for clueing me in. I'll try to remember that, but not being a thinking person, I might have difficulty. You know how it is, oh, wait, no you don't because obviously you're a thinking person who can't manage to find one thing to complain about in the idea that wasting food is stealing. As if, if I only wouldn't buy too much food, the poor would magically have it. Yes, we absolutely live in a culture of waste, and a culture of throw-away products. But that culture is not what creates the poor, and conserving is not what will help the poor, in my totally thoughtless opinion."

To this person, the article was about the feelings he had regarding the poor not having enough to eat, and the wealthy having more than they need. That was all that mattered. But to me, what mattered was the word "stealing." That was what elicited my response to the Pope. I balked at the idea that wasting food was stealing. Because it absolutely is not. I was only arguing that *word*. But this person was arguing his feelings about the poor.

It just didn't work. It can never work. I can't argue with someone who can't even see what the argument is about.

I realized that my "friends" list on my regular Facebook page and my "likers" on the atheism page were, for the most part (by far), liberals who, though they're certainly not alone in it, think with their emotions and not their intellects, or the facts. And the funny thing is, this makes me more liberal than a lot of the liberals I know. During the gay marriage flurry, I posited that marriage equality was for everyone, not just gays. Plural marriage should also be legal. But some of the liberals thought I was out of my mind. They had an emotional reaction to plural marriage, probably because of their tiny amount of misinformation and, most definitely its religious affiliation, and so could not get past their feelings to accept what real freedom must mean: we ought to be able to enter into marriages with any other sentient adults without interference from the State.

I have said, occasionally, that my politics align most closely with Libertarianism. I have, however, not gone so far as to claim that I am a Libertarian. Because I don't like a lot of Libertarians (they can't reason any better than other people) and certainly not Libertarian politicians–I can't say I agree with each and every point in their platform. I had an altercation with a woman some time ago that per-fectly illustrates how people think, and especially how liberals view Libertarians. I made a status update that simply said: "My views are too complex and thoughtful to be reduced to an emotionally charged sound bite, to be cut, pasted, and spread like a virus, in an attempt to subtly shame anyone who dares not participate."

Clearly, I was getting tired of the sound bite nature of Facebook [and it sounds like this was referencing one of those viral "share on your wall or I'll know you're evil" memes]. But this woman with whom I couldn't recall any previous interaction responded by saying she wrote out a response explaining how I was wrong, but wasn't going to post it, because doing so would be useless, much like arguing with Rush Limbaugh. She'd apparently read somewhere that I agreed with a lot of Libertarian principles. So, she wanted me to know that she wouldn't bother to respond. Seriously. You can read the altercation at atheistview.com under the "Why I Quit Atheism" link.

This was not the only problem I encountered being a socially liberal, fiscally conservative a-theist [And don't think you know what I mean by ficscally conservative, because you don't). My wall was constantly filled with statements of bigotry and hatred toward conservatives, namely Republicans and Libertarians, known to most of my liberal "friends" as Republicunts, Repubtards, and the childishly selfish. [They like to say Libertarianism is for bright-eyed, immature college students; something you grow out of.] Ayn Rand was called every vicious name in the book by people who had almost certainly never read her philosophical ideas, because they clearly didn't understand them, and most often attacked her as a person instead. There were constant diatribes against capitalism, as if we actually live in a true

327

capitalist society instead of a corporatocracy. [We used to have government-controlled capitalism, which is still not capitalism.]

I formed new standards for "unfriending." Anyone who called Ayn Rand a cunt was gone. Look, I'm not saying I like the woman. I don't know much about her at all. But I object to people calling a strong-minded woman a cunt simply because they don't agree with her politics. And then, anyone who called *any woman* a cunt was gone. Anyone making bigoted and hateful statements about large groups of people was gone. Many were ...gone.

I have family who are still Republicans. Sure, I can't understand it completely, but I'm not going to stomp my feet and call them names. I used to be a Republican myself and only left when they started going batshit crazy–due, in my opinion, to religion. [Of course, this was before Donald Trump and the new Republican insanity took over the party.] Every now and then someone on Face-book would post the question, "How can an atheist possibly be a Republican?" As if they couldn't fathom the fact that most people don't fit ideally into either party and choose the one they can stomach the best. And they apparently don't know about the existence of decent social liberals who are also fiscally conservative–they call them Libertarians as if it's a slur, and lump them all in together because it makes their world neatly compact. [Not to forget that Republicans use the word Liberal as a slur as well.]

Of course, they're also asking how blacks and gays can be Christians, trying as hard as they can to deny the enormous propensity for hope and fear and the need for belonging, in the human animal.

And so, there I was, arguing once again with someone who couldn't understand something as simple as the meaning of the word "steal," and was emotionally committed to the idea that his not finishing his Big Mac was stealing from the poor homeless man down the street. The guilt! And he dared to tell me he was the thinking one in the discussion.

I'd had it.

I didn't want to talk to unreasonable people anymore.

I quit.

And then I remembered Laura Riding Jackson. The lecturer told us that day that Jackson renounced poetry at some point in her life because it had failed in its mission. Call me skeptical, but I am fairly sure that poetry has no mission. Jackson disagreed. The speaker read a few paragraphs from Jackson's treatise explaining why poetry had failed. When he was finished, he sighed and admitted he didn't understand any of that and he often had to leave interpretations of her essays and poetry to people smarter than himself.

I didn't understand it either, and when I was asked to speak to that group of atheists, and so reread my article, "The Honesty of Atheism," I finally put it all together.

I finally got it.

Jackson chose the exact words she felt conveyed her reasons. And she *failed to communicate*.

Yes. Words have precise meanings. As an author, I must choose the right word. Not just the right word for its meaning, but right for the sentence, the paragraph, the novel, the tone, the voice–my audience. I can't just insist that this word is the only word that means what it means and therefore, I must use it. It's no good to use the precise word if people can't understand what I'm saying. While I stand by my article on the honesty of atheism, while I agree with it completely, I understand that it's meaningless. Because people don't care.

Too many people think with their emotions instead of using their sense of reason. When the Zimmerman verdict came in, my Facebook wall was flooded with outrage. Never mind the truth. Never mind the actual facts of the case; and never mind the fair application of the law. I "unfriended" more than fifty people who were thinking with their emotions instead of seeing objective reality. Why? Because they were upset that Trayvon Martin was dead.

I was upset about that, too! I was horrified by what had happened. But I didn't let those emotions guide my thinking, or my search for the facts. I didn't let a media more concerned with ratings than truth tell me what was true. And I couldn't reason with any of those who were crying out injustice, when in fact, justice and the law were adequately applied. I can't argue with emotions.

I am not immune. When the Newtown school shooting happened, I was incredibly upset–sick with it. And I am still working out my position on the issue of guns in America. I struggle to leave my emotions out of it, to set my fears aside, but I strive to remind myself that freedom, above all, is paramount. It's just like Benjamin Franklin said (and my husband dared to remind me during my period of anger and emotion): "They who can give up essential liberty to obtain a little temporary safety, deserve neither liberty nor safety." [*I no longer feel this way. The idea that "freedom is paramount" is a lovely idea, but it can't work because we live in a society. Of humans. The idea that a gun should be easier to obtain than a driver's license is ridiculous.*]

And so, the moral of the story is this: No matter who they are, no matter what they believe or don't believe, most people don't want honesty and precise word usage and logic and reasoning. People too often think with their emotions, not their intellects. Objective reality, facts, evidence, the law, justice, and freedom are all too often cast aside in the rush to assuage feelings.

They just want to feel.

They want to feel alive. They want to feel important. They want to feel right, and justified, and useful. They don't care about words and reasoning and what's right or wrong. They only care about how it feels.

I can't argue with that. I don't *want* to.

So, I quit. I quit trying to reason with people who didn't want to reason. It wasn't good for me and it wasn't good for them.

I quit atheism.

And by that, I mean that atheism can no longer be a defining characteristic for me. It says absolutely nothing at all about who I am. But I don't want to stop learning. Not having to be acquainted with people for whom I'm not a good "friend" fit doesn't mean I'm not paying attention to the world. Just like not wanting to see pictures of suffering animals almost daily doesn't mean I don't occasionally read about, and make myself aware of, the situation.

I have come to realize that you don't learn by arguing with people who don't share your passion for reason and preciseness of language. You learn by talking with intelligent people, reading their books, reading articles and discussions, etc.. So I didn't give up learning. And I'm still an atheist. But from what I've seen of the atheism community (do I need to mention the feminism fiasco and atheism+? And they can't even come to terms with the definition of atheism), I just don't fit in there.

I don't fit anywhere. I never have, and I guess I never will. There is no club, no political party, no group into which I would put myself. And I'm just not the type of person who doesn't mind aligning herself with a group even if she doesn't accept all of its values and views. To me, that would debase my own. I'm just not willing to sacrifice my viewpoint to any group, or mob, to belong.

So, I'll just stop trying. I emailed the leader of that atheist group and declined to speak to them. I have no interest in atheism, anymore.

Now I'm just looking for awe, education, reason, logic, science, nature, art, literature, fun...cats and chocolate. I think those things will do me just fine.

*Facebook.com/AtheistView
**You can find my list of current blogs at diannanarciso.com

Chapter Seventeen

Confessions of an Exhibitionist

The Internet is a strange place. It used to be that when you made an ass of yourself, if you were an ordinary person, you did the ass-making in front of a fairly small audience. The story might get around, but there was rarely any physical evidence of your make-assery and you were very likely to live it down and go on with your life. Now an ordinary person can make herself ridiculous in front of the entire Internet and never live it down. *Never*.

I try not to imagine what I would have done on the Tubes if they existed when I was a teenager. There would definitely have been a lot of maudlin whining and moping and bad poetry about lost love and anguish over the minutiae that dominate an unworldly teenager's life. There would have been chick fights that wouldn't end because the Internet is forever. I'd probably have my ass kicked a lot over things I said on Facebook. I'm sure it wouldn't have been pretty.

Here's the question though...I mean, I get that back then, I would have tried to communicate my awful angst to the entire world, but now, I'm actually a very private person. I know, right? It makes no sense at all. Why would an otherwise private, mind your own business type person expose herself on the Internet...especially as an atheist?

Part of it is the Internet itself. Ordinary people can suddenly have an audience; they can be heard. And a lot of us are clamoring to be heard. We have a need to be. Sometimes it seems like the entire world is shouting their stuff, doesn't it? (As an aside of sorts, did you know that there are people who, while they are in a financial position to be, aren't on the Internet? There are people with email accounts who don't check for incoming messages several times a day. I'm not sure what that's all about.) As soon as the Internet became a thing, I was on it. The Internet came about at the same time I realized atheism. It was almost as if I was supposed to start making an ass of myself on a regular basis (in public, that is). I had a voice and I was ready to use it...strike that. I wasn't ready. I was still pretty immature, but I didn't let that stop me.

I struggled for a long time with speaking my mind. I don't like confrontation. My feelings were hurt easily. It got to a point, before I wrote *Like Rolling Uphill*, that whenever I'd respond to someone about atheism, religion, evolution, and that whole range of debate, I'd get a queasy feeling; I'd try not to look for a rebuttal because I didn't want to get yelled at. And after the publication of my book, I backed off the debates. As you can see from the essay, "Why I Quit Atheism," it didn't help. I was still arguing my viewpoint, just with different people.

So, yeah, I quit. I decided that if there is a general atheism "community," which I really don't think can be said to exist, I wasn't a part of it. I don't think atheism should be a community. I don't think we ought to form communities based on belief or lack of belief. What religious people do is cluster in groups where they feel comfortable. The problem is that leaders then use that group to dictate to its members how to think, believe, and live. Then they split off from each other into smaller groups because there are challenges to that dogma.

When we start thinking of atheism as a community, the same thing happens. A group calling themselves Atheism Plus came out of a squabble over feminist complaints about lack of rules governing male behavior at atheist conventions, basically. They claimed they represented atheism *plus* progressive notions of liberalism, social justice, and feminism. They proceeded to denigrate anyone who wouldn't join. If you weren't *with* Atheism Plus, you were against social justice and a misogynist. Questioning their methods or their ideology was forbidden. People were banned from their forums. The entire episode served only to prove that atheism is not equal to rationalism; atheists can be just as emotionally charged, illogical, petty, and controlling as religious people.

So, I say 'no thank you' to an atheist "community." But, if I quit, why this second edition? Why am I essentially back...if I ever really left?

I said, when I quit, that atheism couldn't be a defining characteristic for me anymore. But as it turns out, that isn't true. It can't be true, really. Because I am an atheist. I can't *not* be an atheist, because I don't believe in any gods. Atheism isn't something you can quit because it's just a description of yourself and has no ideology attached to it. You can quit political parties, you can change world views and philosophies of life, you can quit friends, lovers, and spouses. But you can't quit atheism unless you somehow manage to believe in the god or gods you didn't believe in before.

I also said I didn't care about atheism anymore, but that's not exactly true either. It's not atheism I care about so much as the rights of atheists. I care about the rights and freedoms of everyone, actually—yes, even the rights of religious people. One of the most frustrating things about fighting for separation between religion and government is arguing with Christians who don't understand that secularism protects them just as much as it does me.

If we lived in a world in which being an atheist didn't matter, a world in which nobody cared, in which atheists were treated no differently from theists, and religion wasn't being forced into government, into women's lives, into my life, I would never have felt *different*. I wouldn't have felt like I had to defend myself or my rights. If we lived in a world like that, my being an atheist wouldn't be an issue.

But we don't live in that kind of world. And while The United States is growing more diverse, religion and religious people are constantly trying to get us "back" to some "better" period of time when there was Christian prayer in schools and if a woman wanted an abortion she had to get one in a dirty hotel room by someone who may or may not have been an actual doctor. They want to go back to a time when women were content being "the Missus." Women who wanted to work had to be happy as secretaries, teachers, or nurses. They want to return to the era when the only people who really mattered were white and schools were segregated by race. And if you don't think that my being an outspoken atheist has anything to do with that, you're wrong because that white majority was Christian. It was Christians who segregated the schools; Christians formed the KKK and hung young black men without cause. Christians, I'm sorry to say, have a long and dirty history of bigotry and of forcing everyone to live according to their rules. It's certainly Christians today who are losing the battle against the right of gays to marry.

Where I live, the city's official website has a photograph of an American flag with sunshine peering through it in such a way that it forms a cross. The page is dedicated to local men and women serving in the military. It includes the phrase "In God we Trust." In November, 2005, Space Coast Freethought Association protested this promotion of the Christian religion on the website that was supposed to represent all the people who live here. I spoke personally with the mayor and he claimed the picture was taken locally and it was a coincidence that the sun made a cross. That wasn't true.

The picture was taken in Yuma, Arizona on September 12, 2001, the day after the terrorist attacks that shocked our nation, and was passed around the Internet with variations of accompanying text. The worst that I saw said this: "...it seems, dear friends, that we are truly, 'one nation under God,' whether they want to believe it or not!"

This picture's inclusion on the city website is an affront to nonbelievers, but nobody cares about the atheists who live here, much less about local non-Christian members of our military. Nobody cares about the Muslims or the Jews or the Wiccans, either. (The mayor at the time was Jewish and he said the picture didn't bother him; apparently, if it didn't bother him, it shouldn't bother anyone. But a lot of things don't bother politicians when their tax-paid jobs are involved.) Our city government doesn't care about diversity. [*As of 2021, the city's updated website has a much more professional look and these complaints no longer apply.*]

Where I live, in 1996, a Wiccan priestess from my city traveled to another in our county to give the invocation at a city council meeting. She was invited by a council member. When she gave her invocation, most of the council stood and turned their backs on her, some even left the room. After the invocation and the reciting of the Pledge of Allegiance, more than one hundred Christians stood and said the Lord's Prayer as protest. The council member who'd invited the priestess ended up resigning her position over the controversy. This is the way many Christians handle freedom of religion. You see? It's not freedom for all, just for themselves and their kind.

You think that was a long time ago? This year,

2014, an atheist group asked to give the invocation at a county commission meeting. Not only were they denied, but in the discussion of the request, the commissioners made it clear that the invocation must invoke "a higher authority which a substantial body of Brevard constituents believe to exist." Freedom of religion is only for the majority where I live. They were kind enough, however, to vote unanimously that remarks by atheists or the nonreligious could be made during the public comments period. Sweet. Separate but equal, right?

Where I live, the school board was just fine with putting a diverse population of high school students in the county's largest Christian church for graduation ceremonies. When I found out about it, my oldest son was in high school and I complained. The principal of his high school didn't care. The school board didn't care. In fact, the superintendent responded to my complaint by saying that no *reasonable* person would see the ceremony as promoting Christianity. That's right, only unreasonable people care about freedom of conscience. Never mind the fact that the county was putting Muslims, Jews, atheists, Wiccans, and others into the position of choosing between entering a religious sanctuary for an important ceremony, and engaging in the critical moment of said ceremony while standing in front of an enormous cross, or staying home. No one should be compelled to enter a church, much less take part in a major life ceremony in one.

The next year, a student at my son's school contacted Americans United for Separation of Church and State and together they filed a lawsuit against the school board. I joined that lawsuit. And we won. *Of course we won.* But very few people could understand the problem with taking a secular student body and making them go to church for a solemn ceremony.

"What's wrong with it?" A woman asked me as we both stood at the church, peering through a window at the sanctuary.

"It's a church," I said. Like, duh.

A local conservative radio commentator wanted to know if we atheists were like vampires and our garlic was churches. Christians lose their perspective when someone protests their arrogant intrusion into our lives. Just think about it. These same people, if they could stand to admit it, would complain if the high school in question held its graduation ceremony in the auditorium of a rival high school and students had to walk in front of an enormous cutout of the rival mascot to get their diplomas. They'd say, "You're going to cover the bulldog, right?"

And of course these Christians would scream foul if it was the Wiccans or the Muslims who had the big building and their precious Christian children were made to enter those sanctuaries and get diplomas in front of symbols of those faiths. What if the atheists had a big building with a big sign behind the stage that read, 'No Gods, No Masters'? You can bet they would protest holding graduations there. But because it's a Christian church, not one of "those" religions or those evil atheists, *what's the harm*? And isn't it funny that when they want you to graduate in it, or they want to bring public school kids into it to see a play, or they want us to vote in it, then it's just a building. *What are you complaining about; what are you, a vampire?* But when someone protests in front of it, or talks smack about it, suddenly it's a sacred, holy place and we have to respect it. [Cue: Golden Earring, "Twilight Zone."]

Sadly, Christians don't stop when they're defeated. They can't see that what they're doing is wrong, that they're forcing other people to participate in their delusion and violating our rights. Instead, they just keep plugging away, and keep running for office for the purpose of Christianizing us all, and keep lobbying for changes on the Supreme Court for no other reason than to establish a theocracy. They won't stop infusing their religion into our government and our lives. So one day, another lawsuit will take place and because they've so invaded our government, and so fundamentally warped the ideals of freedom, they just might win.

They already changed our nation's motto from *e pluribus unum* to 'In God we Trust' and put it on our money. They put 'under God' into the once secular Pledge. They made Christmas a national holiday and promote national days of prayer. Sure, we managed to end prayer in schools and we've made some small progress with their constant intrusion into our lives, but they're pushing back hard. Before you know it, we'll be graduating high school students in churches. Abortion will be illegal (they've already succeeded in making it extremely difficult to get one). Gay rights will be rolled back, no more gay marriage. Pot will once again be criminalized where it wasn't before. Prayers at public meetings will be all Christian, all the time. Schools will stop teaching theories of evolution in science class (not that they're really teaching them now). Kids will be forced to stand and recite the Pledge of Allegiance in schools and adults will be forced to do the same at government meetings. The Ten Commandments and the Lord's Prayer will be posted all over the place. But not to worry, everyone will still get to own guns and carry them around in public.

So that's it. That's why I can't quit atheism. And that's why I'm still writing about religion. That's the answer to the questions: Why do atheists even care? Why don't they just shut up about religion and God? Why are they so angry and mean?

Atheists care what people think and believe because it affects us. If Christians were content to believe what they do, and smart enough–compassionate and empathetic enough–to let others live their lives as they see fit, this book wouldn't exist. But too many Christians are hell bent on forcing the rest of us to join them in their delusions. They are too shortsighted to understand that if the government can force Christianity onto everyone, it can force a particular version of Christianity on us...and it might not be theirs.

And that's why I'm out there making an ass of myself on the Internet. I was forced into it by the outrage of living in a society dominated by Christians. I'd like to be able to say it doesn't matter what you believe. But the truth is, it does. Religion, besides being manmade and ridiculous, attends too much to that core fear in humans and leads them too easily to start dictating to the rest of us how we should live. As far as I'm concerned, the religious deserve all the snarking they get.

So I'm an exhibitionist. I have stuff to say and I'm going to say it. Because I'm right about some very important things. I'm right that only a secular government that stays out of religion can possibly represent a religiously diverse society. That means no religious commandments, scriptures, or tenets posted on public property; no prayers at government meetings; no mention of any gods on our money, in our Pledge, in our oaths; no voting in religious buildings; no use of religious buildings for any government or public meetings of any kind; no prayer in public schools; no religion taught in schools except in history classes in upper grades—yes, that means no Christmas trees, no Hanukkah, no Easter egg hunts; science standards for schools written by scientists; no churches or religious sects of any kind coming into schools with clubs or assemblies—and that includes Cub Scout and Boy Scout groups run by churches; no promotion of any religion by the government; no national days of prayer; no prayer proclamations by any government entities. It means a government that allows us to decide when and how to engage in religious rites and rituals all by ourselves—a government that respects our individual liberties and doesn't assume Christianity as the default religion.

If you don't agree that a secular government like that is the best form of government, you are *wrong*. It's that simple. *You. Are. Wrong.* You don't understand freedom. And you are the problem. You are why religion sucks. You are why people think of bigotry and hate when they think of Christianity. You are why so many Americans feel like second-class citizens. And because your inability to understand the simplest ideas of freedom negatively affects me and my rights, I'll keep being an exhibitionist.

I care what you think, all right; I just don't care what you think of me.

Books by Dianna Dann Narciso

Fiction by Dianna Dann
Camelia
Always Magnolia
Bury Me

Romantic Comedy by Dianna Dann
Bookish Meets Boy
Pari and the Ghost Whisperer

Fantasy by Dana Trantham
Children of Path: The Kell Stone Prophecy Book One
The Wretched: The Kell Stone Prophecy Book Two
Mark of the Faire: The Kell Stone Prophecy Book Three
The Kell Stone Prophecy: Complete Trilogy

Paranormal Humor by D.D. Charles
Zombie Revolution

Children's Fiction by Dana Trantham
Wayward Cat Finds a Home
Wayward Cat Saves the Day
Zombie Cats
Franken Lizard

For more, visit
waywardcatpublishing.com